Claire —
Happy
micro waving —
Carolyn /95

Definitive
Microwave Cookery II

by

Carolyn Dodson

Dedication

Lovingly, I dedicate this book to my mother, Velma Scott, who not only taught me to prepare good 'home cooked foods' and enjoy the simple things of life, but who always encouraged and supported me in whatever I undertook.

Acknowledgments

To Art Scott, who came to my kitchen set at the T.V. station to take the photographs for the book cover.

To Pam Porvaznik, who supplied me with the proper words when mine escaped me.

To my loyal Tupperware friends who have always believed in my techniques and recipes and kept asking for another book.

To all those who gave me the encouragement I needed to 'keep cooking' by attending lectures, demonstrations or tuning into my television segments.

To all of my wonderful friends that tasted those 'questionable' recipes and gave me their valuable input.

To Evelyn Hoefler, my 'like a daughter', who laughed, cried and supported me during those long weeks away from home.

To David Crain, my 'like a son', who never failed to help me whether it was doing dishes, going to the warehouse for books or taking me to the airport at any hour.

To my son, Scott Duncan, who although a long way off in California, has always been there for me when I needed love, support and a 'fan'.

And to my wonderful husband, Bill, who has never complained about my long hours at the computer, the long meetings with corporate executives throughout the world, which often included tasting 'exotic' and unfamiliar foods nor about the many nights spent at presentations rather than with him, Most of all, however, for his unconditional love and his complete faith in me.

ISBN: 1-8823303-0-7

Published by the Magni Company
P.O. Box 849
McKinney, Texas 75070
Printed in the United States of America

INTRODUCTION

DEFINITIVE MICROWAVE COOKERY II represents the second in a series of cookbooks aimed at making the microwave the most user-friendly appliance since the toaster.

Recognizing that today's cook can be from both genders, involved in multiple activities, on career paths with even less time in the kitchen than any past generation, my mission is to bring the cook back to the basics. I incorporate in this cookbook all the things my mother and Great Plains Grandmother taught me and how these often forgotten "home cooking" techniques translate to the modern technology of today.

Included are original recipes that range in taste from the highly-creative spare-no- expense guest menu to the ultra-simple, nutritious family fare. It is so easy to be successful in the kitchen! Low fat, healthy meals made from fresh ingredients become no fuss masterpieces with little or no effort.

Imagine a perfect beef Stroganoff on a fluffy bed of wild and white rice. I'll show you how to cook with ease.

Or if you want to impress the boss or simply pamper yourself, try the Williamsburg Trifle. Made as easily for 50 as two! Layers of chocolate cake, chocolate almandine pudding, real whipped cream, pecans and cherries served in an exquisite crystal bowl.

For those who are counting fat grams but want a memorable menu for family or friends, check out the recipe for Chicken with Lobster made with a paprika and sour cream sauce, always a favorite with my catering clients. A touch of celebrity? How about Sinatra Pasta Salad, a combination of spaghetti, bean sprouts and water chestnuts in a tangy mustard sauce which I made especially for "Ole Blue Eyes" when he was visiting friends of mine in Wichita. Sinatra liked it so much his wife Barbara took the recipe home.

I take the microwave beyond food in this book. There are recipes for, lip gloss, liquid soap and even doggie cookies for your canine friend. All made in the microwave.

Definitive Microwave II is packed with a world of information for a healthier lifestyle and even nutritional analysis with every recipe. There are household and cooking tips and information along with charts and illustrations.

It is not necessary to sacrifice quality or taste when cooking in the microwave. *Definitive Microwave II* will teach you to take basic conventional techniques which everyone should know before they cook and apply them to microwave cooking so even a "novice" will become an accomplished cook.

Enjoy and....

       Happy Microwaving,

              Carolyn

Contents

MICROWAVE INFORMATION

HOW A MICROWAVE WORKS

A microwave contains a "miniature radio station" or magnatron tube which sends out microwaves or radio waves about five inches long and as big around as a small finger. These microwaves cross the top of the oven where they either "dump" into the oven cavity and a turntable moves the food through the stream of microwaves or they "hit" a stirrer fan and bounce down and around in the oven. One of these two things must happen to cook food evenly.

Microwaves "bounce" off of metal... therefore, we cook in a six sided metal box so they won't get out into the room to you. This makes them very safe to use. They pass through paper, plastic or glass like sunshine goes through a window pane with no effect at all. Therefore, we cook in utensils made from these types of materials. The microwaves are attracted like magnets to the fat, sugar and water within the food. Water molecules are very good absorbers of microwaves, sugar and fat are better and salt is best. Thus, foods high in fat, sugar and salt will cook faster than foods made up primarily of water.

The microwaves "wiggle" into the food, penetrating the food approximately one inch in all directions (top-bottom-sides) causing molecules to vibrate against one another at the rate of 2 1/2 billion times a second. The friction caused by this vibration produces the heat that cooks our food. Heat from the vibrating molecules on the outer 1-1 1/2 inches must go somewhere so by "conduction" it moves inward layer by layer. Microwaves do not actually touch most of the food they cook. They penetrate only its surface and the vibrating molecules near the surface then agitate the deeper molecules. Cooking of larger, more dense foods is started on the edges and the heat is conducted to the center.

Stirring will help food cook more uniformly as it redistributes heat from the outer layers of the food to the inner layers. Arrangement of the food, dish style, denseness of the food, etc. are also important to microwave cooking. (See "What Affects Microwave Cooking") Furthermore, microwaves have no effect on ice until the ice begins to melt. Then, the water will attract the microwaves.

MICROWAVE SAFETY

Radiation is the flow of energy through space. Examples of this: Light and warmth of the sun, ordinary light bulbs as well as the warmth of a fireplace.

People who worry about the safety of microwave cooking mistakenly associate microwaves with nuclear radiation. They are, however, vastly different. Microwaves are virtually identical to radio and TV waves. These common waves have little energy. Other less common waves such as Xrays carry more than a million times more energy than microwaves. Radio frequency radiation is, on the other hand, emitted from the human body at total energy levels greater than that total emitted from a microwave oven which is operating within government standards.

Too much radiation of any kind, including microwaves, could be dangerous. For example, excessive sound waves bring hearing loss and overdoses of ultraviolet light cause sunburn. The government sets rigid safety standards for microwave ovens. The standards adhered to are approximately 1/10,000 of the level known to cause harm to humans.

The microwave oven has been in use since the late 1940's. With millions of such ovens in homes today, federal health officials have repeatedly stated, "There hasn't been a documented case of human injury." In fact, James A. Van Allen, who discovered radiation belts around the earth, says, "In my judgement, the likelihood of microwave oven hazard is about the same as the likelihood of getting a skin tan from moonlight."

TEST FOR HOT SPOTS IN YOUR MICROWAVE

Cover the bottom of your microwave oven or turntable with a dampened paper towel. Turn on the microwave for 1 minute at 100% power. The dried and damp areas show the cooking pattern or hot and cold spots of your oven. Severe problems should be corrected by a service representative. If the hot/cold spots are not severe, learn to use these to your advantage. Harder to cook foods or larger portions of food should be placed in the warmer areas. Portions which cook easily should be placed in the cooler areas. Example: A leg of lamb roast. Place the small end of the leg in the cool area; the large end of the roast in the warm.

TEST FOR POWER FLUCTUATION IN YOUR HOME

The power supply to your home may vary throughout the day, thereby affecting your microwave cooking times. Bring a cup of the same temperature water to a boil in your oven at three different times during a day other than a weekend or a holiday. For example: 8 a.m., 12 noon and 5 p.m. You will see that times may vary. This shows the "peak " times of power usage. It will usually be the same time each day other than holidays or weekends when schedules may change. Therefore, it may be necessary to adjust the cooking time upward or downward by a few seconds to achieve similar results of certain foods being cooked. With delicate foods, such as cakes or foods that cook only a short time, knowing this can really make a difference in the quality of the food. It also explains why food cooked exactly the "same way" sometimes will not turn out the "same way". For example: a poached egg may take 40 seconds in the morning and 1 minute 15 seconds in the evening to get the same result.

CORRELATION OF CONVENTIONAL AND MICROWAVE TEMPERATURES

Better results occur with foods cooked in the microwave if they are cooked at similar levels of "heat" (power level) as those cooked by conventional methods.

TEMPERATURE CORRELATION

Based on a microwave with 650-700 watts of power, the scale below shows how you can learn to relate your microwave "percentages of power" to your conventional" degrees of heat." To determine accurate wattage of your oven, refer to *Microwave Wattage* Section. After this has been done, use the following chart as a guide:

100%-90% power =	425-500 degrees, deep fat fry, broil or having the burner on top of your stove on "high"
80% power =	375-425 degrees.
70% power =	350-375 degrees or "medium high" stove-top.
60-50% power =	300-350 degrees or "medium" stove-top.
40-30% power =	225-300 degrees or "medium low" stove-top.
20% power =	200-225 degrees.
10% power =	150-200 degrees or as low as you can turn the burner on top of your stove without it going off.

If your microwave has power levels listed by words such as Simmer, Roast, etc., look in your owners manual as it will give you the percentages for each position or look at your microwave controls and picture them, high to low as you would your conventional oven dial (Broil—150 degrees). Then refer to the *Temperature Correlation Chart.* You will see that by relating microwave and conventional temperatures, you will be able to adapt your "conventional" recipes to microwave more easily. (See *Microwave Information for Recipe Conversion.*)

MICROWAVE WATTAGE

Microwave oven power is measured in watts and indicates the cooking power of your oven. Generally speaking, ovens labeled with more watts of power will cook food faster than ones with lower wattage. As I have based most of my rules on a 650-700 watt oven, it is important to explain a recent change which has taken place in microwave wattage tests.

Before last year, most U.S. ovens were rated by microwaving two liters of water for a specific time. This is the test I refer to when talking about 650-700 watt ovens.

Recently most manufacturers have started using a standard formulated in Europe in which one liter of water is microwaved. The same ovens rated by this procedure earn higher wattage numbers without actually cooking faster. For example, an oven rated 700 watts by the U.S. procedure is now rated 800 watts.

To further complicate things, a few new ovens cook faster because of redesigned systems. A few ovens have as much as 1000 watts of power when tested by either procedure. Although foods will cook in any oven, to cook properly it is necessary to determine the wattage of your oven. Use the following consumer *Time To Boil Test* formulated by the International Microwave Power Institute to test your oven.

Time To Boil Test

From a container of half ice and half water, measure exactly 1 cup of water (no ice) into a 1 cup glass measuring cup. Place in center of microwave oven. Heat on high power for 5 minutes or until water begins to boil. If water begins to boil in less than 3 1/2 minutes, consider your oven "high power"; If longer, the oven is "low power."

When using recipes and package directions, set a "high power" microwave oven for the minimum time recommended. If your oven is "low power," it will probably take the longer time. However, always check for proper doneness by using indicators as recipes and packages direct.

The following tests are tests that I have used in the past to test oven wattage and relate temperature to wattage output. They may help you also. 1 Cup (8 oz.) of room temperature water (approximately 75 degrees) will boil in:

A. 2 minutes if 700 watts or higher and is equivalent to 550 degrees or higher when at 100% power.

B. 2 1/2 minutes if 650 watts and is equivalent to 500 degrees when at 100% power.

C. 3 minutes if 600 watts and equivalent to 450 degrees when at 100% power.

D. 3 1/2 minutes if 500 watts and equivalent to 400 degrees when at 100% power.

E. 4 minutes if 400 watts and equivalent to 350 degrees when at 100% power.

If water boils more quickly than in 2 minutes, you are cooking in a high wattage oven and need to adjust cooking times downward.

Hopefully this wattage information will help you relate the "high" power on your microwave. Then refer to *Correlation of Conventional and Microwave Temperature Section* for a guide to temperature levels of the various power levels of your microwave.

You must adapt your recipes according to size and wattage of your oven. Cooking times for various ovens are as follows for each minute cooked at 100% power:

750 Watt/Higher	600-700 Watt	500-600 Watt	400-500 Watt
45 sec. or less	1 min.	1 min. 15 sec.	1 min. 30 sec.

As most recipe books are written for 700 watt ovens, it may be necessary to adjust your cooking times by adding or subtracting necessary seconds as above for each minute you cook your food.

For example: If the 600-700 watt oven takes 1 minute to cook, a 500-600 watt oven would take 1 min. 15 seconds and a 400-500 watt oven would take 1 min. 30 seconds, so adjust accordingly to allow for this time difference.

Make certain, however, that your oven is actually producing "higher" watts and simply was not rated by European standards which give higher wattage numbers without actually producing faster cooking times, before adjusting your recipes.

WHAT AFFECTS MICROWAVE COOKING TIME

In the microwave we cook by time, not temperature (unless using a probe). A few things that affect the cooking time are:

1. Starting temperature of food (cold vs. room temperature or warm).

2. Quantity of food (large amount or small amount).

3. Shape of food (thin vs. thick; circle vs. square, etc.).

4. Shape of container in which food is cooked (square vs. round vs. ring).

5. Composition of food (high sugar-fat content heats faster than lower sugar-fat content; high sugar-fat heats faster than water)

6. Density of food - two foods weighing the same with different densities (amount of air between molecules) cook differently. A dense or compact roast takes longer to cook than a porous loaf of bread of the same weight.

7. Wattage of the microwave oven - low wattage ovens take longer to cook foods than higher wattage ovens.

8. Electric power fluctuation - power supply in your home may vary throughout the day which can affect microwave cooking times.

Other factors:

Since small items cook faster than large items, a good practice is to cook all of one size food at a time.

Fresh vegetables contain more water and cook faster than those that are less fresh.

The shape and size of vegetables and other foods make cooking times vary. Cut those that cook more slowly (dense with less water content) such as carrots into uniform small pieces. Cut those foods requiring less cooking time (porous with higher water content) such as mushrooms into larger uniform pieces. Cooked together these will cook correctly in the same amount of time.

Foods, such as soups, which have a high liquid content take longer to cook than foods which cook from their own moisture content. Liquid ingredients slow down cooking. In other words, one pound of food with 50% moisture will take less time to heat to a certain temperature than one pound of food with 75% moisture. For example: If meat is cooked in liquid, cooking time will be greater than meat not cooked in liquid; a potato cooked in water will take longer to cook than one cooked by itself. Also, if meat is partially cooked prior to adding the liquid, cooking time will be shorter. Combine partially cooked food with hot liquid and the cooking time will be shorter still.

Cooking large food in the microwave

Large foods such as turkeys or roasts, which cannot be stirred, should be turned over "rotisserie style" while cooking. This promotes uniform, even heat in the microwave just as a rotisserie cooks large pieces of meat more evenly on a charcoal grill. In some cases, cooking food in hot liquid will add additional heat to the food's surface causing it to cook faster. You may tenderize muscular cuts of meat such as a pot roast by "slow cooking" in hot liquid. While cooking, these foods should also be turned over to promote even heat.

UTENSILS

Microwave cooking patterns in various types of containers and proper "circle fashion" arrangement of food is illustrated below.

Cooking patterns of different pans

NOTE:

Corners cook 4 ways- from 2 sides, top & bottom. Sides cook 3 ways - from 1 side, top & bottom. Center cooks 2 ways - from top & bottom only.

NOTE:

Sides cook 3 ways - from 1 side, top & bottom. Center cooks 2 ways - from top & bottom.

NOTE:

All sides cook 3 ways - from in/out sides, top & bottom. (Ring shaped pans work well for cakes and other foods since they allow microwaves to reach to food from the top, bottom, inside and outside of the ring. If you do not have a ring pan, an empty glass or cup may be placed in the center of a round dish to create a space, thus enabling the microwaves to penetrate all four ways also.)

Food arrangement for even cooking without stirring or rearranging

NOTE:
Place thicker or more dense food to outside of dish, thinner or more porous portions to the center area of dish (spoke fashion).

NOTE:
When cooking similar sized pieces of food such as rolls or boneless chicken breasts, three or more whole foods, such as potatoes or dishes such as custard cups in the microwave oven, arrange them in a circle (circle fashion) leaving about 1-2 inches between each. This pattern promotes even cooking by giving each food maximum exposure to the microwaves. "Circle fashion" allows the microwaves to reach the food from the top, bottom and inner as well as the outer edge of the circle.

xiv

TESTING UTENSILS

Place the dish to be tested and a small cup of water side by side in the microwave. Turn the oven on for one minute at 100% power. If the water is cool and the dish warm to hot, the dish is absorbing microwave energy. Do not use this utensil in the microwave. If the water is warm to hot, however, and the dish cool, it is a safe utensil to use.

COVERS AND LIDS

There are three basic "lids" or "covers" used in microwave cooking and for "Standing Time" outside the oven (See Standing Time). The uses are summarized below:

Plastic Wrap, Tight Fitting Casserole Cover or Microwave Wrap

Recipes that require cooking techniques needed to produce moist foods or recipes using terms such as "tightly covering", "steaming", "moist", etc.

Wax Paper, Microwave Wrap or Vented Casserole Cover

Recipes that require cooking techniques needed to produce neither moist or crisp foods or terms such as "crack the lid", "allow some steam to escape", "partially cover", etc.

Paper Towels

Recipes that require cooking techniques needed to produce a dry or crisp food or terms such as "dry heat", "crusty", "crisp", "absorb excess moisture", "no lid or cover", or to simply prevent splattering and hold in heat. There is also a new product, "Microcrisp" that actually promotes browning and crisping in the microwave.

SHIELDING

Never run a microwave oven empty or with too much shielding. Damage could occur. Small pieces of foil, however, may be used to cover various parts of food to keep them from overcooking. This is known as shielding. For example: The wings, breast bone and leg ends of a chicken or turkey may overcook if not protected or "shielded" for part of the cooking time. An aluminum foil ring or "donut" may also be placed on cakes, egg dishes, etc. to promote more even cooking. Covering corners of square dishes with small pieces of foil will prevent overcooking of corners. If sparks are seen, remove foil from the microwave. There must be enough water (food) to attract the microwaves. If there isn't enough water (food), there will be "arcing" or sparks. The food mass must be substantially greater than the amount of foil used (80% food volume—no more than 20% foil volume.) When shielding, place foil smoothly over the food it is protecting. Do not allow the foil to touch the side of the microwave oven, which is also metal, as this will cause arcing.

SIX MINUTE PER POUND RULE

With only a few exceptions, most foods (meats, poultry, vegetables and fruit) will cook to done in a "full size" microwave (650-700 watts) at 100% power in 6 minutes per pound. An exception to this is fish and seafood which take 3-4 minutes per pound.

For cooking foods at other than 100% power, see *Lowering Cooking Temperature in Basic Precepts of Meat Cookery Section.*

STANDING TIME

Six minutes a pound at 100% power plus standing time will cook most foods to done. 80% of the cooking occurs in the microwave while it is on. 20% takes place in or out of the oven after the oven turns off. This happens whether you want it to or not. Somewhat similar to an automobile putting on its brakes and coming to a stop down the road, the water molecules inside the food which move 2 1/2 billion times a second must come to a gradual stop... or later "down the road". We must allow for this or foods will overcook. Always cover food which is taken out of the oven for standing time. Cover with the proper "lid" or "cover" according to the texture desired (crisp, moist, etc.). Heat will stay inside the dish and food will finish cooking properly. Cover or it is like cooking the last part of the conventional cooking time with the oven door open. Standing time allows cooking to continue or "ongoing" cooking to complete which is critical to cooking good food in the microwave. If food is cooked to done, it will be "overcooked" after the standing time and "ongoing" cooking is finished.

BROWNING AND CRISPING

Meats containing fat will brown when cooked in the microwave as fat comes to the surface (protein plus sugar plus heat = brown) and will caramelize. Crisp crusts like foods that are deep fat fried cannot be achieved in a microwave. Extended cooking time, however, produces high enough heat that browning will occur. Meats with high fat content brown the most. Meats cooked 6 minutes or less or with little fat content (such as fish or poultry without skin) will need spices or sauces to give them the "golden brown" look. To make food aesthetically pleasing or "brown", you may use soy sauce, teriyaki sauce, Worcestershire sauce, butter-paprika mixture, pepper-paprika-parsley-thyme spice combo, gravy mixes, crumbs, seeds, wheat germ, sugar, Micro Shake or other available browning products including Microcrisp wrap which is new to the market. Browning dishes, which are preheated to a high temperature and used for browning foods in the microwave, are available and may also be used.

DEFROSTING

Proper time for defrosting is dependent on the type and size of the food. Always cover while defrosting. The bigger the piece of food, the lower the temperature or power level should be to prevent "cooking". Also, a very porous type of food will defrost more easily than a dense one. The following chart should be helpful for defrosting:

1" thick	6 min. per lb. at 50% power
1 1/2 - 2" thick	7 min. per lb. at 40% power
2-3" thick	8 min. per lb. at 30% power
3-4" thick	9 min. per lb. at 20% power
Over 4" thick	10 min. per lb. at 10% power

Defrosting frozen casseroles take approximately 15 minutes per quart at 30% power. Defrost before cooking.

Defrost breads at 30% power. Wrapping in paper towels prevents sogginess. Placing on a microwave rack will allow air to circulate around them also.

Defrosting by microwave preserves vitamins. Water soluble nutrients have less time to dissolve.

Remember you may "shield" while defrosting to prevent food from cooking during the defrosting process.

REHEATING

Reheating at 100% power causes foods to heat unevenly. Reduced power levels produce better results. 70% power is good for soups, casseroles, meats and plates of leftovers. 50% power is better for large or layered casseroles.

Choose 50%-70% power according to food type. Arrange harder to heat portions to outside of plate and porous, easier to heat food to the inside or center of the plate. This type of arrangement makes it unnecessary to rearrange or stir. Cover according to the texture you desire. (Example: moist food = microwave wrap or plastic wrap; dry or crusty texture = paper towel.) Cook about 6 minutes per pound at 50% power. Stir if necessary.

A few frozen foods such as pasta and soup may be reheated without defrosting. Stir these as they heat.

To determine if food is thoroughly warmed, place your hand on the bottom of the container. Your hand may be held on the bottom of the container for about 2-3 seconds before the container becomes uncomfortable to the touch if thoroughly warmed.

Dense foods such as meats and baked potatoes take longer to heat than porous items such as bread products, rice and pasta.

Microwave energy is instantly attracted to foods that have a high concentration of fat or sugar. For example, a sweet roll will get hot faster than a plain dinner roll.

The cooking container you choose will help or hinder uniform reheating efforts. Very thin layers or very deep layers of food will contribute to uneven cooking.

To reheat bread use the following chart as a guide:

Unsliced bread	1 loaf	30 seconds	100% power
Sliced bread	2 slices	10 seconds	100% power
	4 slices	20 seconds	100% power
Buns and Rolls	2	20 seconds	100% power
Donuts	2	15 seconds	100% power
Sweet Rolls	2	20 seconds	100% power

CONVERTING RECIPES

Look for recipes that will convert well. For example: Recipes that call for "moist cooking", "stirring", "covering", "steaming", "sauces", etc. will convert from conventional to microwave easily. Stay away from those that suggest "crusty", "crisp", "golden brown", etc. They may not convert well. 85% of all conventional recipes will convert, many having superior quality to conventionally cooked foods.

Adjustments for Ingredients

1. Reduce the "least rich" liquid ingredient in the recipe by 20-25% as it is not needed. There is no dry heat to cause it to evaporate. (Example: A Packaged cake mix calls for eggs, oil and water... water is the least rich so use 3/4 cup of water instead of the 1 cup called for.)

2. Cut back on spices and herbs by 20-25%. Flavors will be more intense as they won't "burn up" and will be stronger than they are when cooked conventionally due to hot air and long exposure to heat. Reduce sauces by 20-25% as they will not reduce in volume while cooking in the microwave as they would if cooking conventionally.

3. Increase leavening (such as baking powder or baking soda) by 10% when baking from "scratch" (not a prepared mix). Let batter stand for a minute or two before baking. As the microwave oven cooks much more quickly than a conventional oven, this will give the "chemical reaction" of the leavening a "head start" so your food will receive its full benefit.

4. Fat and oil in most recipes, other than cakes and baked goods may be reduced by 10% or more, as adding fats causes more intense heat and affects cooking time. Fats should be trimmed from meats so they will not attract the microwaves.

When cooking vegetables, fruits, main dishes and soups in the microwave, fats used to prevent sticking in conventional cooking may be eliminated from the recipe. They are not needed. Instead use small amounts of butter or fat as you would vanilla, for flavoring only. These steps will reduce fat grams in your foods for a healthier diet.

xviii

5. Whole foods such as potatoes or pieces of vegetables and meats that are to cook together should be as equal in size and shape as possible. Cut vegetables into uniform pieces according to their denseness . Microwaves have no intelligence level and cannot distinguish between something that is large or small. Therefore overcooking of small pieces may occur before the large pieces are done.

Also, cut the pieces of vegetables or fruits, etc. according to their denseness. The more dense the food, the harder it will be to cook; the more porous the food, the quicker it will cook. Therefore, if cooking together, make certain that you have "small" dense pieces and "larger" porous pieces so they will cook uniformly and finish cooking at the same time without overcooking either.

Another factor which presents itself in microwave cooking and the heat intensity at which foods cook is the water, sugar and fat content within each food. For example: Water heats "fast" (212 degrees); Sugar heats "faster" (260 degrees); Fat heats "fastest" (300 degrees). Therefore, fat, having the hottest heat intensity will cook and attract the microwaves before sugar and water. Sugar, which has the next hottest heat intensity, will attract the microwaves before water.

6. Cornstarch sauces thicken more rapidly and need less stirring than flour based sauces.

7. An electric mixer is useful to "blend", but it is not needed for "whipping in air" for fluffiness which is necessary in some conventionally cooked foods. Microwaved eggs and baked goods such as cakes will have about 1/3 more volume than conventionally cooked products as no "hard, dry" crusts form to hold down the volume or fluffiness as with conventionally cooked foods.

Choosing the Right Containers and Covers

1. Pick a microwave container slightly larger than needed in conventional recipes. This will allow for expansion of food, which occurs in some microwaved foods, and for stirring. Choose a container about twice the size of the food to be cooked.

2. Cover the container according to the texture desired (See Covers and Lids). If food is not covered during cooking time, make certain you cover it if you remove it from the oven for standing time. Again, cover it according to desired texture. This will keep the "heat" inside the food so it will finish cooking properly.

Cooking Times, Temperatures and Techniques

1. Refer to *Correlation of Conventional* and *Microwave Temperature* and *Covers and Lids* Sections to help you correlate temperatures and covers with those used in the conventional recipe.

2. Microwave cooking time should be reduced to 1/4 of the conventional cooking time. This will work in 80% of the recipes you convert. The others will require more time as they will probably be more moist or rich. Therefore, add cooking time and check product every 30 seconds or so until done.

When in doubt, always undercook as more cooking time may be added if needed. Once overcooked, food is ruined. Example: If a conventional recipe cooks for 1 hour at 350 degrees, covered tightly, the converted microwave recipe would cook for 15 minutes at 70% power covered with plastic wrap or a tight fitting casserole cover. Food would then be allowed to "stand" a few minutes for ONGOING COOKING to complete. 20-25% of the total cooking time is a good rule of thumb. If cooking time is 10 minutes, standing time will be 2 1/2 minutes, covered properly.

3. Take advantage of the microwave cooking pattern by arranging food properly. Rearranging and stirring will not be necessary (See Utensils).

Special Tips for Converting Recipes

1. Substitute quick cooking rice for converted rice or use cooked rice.

2. Remember that smaller quantities are what save time in the microwave. Larger quantities will lose the time saving advantage, but will still save electrical energy costs and clean up time.

3. Coat greased pans with nuts and crumbs for a "crusty" look.

4. For egg baked mixtures such as custards that should not be stirred during the cooking time, heat the milk before adding the eggs.

5. Add cheese and other toppings toward the end of the cooking time so they will not become tough or soggy.

6. Avoid flour coatings on meat They will not brown and will get soggy if liquid is added.

7. For pies, cook the crust before filling. It will not become soggy during cooking.

FACTORS THAT LESSEN COOK TIME: High water content, sugar, oil content; small pieces; porous and tender texture; warm starting temperature.

FACTORS THAT LENGTHEN COOK TIME: Low water content or addition of water, low sugar and oil content; large pieces; dense and rough texture; cold starting temperature.

Use techniques similar to those used in conventional cooking when cooking converted recipes in the microwave. If you are unfamiliar with conventional cooking techniques refer to *Cooking Methods in General Information* or to a conventional cookbook. Simply ask yourself—"Do I cook this recipe on high heat or low heat?" You would then select the suitable "temperature" or power level for the type of food being cooked. Continue to ask yourself questions and compare the methods to conventional cooking methods. "Do I cook it covered or uncovered?", etc. Don't worry about the exceptions. Do it the same in the microwave as you would conventionally. Think conventionally—cook microwave!! Food is food, so we handle it the same no matter the cooking method —your results will be much better.

CONVERTING RECIPES—*High Altitude Adjusting*

General Tips 5000 feet or above

1. Because air is thinner at high altitudes, foods that rise, foam or puff will often expand more. Larger containers are needed.

2. Water boils at lower temperature so increase cooking time for foods cooked in liquid such as rice, stews, etc.

3. Add an extra tablespoon of liquid to meats and other non-baked goods immediately after cooking to keep moist.

4. Foods will cool more quickly at higher altitudes. They may need to be reheated after standing time.

5. Whole vegetables should be pierced all over. Beans and carrots will need a tablespoon of water. Crisp frozen vegetables will require a bit less cooking time than if cooked at lower altitudes.

6. Less tender meats, fish and poultry which will be cooked in liquids need 5-10 minutes more to heat the liquid before dropping the temperature or power level for slow cooking to tenderize.

7. Ground meat and poultry may take a few more minutes to cook.

General Tips 7500 and above

1. Cooking speeds up. Faster evaporation, more drying and quicker cooking may occur.

LOWERING COOKING TEMPERATURE

As stated earlier, six minutes per pound at 100% power in a 650-700 watt microwave oven will cook most foods (meat, vegetables and fruit) other than seafood to well done *(See Six Minutes Per Pound Rule)*. Smaller, more porous pieces of food take less time than solid, dense pieces. Use six minutes per pound as your base starting point, however. As in conventional cooking, different foods (meats as well as vegetables and fruit) sometimes take different temperatures to cook properly. Following is the technique for lowering your temperatures or power levels in the microwave when needed to cook foods to well done

100% power = 6 min. per lb.	50% power = 11 min. per lb.
90% power = 7 min. per lb.	40% power = 12 min. per lb.
80% power = 8 min. per lb.	30% power = 13 min. per lb.
70% power = 9 min. per lb.	20% power = 14 min. per lb.
60% power = 10 min. per lb.	10% power = 15 min. per lb.

Remember all of the factors that can affect cooking times in the microwave that were discussed *(See What Affects Microwave Cooking Time)*. For example: Denseness, moisture content, starting temperature, etc. affect cooking of food in the microwave.

PRECEPTS OF MEAT COOKERY

When cooking meat, just as all other foods we cook in the microwave, methods similar to those used when cooking conventionally should be applied *(See Before You Cook and What You Should Know)* .

Tender Cuts

Hotter Temperatures: 70% for large pieces; 100% for small pieces. No Cover Required: Wax paper, microwave wrap or paper towel may be used to help retain some moisture and heat on larger cuts as well as to prevent splatters. *Uniform Size:* Stay away from irregular shapes and thickness. *Similar Methods:* Methods the same as those used when cooking conventionally. (For example: In conventional cooking, a standing rib roast is cooked on a rack, uncovered, in a hot oven..... In the microwave use a rack and a higher power level, uncovered or covered only with microwave wrap to prevent splatters and keep in heat.)

Less Tender Cuts

Lower Temperatures: 30-50% preferred. Muscular roasts depend on a slow cooking process and liquid to tenderize connective tissue. Cook covered or in cooking bag. *Uniform Size:* Again, stay away from irregular shapes and thickness. Turn Large Cuts: Turn, at least once, (rotisserie style) during the cooking period. *Similar Cooking Methods:* Like methods to those used when cooking conventionally. (For example, ask yourself... When cooking conventionally do I cover? Add liquid? Use high heat or low? When method is determined, use that same method in the microwave.)

Using the *Correlation of Conventional and Microwave Temperature Chart,* choose the same temperature (power level) to cook your food in the microwave as the recipe suggests you should when cooking conventionally. Follow your conventional recipe and convert temperatures to microwave power levels. Think conventionally—cook at similar levels of heat (Example: 70% power = 350-375 degrees).

Beef Roasts

When microwaving beef roasts, tender cuts of beef such as sirloin tip, top round and eye round cuts do extremely well and stay juicy when cooked without liquid. More muscular roasts such as chuck and brisket do well also, but need to be cooked in liquid. For both types, select uniform shaped roasts which are marbleized throughout. Those with uneven shapes will not cook as evenly. Also, at least 1/3 more fat is extracted from meat cooked in the microwave than those cooked conventionally. The microwave, however, does not extract meat juices. The key to tender beef roasts is low heat, preferably 30%. High heat does not allow adequate time for the development of tenderness and flavor in many beef cuts. Although this slow cook method takes longer, it still saves considerable time over conventional methods.

Various Degrees of Doneness

For meats you wish cooked to various stages of doneness, (rare to well done) such as tender or semi-tender roasts, steaks and chops, the time is as follows (650-700 watt oven):

Well Done = 100% for 6 min. per lb.

Medium = 100% for 5 min per lb.

Rare = 100% for 4 min. per lb.

You may also wish to lower the temperature, but achieve a different degree of doneness. The following is an example of the method to use. Pick the degree of doneness desired such as MEDIUM. Use the chart for lowering temperatures *(See Lowering Cooking Temperatures),* but substitute the required minutes for the degree of doneness as the top of the chart opposite 100% power. Then lower to the desired heat (500 degree =100% power to 150 degree =10% power). For example to achieve medium:

100% power = 5 min. per lb. = Medium

90% power = 6 min. per lb = Medium

80% power = 7 min. per lb. = Medium

and on down the scale.

For roasts, start all roasts, whether on a rack or in liquid at 100% power for 5-15 minutes. This "sears" in juices or brings liquid around the roast to near boiling. Then use the following as a guideline:

30% power	(Rib Eye, Loin, Eye Round, Tip, Rump, Top Round)	16-22 min. per pound
	(Chuck, Brisket in liquid)	30-45 min. per pound
50% power	(Rib Eye, Etc.)	8-12 min. per pound
	(Chuck, Brisket in liquid)	45-60 min. per pound

In microwaved meats and poultry not cooked in liquid, 20-25% of total cooking takes place after the oven shuts off *(See Standing Time).* This is called ONGOING COOKING. Learn to allow for this time. Check large pieces of meat or poultry in several spots with a meat thermometer to assure that the proper internal temperatures have been reached. Temperatures will rise 10-15 degrees during standing time. Therefore, undercook slightly to achieve the desired final temperature. Of course, you must keep meat covered or in the warm oven during this time to keep the heat inside.

Example:

Rare = 130 degrees before standing, 140 degrees after standing.

Medium = 150 degrees before standing, 160 degrees after standing.

Well = 160 degrees before standing, 170 degrees after standing.

Standing Time

As you can see, undercook by 20% -25% to allow for this. Food is 80% done when the microwave shuts off. I have taken this into consideration in the 6 Minute Per Pound Rule. Cook the proper length of time, then "tent" or cover the meat. Let stand 25% longer. This allows the continuation of the ongoing cooking procedure and for heat to distribute evenly.

Other Meat Information

Meats with natural fats will brown if cooked longer than 10 minutes. Fat will rise to the surface and caramelize. Recently, it has been determined that meats cooked in the microwave are healthier for us than meats cooked by other cooking methods. More fat is drawn off, therefore reducing fat in our diets. Also, conventional frying, broiling or barbecuing of meat, chicken or fish produces potential cancer-causing substances (heterocyclic aromatic amines which are caused by a reaction between the two substances amino acid and creatinine). Microwaving virtually eliminates this hazard.

SLOW COOKING

Unlike tender cuts of meat, roasts, briskets and other muscular meats need liquid to tenderize. When liquid is added around such meats, the liquid should be brought to a boil at 100% power. Power should then be reduced to 30% or 50% and meat slow cooked for 50-75 minutes per pound, covered. Turn over once or twice. It takes liquid and moisture to break down the connective tissue in less tender meats. It is important to cook a longer time at a lower temperature.

Other foods containing large amounts of liquid such as soups, stews, sauces, etc. should be brought to a boil at 100% power and then power should be reduced to 30-50% and slow-cooked for about 1/4 of conventional time. (Example: Spaghetti Sauce (Conventional Directions): Brown meat, add liquid and simmer for 3-4 hours; Spaghetti Sauce (Microwave Directions): Brown meat ; add liquid and bring to a boil. Reduce heat to 50% power and simmer for 1-1 1/2 hours.

DEALING IN MULTIPLES WHEN COOKING IN THE MICROWAVE

When the *Six Minute Per Pound Rule* discussed earlier is not used, the following rules should apply when cooking multiples of food.

Individual Food Items

1. Determine the time for cooking one food item such as a piece of chicken, potato or a single ear of corn-on-the-cob, etc.

2. Double the time to cook two pieces of the chosen food.

3. To increase the items by more than two, double second item and for each additional piece of food added use only one-half of the cooking time of the first item.

Example: One corn-on-the-cob = 3 minutes

Two corn-on-the cob = 6 minutes (time doubled)

Three corn-on-the-cob = 7 1/2 minutes or First Item + Time Doubled for Second Item + 1/2 first item for Third item. (Use this procedure for additional items also.)

Foods Made By Recipe

1. Cook recipe by time given in cookbook.

2. When doubling a recipe for a casserole, soup, etc., add one half of the cooking time of the original amount.

Example: Double Recipe = Time of First Recipe + 1/2 Time of First Recipe or 1 1/2 Times First Recipe

Recipe 1 = 30 minutes

Doubled Recipe = 30 minutes + 15 minutes or 45 minutes

MICROWAVE HINTS

Arranging—Stirring—Turning

1. Whenever possible or when casseroles do not become "set" or firm while cooking, stir once or twice. Bring the outer ingredients to the center and the less-cooked centers to the edge of the dish. This will ensure even cooking.

2. Although most foods cook around the edges before the centers get hot, here are a few exceptions when centers may get hot or done before the outside edges:

   a. For example, high sugar centers of jelly doughnuts will get hot before the cake   part since microwaves are quickly attracted to the sugar.

   b. As microwaves are very highly attracted to fat, the same is true with high-fat foods. For example, the egg yolk with high fat content will cook before the white is set.

Browning—Preparing—Toasting

1. Try sprinkling meats with brown gravy mix or bottled browning sauce for great brown color and flavor. Don't add salt as it dehydrates and toughens.

2. Toast shredded coconut by spreading 1/2 cup in a pie plate. Cook, uncovered, 3-4 minutes at 100% power until golden, stirring once or twice. Remember that coconut can burn, even in the microwave.

3. To toast almonds in the microwave oven, place them in a glass dish, microwave at 100% power for 4-6 minutes, stirring several times.

4. To prepare muscular meats for stews and other casseroles, prick meat with a fork or hammer slightly to break up connective tissue. Meat will be more tender.

5. Peel garlic cloves easily by placing the cloves on a rack and heating in the microwave (30 seconds per clove) at 100% power. Garlic will slide out of the skin.

6. With a little practice, it is easy to make complete meals in the microwave.

    a. Microwave food that requires the longest cooking time first (roasts, casseroles, etc.). These can always be reheated.

    b. Cook foods needing less cooking time (vegetables, fish, etc.) closer to serving time.

    c. At the last moment microwave small items (bread, rolls, etc.) and quickly reheat foods cooked earlier in the day.

You may partially microwave one item while you prepare another. Take out the first item while you cook another. Return the first and complete the cooking time. As a consultant and proud participant in the development of a complete meal "Stack Cooker", I might also suggest you contact a Tupperware Distributor and inquire about these wonderful products.

7. To speed up outdoor barbecuing, start your food in the microwave and finish on the barbecue. Cook meats 1/2 of the cooking time (based on 6 minutes per pound) at 100% power. Immediately place on the grill to finish. Do not let food cool off as this will not allow proper internal temperatures to be reached to deplete bacteria.

8. To peel onions more easily, place them in a covered container and microwave for 1-2 minutes at 100% power. This also helps remove the "hot" flavor from onions you plan to serve uncooked.

9. To speed up cooking of dried beans or peas which have not been soaked overnight, cover them with cold water and bring to a boil at 100% power for about 10 minutes. Reduce power and cook at 30% power for 30-40 minutes. They will be ready to use. For even more tender beans, bring them to a boil. Turn off heat and let them stand in the hot water for 30 minutes. Bring them to a boil one more time and they will then be ready to cook.

Heating—reheating—freezing—defrosting

1. Make several batches of pancakes the conventional way and freeze leftovers in 2-3 stack packages. When ready to use, cover loosely and warm each portion for 20-30 seconds or until hot at 100% power. Serve with syrup which has also been heated in the microwave.

2. Small amounts of food or sauce come out of jars and containers more easily if heated 10-20 seconds at 100% power. Saves lots of food!!

3. Small amounts of vegetables may be blanched in the microwave. Properly prepare vegetables, (chopped, whole, etc.). Figure how long it would take to cook them in the microwave at 6 minutes per pound at 100%

power. Take half of this time. Microwave, covered, stirring or rearranging halfway through. Plunge immediately into ice cold water to cool. Drain, pack and freeze. More nutrients, especially Vitamin C, are retained when microwaved than when conventionally blanched.

4. Place wet finger towels in a nonmetallic basket and heat in the microwave for 1-2 minutes at 100% power. This is especially nice to offer guests before or after dinner if a drop of vanilla, almond or other extract has been put in the water before heating. Gives such a nice scent.

5. A warm compress may be made by heating a wet wash cloth for 15-30 seconds at 100% power.

6. A hot compress may be made by heating a wet wash cloth for 30-45 seconds at 100% power.

7. Warm refrigerated cheese for various uses. Use the following time guide:

   a. Cheese for slicing: 30-60 seconds at 50% power.

   b. Softening cream cheese: To prevent curdling, soften at 30% power if straight from the refrigerator. Check every 30-60 seconds according to amount being softened.

   c. To restore full flavor to refrigerated cheese, heat 4 ounces for 10 seconds at 100% power.

8. Baby milk in glass bottles (plastic is not recommended) as well as baby food may safely be reheated in the microwave if correct timing is used. Never feed milk straight from the microwave. Allow standing time as milk will continue to heat after oven turns off. Be careful there is no steam build up in food or bottle that might cause burns. Shake the milk or stir the food to ensure even heat distribution. Test it yourself before serving to baby. Reheat at 50% power to prevent rapid rise in temperature. It only takes 40-50 seconds for 8 ounces of milk to reach body temperature. It is far safer to feed milk or food too cold rather than too hot.

9. Brandy and liqueurs may be carefully warmed in the microwave for flamed desserts. Place 2 tablespoons of brandy or liqueur in a small, heat-proof bowl. Heat at 100% power for 30-40 seconds, remove from oven and ignite with a taper. Carefully pour over the dish to be flamed. You may also soak a sugar cube in brandy, place on top of food and light it.

10. Cereal and milk may double in volume when they boil, so use a large enough dish.

11. For your information, a phenomena known as superheating occurs when a very hot liquid shows no sign of boiling. Boil-ups or eruptions may occur if the liquid becomes hotter than 212 degrees. This super heating occurs because a liquid requires points of nucleation within it to boil. (Nucleation is dust, imperfections, etc. in the cooking container or tiny gas bubbles coming out of the liquid as it heats.) Absence will cause superheating. Violent eruptions may occur when one of these agents such as instant coffee, rice, etc. is placed into the super heated liquid (water, broth, etc.). To avoid this, stir while heating or before particles are added. You may also let liquid stand a minute or two in the oven after heating.

Refreshing—softening—crisping

1. Freshen day old rolls or cookies for a few seconds at 100% power. Be sure not to overcook. Cookies will taste "just baked".

2. Dry or crisp older bread for croutons. Microwave 4 cups for 5-7 minutes at 100% power, stirring several times.

3. Freshen chips and crackers by microwaving 2 cups for 1 minute at 100% power, uncovered.

4. Soften frozen ice cream by microwaving for 30 seconds at 100% power to make it easier to scoop. Also, place a scoop of ice cream on "yesterday's pie". Heat for 10-15 seconds. The pie will be "fresh and warm" and the ice cream will not be melted.

5. To soften tortillas, place 4-6 tortillas between dampened paper towels and microwave at 100% power for 20-40 seconds. Unlike the conventional method of preparation which uses oil, this saves time as well as unwanted fat and calories from our diets.

6. To soften brown sugar that has become hard, place a slice of white bread or an apple wedge with 1 cup brown sugar. Heat in a covered container for 45-60 seconds at 100% power.

7. Soften butter (1 stick) from the refrigerator by heating for 30 seconds at 100% power. To melt butter, heat for 1 minute at 100% power. Clarify butter by melting 6-8 ounces of butter in a 2 cup microwave safe container on 30% power for 2-3 minutes or until completely melted. Let stand for 3-4 minutes then remove the foam and slowly pour off the yellow oil or clarified butter.

8. To keep microwaved cakes fresh, put an apple, cut in half, in the storage container with the cake.

9. When microwaving chocolate, don't cover chocolate as it will stiffen and moisture will develop. Melt at 50% power, stirring half way through. It takes about 2 minutes at this power to melt 3-4 ounces of chocolate. The chocolate does not actually "melt"... it retains its shape but will change from dull to glossy and will liquefy when stirred.

10. Crystallized honey may be clarified by microwaving for 1-2 minutes at 100% power. Be sure to remove the metal lid before heating.

MORE MICROWAVE HINTS

1. When thickening casseroles, add thickening just before the end of the cooking time (about 5-7 minutes) to prevent them from becoming gummy.

2. When thickening, cornstarch gives less gluey results than plain flour.

3. To clean a microwave, place 1 cup of water with 1 teaspoon of vanilla or almond extract in the microwave. Heat for 2 minutes at 100% power. Use a dry cloth to wipe out the inside of the oven. A pleasant smell will remain, too!!

4. Remove nut shells easily by placing 2 cups of nuts and 1 cup of water in covered glass casserole and heat for 1-2 minutes at 100% power.

5. If a fire should start in your microwave, press STOP and turn off the power at the wall switch. DO NOT OPEN THE DOOR. Fire will extinguish itself.

6. To dry glue quickly, place the freshly glued items in the microwave a minute or two at 100% power. Don't leave too long as paper and wood can burn if overheated.... **Do not place metal objects in the microwave.**

7. The flavor of wine is "brightened" or highlighted with a short cooking time in the microwave so adjust the quantity to your taste. Always use good quality wine.

BEFORE YOU COOK—
AND WHAT YOU SHOULD KNOW

Microwave cooking is somewhat different from conventional cooking, but many of the terms and techniques are the same. Since I advocate "conventional thinking" throughout my book, I am setting out a few "conventional basics" for those cooks who are just beginning or those that are not familiar with those "conventional basics".

Cooking success comes easy when you start with a good recipe and follow it to the letter.

HOW TO FOLLOW RECIPES

Make it a habit to take these steps every time you try a new recipe:

1. *Read the recipe before you begin.* Be sure you understand all cooking terms used *(See Cooking Terms Section).*

2. *Check the ingredient list.* Make certain you have everything you need, in the amount called for and assemble the ingredients.

3. *Do not substitute key ingredients if you are a beginning cook.* That goes for product forms and package size, too. Example: Pudding mixes come in two sizes (regular and family) as well as two types (regular and instant). Using either the wrong size or kind might result in a disaster.

4. *Check the utensils you will need.* Assemble items for measuring, mixing, cooking and serving.

5. *Do as much advance preparation as possible.* Chop, cut, melt or otherwise prepare ingredients before you start to assemble recipe.

6. *Measure accurately. (See How to Measure Ingredients).*

7. *Mix carefully.* Ingredients are combined in different ways (folding, beating, stirring, etc.) to achieve different results. *(See Cooking Terms).*

8. *Clean up as you work.* The less cluttered the work surface, the less chance of making a mistake.

9. *Cook as directed.* Follow suggested time, but be safe, start checking for doneness a few seconds early. Ovens and heating units can vary.

10. *Be careful about doubling or halving a recipe.* Some recipes can be increased or decreased successfully, some cannot. The beginning cook needs to get a bit of experience before trying this.

HOW TO MEASURE INGREDIENTS

Accurate measurements are essential if you want good results. All measurements should be level, unless the recipe directs otherwise.

Pay special attention to wording used in your recipes: For example, 1 pound shelled, deveined shrimp is a different measurement from 1 pound shrimp, shelled and deveined. There are more shrimp to the pound when they are weighed after the shells are removed than before and this could affect the number of servings.

Use the right measuring equipment: For dry ingredients, use a set of graduated measuring cups, consisting of 1/4, 1/3, 1/2 and 1 cup measures. For liquids, use a liquid measuring cup—glass or plastic with a rim above the cup line to prevent spilling. The cup should be marked for smaller measurements also. Measuring spoons are used for both dry and liquid ingredients. A standard set includes 1/4, 1/2 and 1 teaspoon and 1 tablespoon measures.

To Measure Liquids: Place the liquid measuring cup on a level surface. Lower your head so that the desired line of measurement is at eye level. Slowly pour liquid into the cup until it reaches the desired line. If using measuring spoons, pour the liquid just to the top of the spoon, not letting it spill over.

To Measure Dry Ingredients: Spoon lightly (or pack lightly if brown sugar) the ingredient into the measuring cup or spoon. With the edge, not the flat side of a straight edged knife, level off the top.

a. Flour: Do not sift today's finely milled all purpose and cake flours. Measure and use them right from the package or canister. Lightly spoon the flour into the cup and level off.

b. Granulated sugar: Lightly spoon the sugar into the measuring cup and level off with a straight edge.

c. Brown sugar: Pack lightly into the cup with the back of a spoon and then level. When properly packed, it will hold its shape when inverted from the cup.

d. Confectioners' sugar: Because this type sugar sometimes become lumpy, many recipes call for sifting. In that case, sift and then measure the same way as granulated sugar. If the recipe does not specify sifting, measure it and then sift if necessary to sift out lumps.

To Measure Shortenings:

a. Liquid shortenings, such as salad oil or melted butter, should be measured as liquids.

b. Solid shortening such as vegetable shortening, peanut butter, etc. should be spooned from the container and packed firmly in graduated measuring cup or spoon to the top. Level with the edge, not the flat side of the knife.

c. Butter and margarine: Each 1/4 pound stick measures 1/2 cup. The wrapping is usually marked in tablespoons for measuring smaller amounts. Use regular, not whipped butter or margarine in recipes since air is incorporated in the whipped product.

KNOW YOUR INGREDIENTS AND HOW TO USE THEM

Here are a few of the more common ingredients used in recipes:

Fats and Oils

Fats are solid at room temperature and are made from vegetable, animal products or both. Oils are fats that are liquid at room temperature and are usually of vegetable origin. Drippings are fats usually obtained by cooking fat meats (bacon, pork, beef, etc.)

Leavenings

Leavenings are substances that form bubbles of gas (carbon dioxide) or physical leavenings like steam and air. The gas, air or steam expand when a batter is heated making it light and affecting texture.

Yeast is a tiny plant that produces carbon dioxide from sugar when temperature and moisture are favorable for its growth. (Yeast comes in two forms... active dry and compressed).

Baking soda is an essential ingredient to baking powder or may be used as a leavening itself. It gives off gas when mixed with a food acid such as buttermilk, sour milk, vinegar, etc. One-fourth teaspoon baking soda plus 1/2 cup sour milk is equivalent to 1 teaspoon baking powder (double acting).

Baking powder makes many foods rise when baked, etc. Baking powder is a combination of baking soda, a dry acid and starch. There are two types— Double acting and Quick acting. Labels should clearly indicate the type it is. Double acting causes two reactions... the first during mixing, the second during baking. Quick acting bubbles only once and should be baked immediately so that the leavening action is not lost. Normally these two cannot be interchanged.

Eggs

Slightly beaten eggs are whole eggs beaten with fork only long enough to break up yolks and have streaks of white and yellow.

Beaten eggs are whipped until whites and yolks are blended.

Well beaten eggs are whole eggs beaten until light in color and texture.

Well beaten egg yolks are beaten until thick and literally lemon-colored foam is formed.

Stiffly beaten egg whites are beaten until peaks stand up straight, but still moist and glossy.

Soft peak egg whites are beaten until peaks droop and do not stand up straight.

Sugar

Sugar is the term that refers to beet or cane granulated white sugar. The most commonly used sugar for table and recipes.

Confectioners' or powdered sugar is granulated sugar crushed to make very fine, soft sugar.

Brown sugar is refined less than granulated. Molasses accounts for the color. Dark brown sugar contains more molasses and has stronger flavor than light brown sugar. They usually should not be interchanged in recipes because of this flavor difference. Granulated brown sugar is dry and pourable but should not be used as a direct substitute for regular brown sugar.

Raw sugar is unrefined crystalline sugar. It consists of coarse, sticky brownish-yellow crystals. Cannot be substituted for granulated sugar in most recipes.

Thickening Agents

Flour may be thoroughly blended with fat before liquid is added. Or it may be blended with cold liquid or with sugar before mixing with hot mixture.

Cornstarch may be blended with cold liquid or with sugar before adding to hot mixture.

Arrowroot cooks at a lower temperature and for less time than flour, etc. Ideal for sauces and custards containing eggs or other highly sensitive ingredients.

Tapioca (Quick cooking) needs no soaking. When used for thickening it may be added to recipes and heated to boiling and cooled without stirring. Tapioca also absorbs foods liquids.

Eggs are slightly beaten when used for thickening. To add them to a hot mixture, stir small amount of hot mixture into eggs, then stir egg mixture into remaining hot mixture.

The proportions for White Sauce (Medium Consistency) is as follows:

1 cup liquid + 2 T. flour (30 calories)
1 cup liquid + 1 T. cornstarch (30 calories)
1 cup liquid + 1 T. arrowroot (29 calories)
1 cup liquid + 4 tsp. tapioca (43 calories)

Flour

All-purpose flour, sometimes called general purpose flour is used in most general baking and as a thickening agent. It is made from hard or soft wheats or a blend of the two.

Cake flour is blended from soft wheats and has a softer texture than all purpose flour.

Self-rising flour is all purpose flour to which leavening agents and salt have been added in proportions suitable for general baking—not however for yeast breads and egg leavened cakes such as angel food.

Whole-wheat flour is also called graham flour. It contains all the components of the entire, cleaned wheat grain in the same natural proportions.

Other flours which are not so common are buckwheat, corn, potato, rice, rye and soy. These are used in special recipes and in special diets.

Milk and Cream

Milk is available fresh, cultured, canned and dried.

Fresh milk products include whole milk which contains not less than 3.25 percent milk fat or butterfat. Low-fat milk has between .02 and 2 percent milk fat. Non-fat milk contains no more than 0.1 percent of milk fat and skim milk has most of the fat removed. Half and Half or Light cream has much more fat than regular whole milk and is used to give richness and flavor. Whipping cream contains 30-40 percent fat, much more than Half and Half.

Cultured milk products include buttermilk, yogurt, sour cream and sour half and half. Buttermilk is thick, smooth, mildly acid. It is made by adding bacterial culture to fresh milk. Yogurt is thick, custard-like, mildly acid, usually made by fermenting partly skim milk. Sour cream is commercially cultured light cream. It has a thick texture and a rich, zesty flavor.

Canned milks include evaporated milk, which is whole milk with 60% of the water removed. When mixed with an equal volume of water it can be used in recipes calling for "milk". Undiluted, it can be used in place of cream. Sweetened condensed milk is concentrated whole milk with about half of the water removed and contains about 40 percent sugar. It should not be substituted for either fresh or evaporated milk.

Dry milk is whole milk with most of the water removed. Nonfat dry milk has also had most of the fat removed and contains no more than .20 percent fat by weight. Dry milk may be reconstituted with water according to package directions and used in recipes calling for "milk".

Vinegar

Vinegar is an acid liquid used for flavoring and preserving.

Cider vinegar is made from apple juice and has a mellow fruit flavor. It is an all-purpose vinegar and used in general cooking.

Distilled white vinegar is another all-purpose vinegar usually made from grain alcohol. It is especially good for canning and pickling since it does not alter the color of the food.

Special vinegars: Mixed herb or salad vinegars are blended vinegars which may be flavored with a combination of herbs such as basil, rosemary, tarragon and thyme. Wine vinegars made from red or white wine have a tangy flavor.

COOKING TERMS AND TECHNIQUES

Bake: To cook food covered or uncovered in an oven-type appliance.. For meats cooked uncovered, it's called roasting.

Barbecue: To roast or broil food on a rack, spit or under a heat unit. Food is usually brushed with a highly seasoned sauce as it cooks.

Baste: To moisten foods during cooking with a special sauce. Helps prevent dryness.

Beat: To make a mixture smooth with rapid, regular motion using a spoon, wire whisk, or mixer.

Binder: Eggs, starch or fat used to hold a mixture together.

Blanch: To scald, either to loosen the skin from some foods or to precook for a short time before canning or freezing.

Blend: To thoroughly mix two or more ingredients until smooth and uniform.

Boil: To cook in liquid in which bubbles rise constantly to the surface and break.

Bone: Remove bones from meat, fowl or fish.

Braise: To cook food slowly in a small amount of liquid in a covered container.

Bread: Coat with crumbs before cooking.

Broil: Cook by direct heat as over coals on a barbecue.

Candied: Cooking in syrup or sugar

Caramelize: Melting sugar slowly on low heat until it develops characteristic flavor and becomes brown in color.

Chill: To refrigerate food or let it stand in ice or ice water until cold.

Chop: Cutting small pieces with knife or food processor.

Coat: To sprinkle food with, or dip it into flour, etc. until completely covered.

Cool: Removing from heat and allowing food to come to room temperature.

Cream:

1. To make soft, smooth and creamy by beating with spoon or mixer.

2. To cook food in or serve with a white or "cream" sauce.

Crisp-tender: Food cooked (as vegetables) until they begin to soften.

Cube:

1. To cut food into small cubes (about 1/2 inch).

2. To cut meat or the surface of meat into a checkered pattern to increase the tenderness by breaking tough meat fibers.

Cut in: To distribute solid fat in flour or flour mixture by using pastry blender or two knives scissor fashion until flour coated fat particles are of desired size.

Deep-fry: To cook in hot fat deep enough for food to float on it.

Dice: To cut food into very small uniform pieces (about 1/4 inch).

Dissolve: To disperse a dry substance in a liquid to form a solution.

Dot: To scatter bits such as butter or margarine over surface of food.

Dredge: Coat with flour or other substance.

Flake: Break into small pieces.

Fillet: A piece of meat, fish or poultry from which all bones have been removed.

Flute: To make decorative edge, usually a pastry.

Fold-in: To combine delicate ingredients such as whipped cream or beaten egg whites with other foods by using a gentle, circular motion to cut down into the mixture, slide across the bottom of the bowl and bring some of the mixture up and over the surface.

Fry: To cook in fat such as deep-fry, pan-fry or saute in conventional cooking.

Glaze: A mixture applied to food which adds gloss and flavor.

Grate: To rub food on a grater or chop in a food processor to produce fine, medium or coarse particles.

Grease: To rub surface of dish or pan with fat to keep food from sticking.

Grill: To cook by direct heat or on a grill type appliance.

Grind: To reduce to particles in food grinder or food processor.

Hull: To remove outer covering or seeds from fruits or vegetables.

Julienne strips: Very thin uniform strips.

Knead: To work a food mixture with a press and fold motion.

Lukewarm: A temperature of about 95 degrees Fahrenheit—neither warm nor cold.

Marinate: Allowing food to stand in a liquid to add flavor or to tenderize.

Mince: To cut into very small pieces, using knife, grinder or food processor.

Mix: Combining ingredients until evenly distributed.

Pan-broil: To cook food, uncovered, on ungreased or lightly greased hot surface, pouring off fat as it accumulates.

Pan-fry: To cook in a small amount of fat.

Parboil: To boil or cook until partially cooked, usually before completing cooking by another method.

Peel: To remove outer covering of foods by trimming away with knife or vegetable peeler, or by pulling off.

Pit: To remove seed or pits from fruits.

Poach: To cook in simmering, hot liquid.

Pot-roast: To cook large pieces of meat or poultry by braising.

Precook: Partially cooking food before final cooking or reheating.

Preheat: To heat to desired temperature before putting food on to cook.

Puree: To press food through a fine sieve or blend in food processor so it becomes a smooth thick paste

Reconstitute: To restore concentrated food to its natural state, usually by adding water.

Roast: Cooking food, uncovered without water (usually in an oven).

Saute: Frying quickly. In the microwave this can be done without liquid or fat—simply cooking fast, covered to cause softening.

Scald:

1. To heat to just under the boiling point.

2. To dip certain foods in boiling water (*See Blanch*).

Scallop: Bake food with sauce or liquid. Usually crumb topped.

Score: Cut narrow slits part way through outer surface of food.

Sear: To brown surface of meat quickly with intense heat.

Shred: To cut food into slivers or slender pieces, using a knife, shredder or processor.

Sift: Putting dry ingredients through a sifter.

Simmer: To cook in a liquid just below the boiling point. Bubbles form slowly and collapse just below the surface.

Steam: Cook in steam. (In microwave cooking water is not normally needed to accomplish this... simply cover food tightly before cooking to produce steam.)

Steep: To allow food to stand in hot liquid to extract flavor and color.

Stew: To simmer in a liquid.

Stir: To mix foods in circular motion.

Toast: To brown in dry heat.

Toss: To mix foods lightly with a lifting motion using two forks or spoons.

Truss: Securing fowl or other meat with twine, skewers, etc.

Whip: To beat rapidly with mixer or whisk so air is incorporated and volume is increased.

Read the recipe before you begin. Be sure you understand all cooking instructions.

Healthy and Lean

T he recipes in this book have nutritional analysis and most have been adapted to be quite "lean" by using many low fat ingredients. This chapter, however, is set up to give you a complete overview of being healthy and eating healthy. The information will help you adjust the recipes even further if desired. Also included is information which should be helpful to those wishing to convert to a healthier lifestyle.

STUDY GUIDE FOR HEALTH

The following "pyramid" is the government's new dietary chart suggested for healthy eating. Through the years, USDA food guides have advised equal quantities of meat, breads, fruits, vegetables and dairy products and have been referred to as the basic 12, 7 or 4. The pyramid does not change what is recommended, but illustrates healthier eating concepts. There is a place for all types of foods unless there are specific health problems. Although the pyramid is just a guide, it will, at a glance, help us understand more about the foods we need, from what groups and in what amounts.

What's a "serving"?

Remember that daily serving sizes may be different than we might personally envision them. What we consider a serving size such as a sandwich, a piece of pizza, a plate of spaghetti, etc. may actually give us several USDA defined servings for one or more of the basic food groups.

Knowing what makes a serving is the best way to determine calories and fat and find your way around the food pyramid. Snack-food manufacturers will tell you the calories in ounces... but how many chips are in an ounce? The government says aim for 3 servings of vegetables a day... but what is a serving?

Let your fist, thumb and palm be your portion guide. Amounts approximate to a woman's hand of average size.

A. A fist = One cup (Your fist is about the same size as a cup.)

B. A handful = One to two ounces of snack food.

C. A thumb = One ounce of cheese.

D. A thumb tip = One teaspoon.

E. A palm = Three ounces.

Suggested serving sizes are approximately as follows:

Meat, Fish, Nuts	2-3 ounces per serving supplies protein, B vitamins, Iron and Zinc.
Dry Beans	1/2 cup, cooked, per serving supplies protein, vitamins and minerals—Thiamin, Riboflavin, Niacin and Iron.
Eggs	1 egg per serving supplies protein and most vitamins and minerals.
Vegetables	1/2 cup cooked vegetable or 1 cup raw vegetable per serving provides vitamins, minerals and fiber—Vitamin A and Vitamin C and is low in fat—eat a variety of dark green, yellow, orange and red.
Fruits and Juices	1/2 cup fruit juice or 1 medium-size fruit provides vitamins and minerals—Vitamin A and Vitamin C and is low in fat and sodium.
Milk Products	1 glass (8 oz.) milk or 1 small piece of cheese (1 oz.) provides vitamins and minerals as well as the best source for calcium.
Bread and Cereal	1 slice bread, 1/2 cup cooked cereal, 3/4 cup (1 oz.) ready-to-eat cereal, 1/2 cup rice or pasta-Rice and Pasta supplies Thiamin, Riboflavin, Niacin, Iron.
Fats, Oils, Sweets	Very small amounts, eat sparingly as few nutrients are provided—no quantity suggested.

Nutrition

Fruits and Vegetables

Washing—Scrubbing vigorously can destroy vitamins and minerals. Rinse fresh fruits and vegetables quickly. Rub gently if dirty, but never soak.

Cutting—Wait until the last possible moment to slice fresh vegetables and fruit because cutting and tearing destroy Vitamin C.

Cooking—Produce has the most food value when it is eaten raw. To minimize loss of nutrients use as little water as possible to cook. Microwave oven cooking is an excellent way to preserve minerals and vitamins because no water or very little is used.

Deep fat frying can destroy nutrients and boiling is least healthful.

Meat and Poultry

Stewing and braising can destroy important Vitamin B. Faster cooking methods such as microwave cooking, broiling, frying help to lock in vitamins.

Rare steak, therefore, will contain more nutrients than a well done one simply because it has been exposed to high heat for less time.

Barbecuing reduces fat content, but microwaving reduces fat content even more. Microwaves are attracted to the fat content before the water content of the food and effectively cooks out excess fat more quickly than other cooking methods.

Other Nutritional Factors

Refrigeration of fresh peas and lima beans in their pods help maintain nutritional value.

Rinsing rice or pasta after cooking causes vitamin loss.

Cooking pasta in salt water may draw out valuable vitamins.

When refrigerating, remember the shorter the storage time and the cooler the temperature, the less vitamins and minerals are lost.

Milk and cream retain more nutrients longer when stored in opaque containers.

Frozen foods stored at 15 degrees or higher can lose vitamins.

Use liquid when serving canned vegetables. Place juices in ice tray and freeze. Store in container in freezer and use for soups, etc.

Cover and store leftovers in refrigerator. Use quickly. Reheating after a few days can rob them of up to half of their original vitamins.

Avoid excessive trimming and chopping and decrease nutrient loss.

Store juices covered, or they will lose Vitamin C.

More About Nutrition and Diet Regarding Microwave Cooking

Microwave off fat in a flash. Because microwaves are attracted to fat molecules before the water content of food, fat melts away before food becomes overcooked.

Vegetables and fruits are more nutritious when cooked in the microwave because no water or very little is added. Also, a number of vitamins rapidly break down with exposure to heat and dissolve into cooking water. Because microwave cooking requires less water and exposes food to heat for a shorter period of time than conventional methods, fewer vitamins and minerals are lost.

Example: In a Vitamin C study, 3 1/2 ounces of microwaved cabbage emerged with 43 mg. of Vitamin C versus 25 mg. of Vitamin C for stove cooked.

Although grains don't necessarily cook quicker than conventionally, grains are microwave stars as they become plump and fluffier.

About Fat

Most Americans get nearly 40 percent of their calories each day from fat, dietitians say. That number should be 30 percent or less. Because fat contains more calories than protein or carbohydrates , people who trim fat can eat more protein and complex carbohydrates and still loose weight.

Dietary Fat—Fat is essential in our diet. All types of fat and oil have the same number of calories: 9 calories per gram. Fat is fat, no matter what its source.

Saturated Fat—Saturated fat can cause blood cholesterol to increase. Saturated fats are found in the largest amounts in meat and dairy products. They are also in hydrogenated oils and coconut, palm and palm kernel oils.

Monounsaturated Fats—Found in the most part in plant oils such as olive, peanut and canola oils.

Polyunsaturated Fats—Found in some oils that are liquid at room temperature such as safflower, sunflower, canola, corn, soybean and cottonseed. Hydrogenation is a process that makes an oil more solid at room temperature. Hydrogenated vegetable oils give processed foods like margarine, bread, crackers a longer shelf life. Hydrogenation makes an oil more saturated and saturated fats can raise your blood cholesterol level.

About Cholesterol

Cholesterol is a fat-like substance found in all foods of animal origin such as meat and dairy, but not in foods from plants. Some cholesterol is needed by the body, but too much can build up in arteries and cause heart disease, etc.

The "Leaning" of America

No need to stop eating any one food. Simply learn to eat lean—and nutritionally. Read nutrition labels on your foods.

1. Begin to cut the amount of fat you eat whenever you can. You can choose low-fat foods more often when shopping for food or eating out or use less fat when preparing foods at home. Be sure to check food labels so that hidden fats and cholesterol such as egg yolk solids, lard, whole milk products, vegetable products such as coconut and palm oils and other foods which cause foods to become more fat saturated.

1*. Eat more complex carbohydrates (70%-75%) such as bread, potatoes, rice, pasta, fruits and vegetables as they are filling and are burned off as energy. Reduce fat intake.

2. Check the fat facts. To determine the percentage of calories in a food that comes from fat:

a. Multiply the number of grams of fat in the food by 9.

b. Multiply the answer in Step 1 by 100.

c. Divide the outcome of Step 2 by the total number of calories in the product.

Example: 2% milk = 5 g. fat x 9 = 45; 45 x 100 = 4500. 4500 divided by 120 calories = 38% of total calories is fat.

To determine the maximum number of grams of fat you should average a day:

d. Figure out approximately how many calories you may healthfully consume on a daily basis.

e. Multiply the answer in Step 1 by .30.

Example: 1800 calories a day x .30 = 540 calories a day.

f. Each gram of fat contains 9 calories so divide the result of Step 2 by 9. Example: 540 divided by 9 = 60 grams of fat per day.

3. Be "salt" smart and limit your sodium intake. MSG, sodium bicarbonate (baking soda and sodium sulfite) are also salts and cause the body to retain water which is very frustrating for those trying to lose weight.

4. Scrutinize sugars. There are eight different names for sugar: dextrose, fructose, corn syrup, corn sweeteners, lactose, brown sugar, honey and molasses.

5. Increase metabolism by exercising.

6. Eat slowly and drink 8-12 glasses of water a day. Include watwer with meals.

7. Make meals appealing and attractive. Food will taste better.

FDA and USDA Definitions of Food Labeling Terms:

1. Free, Zero, No, Without: Means less than 5 calories per serving; less than .5 grams of fat or saturated fat; less than 2 milligrams cholesterol; less than 5 milligrams sodium; less than .5 grams sugar.

2. Low, Little, Few: No more than 40 calories per serving (120 calories per 100 grams for meals and main dishes); 3 grams or less total fat; 1 gram or less saturated fat; 20 milligrams or less cholesterol; 140 milligrams or less sodium; not defined for sugar.

3. Light, Lite: Generally 50 percent less fat, 50 percent less sodium or one-third fewer calories.

4. Reduced, Less, Lower, Fewer: Food must have at least 25% less of the nutrient than the food its being compared to

5. Lean: Less than 10 grams fat, 4 grams saturated fat and 95 milligrams of cholesterol per serving.

6. Extra lean: Less than 5 grams fat, 2 grams saturated fat and 95 milligrams cholesterol per serving.

Tips For Low-Fat Cooking

1. Use the "lean" machine, your microwave oven, to help you prepare low-fat foods. How?

a. Adding fat when cooking is not necessary. Microwave saute—just cover and cook. Then, add chicken broth or small amounts of butter for flavor only.

b. Prepare quick meals in less time than it takes to use more expensive, higher-fat convenience or prepared foods.

c. For quick meals, defrost and reheat leftovers of earlier "lean" preparations without adding fat.

d. Render fat from foods by cooking in the microwave before adding to casseroles.

2. Choose low fat turkey instead of beef or cook beef in colander to drain off all fat. Then rinse in hot water.

3. Choose white rather than dark meat from poultry. Dark meat contains more fat. Also, skin poultry. You may cook with skins on, but don't eat skins. If cooking in sauce, however, remove skin first.

4. When cooking tender meats, use a rack so fat will drip off. Trim visible fat before cooking. Skim off fat before serving stews, gravy, etc.

5. Before breading, dip meats or fish in lemon juice or skim milk instead of egg or sour cream . Use low fat bread for crumbs.

6. Rather than covering foods with sauce, brush them. Top with low-cal salsa instead of cream sauces.

7. Cut back on meat. Add more vegetables other than corn and peas.

8. Use stocks seasoned with herbs and wine instead of cream or butter sauces. To thicken use cornstarch/broth mixture rather than flour/butter roux with milk. Use low fat milk and cornstarch to enrich sauces instead of egg yolk and cream.

9. Choose rice vinegar for salad vinaigrettes. Because it tastes less acidic than other vinegars, you can use more vinegar and less oil. A no-caloric way to zest a salad is to sprinkle with a little garlic salt and add lemon or lime juice.

10. Rinse tuna, canned vegetables and feta cheese to reduce sodium.

11. Add carbonated water to juices to dilute calories.

12. Eat more complex carbohydrates (vegetables, fruits, bread, cereal, rice and pasta). They are filling without the fat and calories.

13. Foods that need a lot of chewing such as raw vegetables and grainy breads are more satisfying and help you eat less.

14. Always stop eating when full.

Modifying Your Recipes

Low-Fat Substitutions you can make and the reduced fat intake:

Original	Substitute	Fat Grams Saved
1 T. mayonnaise	1 T. reduced-calorie mayonnaise	6.0
1 c. whole milk	1 c. non-fat milk	7.8
1 c. sour cream	1 c. non-fat yogurt	32.1
1 c. heavy cream	1 c. evap. skim milk	56.0
1 c. grated cheese	1 c. non-fat grated cheese	80.0
8 oz. cream cheese	8 oz. cottage cheese and	
	1 T. lemon juice (blended)	28.0
1/2 c. oil	1/2 c. Liquid Butter Buds	
	or 1/2 c. apple-sauce	100.7
1 c. cream soup	1 c. broth	16.5
1 c. walnuts	1/2 c. walnuts	47.4
1 lb. ground beef	1 lb. ground white turkey (skinless)	115.2
2 eggs	2 Egg Beaters or egg whites	12.0
1 c. choc. chips	1/2 c. choc. chips	18.0

Other Substitutions To Reduce Fat:

2% milk .... Skim milk
Whipped Cream .... Whipped evap. skim milk
Jam/Jelly .... Low sugar spreads
1 oz. unsweetened chocolate ... 1/4 c. cocoa plus 1 tsp. vegetable oil
Butter or shortening .... Soft tub butter or margarine
Pecans .... Grape-nut cereal
Cream or butter .... Herb seasoned stock

Other Things To Do

1. In many recipes for fruit breads, muffins, bar cookies and the like, the oil or shortening may be reduced by 1/3 to 1/2 without influencing the success of the recipe:

a. Cakes/Soft drop cookies = no more than 2 T. fat per cup of flour.

b. Pie Crust = 1/2 c. margarine for 2 cups of flour.

c. Muffins, quick breads, biscuits = no more than 1-2 T. fat per cup of flour.

2. Make guilt-free brownies by substituting 1/2 nonfat yogurt or applesauce and 3 egg whites in your brownie mix for 1/2 c. oil and 2 eggs.

3. Replace oil, butter and margarine with liquid Butter Buds, low-fat margarine, applesauce or corn syrup. If recipe calls for only oil, substitute 1/2 applesauce and 1/2 non-fat milk to obtain moistness. When mixed with sugar, flour and egg substitute, use corn syrup to replace oil.

4. Without adverse effect, cut sugar content in recipes by 25% and increase sweet spices (cinnamon, ginger, vanilla and almond extract) which are flavorful sugar substitutes. Instead of sugar to sweeten baked goods, use fructose which has the same calories per spoonful but is sweeter. You can use 1/3 as much.

5. Learn to use spices, flavorings, low calorie maple syrup and fruit juices instead of sugar to sweeten.

6. In recipes calling for several eggs, all or part of the yolks can be eliminated without drastically affecting results. Simply add an extra white for every 2 yolks discarded. Also, you may use liquid or frozen egg substitute (made with egg whites rather than yolks) instead of whole eggs.

7. Use egg whites, not whole eggs, for coating meat, fish or poultry.

8. Reduce cheese, nuts and chocolate chips up to 1/2 in recipes.

9. Whole wheat flour can stand in for half the flour called for in most recipes. You get more fiber, vitamins and minerals plus a richer color and taste.

10. Instead of cream to thicken pasta sauce, use chicken broth and 1 tablespoon of cream. Instead of tossing pasta with oil, use a few tablespoons of the water the noodles were cooked in.

11. For creamy sensation without cream and butter, use olive oil, buttermilk, low-fat or skim milk or cottage cheese, pureed vegetables or low-fat yogurt. A new cheese from Vermont, a fromage blanc, can be used in diet sauces. Simply puree and dilute with broth or a vegetable puree. You have a very creamy sauce. For stronger taste or flavor, add only small amounts of hard cheese, such as blue cheese, as these contain 40% fat.

12. Make crustless pumpkin pie or quiche.

13. Use acids such as lemon juice, vinegar, tomatoes, hot pepper—or herbs and spices for flavor.

14. If oil must be used, use spray-on oil for sauteing, for oiling baking pans and for spritzing hot cooked vegetables, pasta or rice and even for dressing salads. Instead of high-fat salad dressing, spray a little oil on the salad mixture, toss, then add vinegar, lemon juice, orange juice or grapefruit juice to taste. Spray vegetables, etc. lightly with butter spray rather than doting with butter.

notes:

_____
_____
_____
_____
_____
_____
_____
_____
_____
_____
_____
_____
_____
_____
_____
_____
_____
_____
_____

Appetizers/Beverages

DID YOU KNOW?

♥ Perk 1 tablespoon of powdered dishwashing detergent and a full pot of water to get your coffee pot really clean.

♥ A thimble over the percolator stem before measuring in the coffee will prevent it from getting clogged... Be sure to remove before perking!

♥ Put a piece of chocolate or a vanilla bean in the coffee filter before you add your coffee... Or add 1/2 envelope of instant cocoa mix to one cup of strong black coffee... Cafe Mocha at half the cost.

♥ A pinch of salt in your coffee grounds before brewing intensifies and improves the flavor. Works in hot chocolate, too.

♥ If a dish is cracked, boil it for 45 minutes in sweet milk and the crack will "weld" together. It will be hardly visible and will be strong enough to stand the same usage as before.

♥ For a quick counter cleanup (vegetable peels, crumbs, etc.), whisk them into a dust pan that has been stuck under the counter edge.

♥ To get a car out of the mud, snow or sand, let a little of the air out of the tires and drive off.

♥ Freshen a stale lunch box by leaving a piece of bread dampened with vinegar on the inside.

♥ Keep a toothbrush by the kitchen sink as it is great for cleaning beaters, graters and other kitchen utensils.

♥ Salting water hastens the boiling process.

♥ Whiten shoe laces by washing them in sour milk.

♥ So the syrup bottle caps will loosen easily, give the top of the bottle a "spritz" of no-stick vegetable oil before putting the cap on the bottle.

♥ To cut costs, keep liquids covered, as they release moisture, causing refrigerator to work overtime.

♥ Store ice cubes in a brown bag. They won't stick together.

♥ Before emptying the vacuum cleaner bag, sprinkle a newspaper with water. When emptied onto the paper there will be no scattering of dust.

♥ Take a vinyl tablecloth instead of a blanket to picnics. Spread vinyl side down to keep out ground moisture.

♥ Dip a new broom in hot salt water before using, as it toughens the bristles and makes the broom last longer.

♥ A tool caddy for gardening can be made from an old golf bag. It has places for tools, towel, etc... even has wheels!

♥ Clean barbecue grate easily by placing cool grate inside a large plastic garbage bag with 1/2 cup powdered dishwasher detergent and enough hot water to cover the grill. Seal, shake and let stand several hours. Rinse thoroughly.

♥ Wax your ashtrays and the odors won't linger, nor will the ashes cling. Saves washing, as they can be wiped clean with a paper towel.

Appetizers

Almond Haystack
Best Beef Dip
Curried Chutney Spread
Franks In Mustard Cream
Mexican Pie
Red Caviar and Cheese Dip
Rose Cheese Ball
Salmon Party Ball
Spinach Dip
Stuffed Cheese Log
Sweet and Sour Chicken
Texas Caviar
Yummy Dip

Beverages

Instant Coffee Mocha
Hot Cranberry Punch
Cappuccino
Banana Punch

Almond Haystack

Serves 40

1 1/2 cups toasted slivered almonds
1 (8 oz.) package light cream cheese, divided
4 cups finely chopped ham
3/4 cup nonfat mayonnaise dressing, divided
1/3 cup sliced green onions including tops
1/4 cup sweet pickle relish

Place almonds in microwave dish. Microwave 4-6 minutes at 100% power, stirring occasionally until lightly toasted. Set aside. Place 4 ounces of cream cheese in microwave dish and soften at 30% power for 1 minute. Stir in 1/2 cup mayonnaise, 1/2 cup toasted almonds, onion and pickle relish. Mix well. Chill. Shape into one large or two small oval shaped mounds. Blend 1/4 cup mayonnaise and remaining softened cream cheese. Mix well. Frost mound with mixture. Chill slightly and cover with slivered almonds. Serve with crackers or party rye bread. (Makes 5-6 cups)

Nutrition (per serving): 74 calories
Saturated fat .... 1 g
Total Fat .... 5 g (60% of calories)
Protein .... 5 g (26% of calories)
Carbohydrates .... 3 g (14% of calories)
Cholesterol .... 12 mg
Sodium .... 300 mg
Fiber .... 0 g

Best Beef Dip

Serves 12

This recipe is good at room temperature also. Remember to cook dishes containing sour cream at lower "temperatures" or power levels so sour cream will not curdle and separate. Also, cold cream cheese should be softened on low power so it will not curdle.

1 (8 oz.) package light cream cheese
1/2 cup nonfat sour cream
2 tablespoons skim milk
1/8 teaspoon Worcestershire sauce
1 (3 oz.) package dried beef
2 tablespoons chopped onions

2 tablespoons chopped bell pepper
1/4 cup chopped pecans

Place cheese in microwave safe casserole. Heat for 1-2 minutes at 30% power until cheese is soft. Stir in sour cream, half and half, Worcestershire sauce and onion. Rinse dried beef under warm water and chop. Mix into cheese mixture and top with pecans. Heat for 3-7 minutes at 70% until mixture is very hot, but not boiling. Serve with chips. (Makes 1 1/2 - 2 cups.)

Nutrition (per serving): 88 calories
Saturated fat	3 g
Total Fat	7 g (71% of calories)
Protein	4 g (19% of calories)
Carbohydrates	2 g (11% of calories)
Cholesterol	19 mg
Sodium	88 mg
Fiber	0 g

Curried Chutney Spread

Serves 20

This is an excellent stuffing for celery or dates. Fat free cream cheese will lower fat grams in this recipe.

2 (8 oz.) packages light cream cheese
1/2 cup chopped toasted almonds
1/2 cup chutney
1 teaspoon curry powder
1/2 teaspoon dry mustard

Place almonds on microwave safe plate. Microwave at 100% power for 3-6 minutes, stirring several times until almonds are toasted. Set aside. Soften cream cheese for 2-4 minutes at 30% power. Mix all ingredients, reserving a few almonds to garnish spread. Chill and serve with crackers. (Makes 2-3 cups)

Nutrition (per serving): 98 calories
Saturated fat	4 g
Total Fat	7 g (66% of calories)
Protein	3 g (12% of calories)
Carbohydrate	5 g (22% of calories)
Cholesterol	17 mg
Sodium	94 mg
Fiber	0 g

Franks In Mustard Cream

Serves 25

Use the lowfat hot dogs and soups that are in the market and reduce the fat grams tremendously. When sour cream boils, it can curdle, cooking longer at lower power will prevent this.

2 pounds regular or cocktail hot dogs

1 cup nonfat sour cream

1 (10 3/4 oz.) can cond. cream of celery soup

1/3 cup prepared mustard

1 teaspoon creamed horseradish

Drain hot dogs and cut into bite size pieces. Mix sour cream, soup, mustard and horseradish. Stir into hot dogs. Heat at 70% power for 12-20 minutes, stirring once or twice until hot and bubbly. (Makes 6 cups)

Nutrition (per serving): 109 calories
Saturated fat .... 2 g
Total Fat .... 6 g (50% of calories)
Protein .... 5 g (18% of calories)
Carbohydrates .... 9 g (32% of calories)
Cholesterol .... 18 mg
Sodium .... 388 mg
Fiber .... 0 g

Mexican Pie

Serves 20

Mozzarella or Monterey jack cheese may be used in this recipe as substitutes or mix the three.

1(8 oz.) package light cream cheese

1(4 oz.) can chopped mild green chiles

1 whole green bell pepper, chopped

1 onion, chopped

1 (16 oz.) can chili without beans

1 (4 oz.) can sliced pitted black olives

1 1/2 cups grated lowfat cheddar cheese

Soften cream cheese for 1 minute at 30% power. Spread cheese in the bottom of 10 inch quiche plate or casserole. Spread chili over cheese. Top with green chiles, green pepper and onion. Sprinkle with black olives and then cheddar/mozzarella cheese. Cover and microwave at 70% power for 10-15 minutes until mixture is bubbly hot. Serve with tortilla chips. (Makes 4-5 cups.)

```
Nutrition (per serving): 108 calories
    Saturated fat ........................................ 3 g
    Total Fat ............................................. 8 g (64% of calories)
    Protein ............................................... 6 g (22% of calories)
    Carbohydrates ...................................... 4 g (14% of calories)
    Cholesterol ......................................... 19 mg
    Sodium ............................................... 232 mg
    Fiber ................................................. 0 g
```

Red Caviar and Cheese Dip

Serves 8

To restore the full flavor of refrigerated cheeses, microwave 3-4 ounces for 10 seconds at 100% power. Heat cheeses for 30-60 seconds at 50% power to make them easier to slice or serve. Cream cheese dips such as this should be heated at even lower power levels to prevent curdling.

12 ounces light cream cheese

2 tablespoons minced green onions including tops

1/4 teaspoon crumbled dried basil

1/8 teaspoon freshly ground black pepper

2 ounces red caviar

Soften cream cheese at 30% power for 1-1 1/2 minutes. Mix onion, basil and cheese. Stir until smooth. Season with pepper and add 1/3 of caviar. Mix until light pink. Transfer to serving bowl. Add remaining caviar, stirring very gently. Cover and refrigerate for at least 8 hours, preferably overnight. Let mixture stand for 30 minutes at room temperature before serving or heat at 10% power for several minutes. Serve with crackers and crudites. (Makes 1 1/2 cups.)

```
Nutrition (per serving): 132 calories
    Saturated fat ........................................ 7 g
    Total Fat ............................................. 11 g (77% of calories)
    Protein ............................................... 6 g (18% of calories)
    Carbohydrates ...................................... 2 g (5% of calories)
    Cholesterol ......................................... 74 mg
    Sodium ............................................... 276 mg
    Fiber ................................................. 0 g
```

Rose Cheese Ball

Serves 15

Cheese may also be shaped into two balls instead of a rose. Roll one in parsley and one in pecans.

1 (6 oz.) jar Old English cheddar cheese
4 ounces blue cheese
1 (8 oz.) package light cream cheese
1 tablespoon Worcestershire sauce
1/8 teaspoon garlic powder
1/8 teaspoon hot pepper sauce
3/4 teaspoon salt
1 pinch crushed red pepper flakes
2 teaspoons paprika
1/2 cup minced fresh parsley

Place cheese in microwave container. Heat for 2-4 minutes at 30% power until cheese softens. Mix cheeses together. Add Worcestershire sauce, garlic, red pepper sauce, salt and red pepper. Blend thoroughly with hands. Shape cheese into a rose with pieces of cheese made into rose leaves. Sprinkle rose with paprika and leaves with parsley. Serve with crackers. (Makes 2 cups.)

```
Nutrition (per serving): 116 calories
    Saturated fat ........................................................ ..6 g
    Total Fat ............................................................. 10 g 74% of calories)
    Protein ................................................................ ..6 g (21% of calories)
    Carbohydrates .................................................... ..1 g (5% of calories)
    Cholesterol ........................................................ 29 mg
    Sodium ............................................................... 357 mg
    Fiber .................................................................. 0 g
```

Salmon Party Ball

Serves 15

1 (16 oz.) can salmon
1 (8 oz.) can light cream cheese
1 tablespoon lemon juice
2 teaspoons minced onions
1/2 cup chopped pecans
1 teaspoon creamed horseradish
1/4 teaspoon salt
1 teaspoon liquid woodsmoke flavoring
3 tablespoons chopped fresh parsley
2 drops red food coloring

Place cheese in microwave dish. Microwave at 30% power for 2-4 minutes until cheese has softened. Drain and flake salmon, remove skin and bones. Mix all other ingredients except nuts and parsley with cream cheese. Chill until firm. Shape cheese mixture into a ball and roll in pecans and parsley. (Makes 2 - 2 1/2 cup.)

```
Nutrition (per serving): 109 calories
        Saturated fat ....................................................... 3 g
        Total Fat ............................................................. 8 g (66% of calories)
        Protein ............................................................... 8 g (29% of calories)
        Carbohydrates .................................................... 1 g (5% of calories)
        Cholesterol ......................................................... 28 mg
        Sodium ............................................................... 268 mg
        Fiber .................................................................. 0 g
```

Spinach Dip

Serves 10

1 (10 oz.) package frozen chopped spinach

4 slices bacon, cooked and crumbled

1 (8 oz.) package light cream cheese, cubed

1/3 cup Picante sauce

1/3 cup chopped green onions including tops

1/4 teaspoon ground cumin

1 tomato, seeded and chopped

1/2 cup shredded light Monterey Jack cheese

Place boxed spinach in microwave container and pierce with fork. Cook at 100% power for 3-5 minutes until hot. Drain well. Mix spinach, cheese, Picante sauce, onions and cumin. Heat at 70% power for 2-5 minutes until cheese melts. Stir in tomato and bacon. Heat additional 1-2 minutes at 70% power until bubbly. Sprinkle with cheese and serve with crackers or chips. (Makes 2- 2 1/2 cups.)

```
Nutrition (per serving): 148 calories
        Saturated fat ....................................................... 6 g
        Total Fat ............................................................. 12 g (75% of calories)
        Protein ............................................................... 6 g (16% of calories)
        Carbohydrates .................................................... 3 g (9% of calories)
        Cholesterol ......................................................... 23 mg
        Sodium ............................................................... 261 mg
        Fiber .................................................................. 0 g
```

Stuffed Cheese Log

Serves 50

This recipe may be halved if desired. Wrap tightly and freeze for later use if desired. To cut fat content of this recipe, use the low fat version of cheese, sour cream and mayonnaise.

2 pounds Velveeta cheese
1 (8 oz.) package light cream cheese
1 cup nonfat sour cream
1 cup nonfat mayonnaise
1 bunch green onions including tops, chopped
3/4 cup chopped pecans
1 (4 oz.) can sliced pitted black olives
1/2 cup chopped pimiento-stuffed green olives
1 (4 oz.) can chopped mild green chiles
1 pinch paprika
1 dash cayenne pepper
1 bunch fresh parsley
2 (16 oz.) packages crackers

Soften cream cheese in microwave for 2-3 minutes at 30% power until quite soft. Mix cream cheese, sour cream and mayonnaise until smooth. Set side. Place cheese in middle of large piece of plastic wrap. Cover with another large piece of plastic wrap and press or roll cheese until it is a large thin rectangle. Down center of cheese rectangle place generous layers of ingredients in following order: green onion, sour cream mixture, pecans, black olives, green olives and green chiles. Fold into thirds, placing one side lapping the other. Roll tightly in plastic wrap. Slide onto large tray or cookie sheet and refrigerate until firm. After firm, unwrap cheese and invert, seam side down on platter. Garnish ends with parsley and sprinkle with paprika and cayenne. Serve with crackers. (Makes 7 cups.)

Nutrition (per serving): 175 calories	
Saturated fat	4 g
Total Fat	9 g (48% of calories)
Protein	7 g (16% of calories)
Carbohydrates	15 g (35% of calories)
Cholesterol	19 mg
Sodium	588 mg
Fiber	0 g

Sweet and Sour Chicken

Serves 40

These wings may be cooked on a microwave rack and basted with sauce for about 6 minutes per pound. This will give a drier, more broiled effect rather than one in sauce. Also, this is a good dish to be served as a main dish if chicken pieces rather than wings are used.

40 chicken wings
14 ounces ketchup
1 (8 oz.) can tomato sauce
3/4 cup apple cider
1/4 teaspoon Worcestershire sauce
1 teaspoon dry mustard
1 teaspoon ground ginger
1 1/2 cups packed brown sugar
1/2 cup sugar
1 clove garlic

Cut off tip of wing and discard. Cut wings in half at joint and place in a large microwave casserole in a single layer. Mix ketchup and other ingredients. Microwave sauce for 8-10 minutes at 100% until hot. Pour over wings. Cook for 5 minutes at 100% power, reduce to 50% power and continue to slow cook for 15-30 minutes, rearranging if necessary until chicken is tender and thoroughly cooked.

```
Nutrition (per serving): 150 calories
    Saturated fat ............................................... 2 g
    Total Fat ...................................................... 8 g (47% of calories)
    Protein ......................................................... 9 g (25% of calories)
    Carbohydrates ............................................. 11 g (28% of calories)
    Cholesterol .................................................. 38 mg
    Sodium ......................................................... 191 mg
    Fiber ............................................................. 0 g
```

Texas Caviar

Serves 15

If you are one of those who are not particularly fond of black eyed peas, this is an excellent way to serve them for New Years' "good luck".

2 (16 oz.) cans black-eyed peas
1 whole tomato, seeded and chopped
1 whole green bell pepper, seeded and chopped
3 green onions including tops, thinly sliced
4 ounces chopped pimientos, drained
1 jalapeño pepper, seeded and minced
3 tablespoons light olive oil
2 tablespoon salsa, medium or hot
2 teaspoons Dijon mustard
2 cloves garlic, minced
1/2 teaspoon sugar
1/2 teaspoon dried thyme

1/8 teaspoon tabasco sauce
1 dash salt
1 dash black pepper

Drain peas and rinse under cold water. Drain thoroughly and place in a large bowl. Mix in tomato, green pepper, onion, pimientos and jalapeño pepper. Whisk together olive oil, salsa, mustard, garlic, sugar, thyme, tabasco, salt and pepper. Pour over bean mixture and toss to mix thoroughly. Chill for several hours. Serve as a dip for chips. (Makes 4-5 cups.)

Nutrition (per serving): 78 calories
Saturated fat .... 0 g
Total Fat .... 3 g (35% of calories)
Protein .... 3 g (17% of calories)
Carbohydrates .... 9 g (48% of calories)
Cholesterol .... 0 mg
Sodium .... 192 mg
Fiber .... 1 g

Yummy Dip

Serves 25

Use less nuts to lower fat grams if desired. When I cater, I put this spread in a fresh pineapple shell for a beautiful presentation. It may also be put into a serving container and used as a dip or made into a ball, rolled in pecans and served as a spread. You may also decorate with olives, pimiento, etc. This keeps very well in refrigerator for days and may be frozen

2 (8 oz.) packages fat free cream cheese
1 (8 oz.) can crushed pineapple in juice, drained
1 cup chopped pecans
1/4 cup finely chopped green bell peppers
2 tablespoons finely chopped onions
3/4 teaspoon seasoned salt

Soften cream cheese for 2-4 minutes at 30% power. Mix in all remaining ingredients, reserving 1/2 cup pecans. Place cheese spread in desired container, garnish with pecans and chill. Serve with crackers. (Makes 3 cups)

Nutrition (per serving): 55 calories
Saturated fat .... 0 g
Total Fat .... 3 g (51% of calories)
Protein .... 2 g (11% of calories)
Carbohydrates .... 5 g (38% of calories)
Cholesterol 0
Sodium .... 149 mg
Fiber .... 0 g

Instant Coffee Mocha

Serves 6

Always keep this on hand for that special drink. This is as good as many of the mixes found in the markets, but much less costly.

4 tablespoons instant coffee
7 tablespoons instant cocoa mix
6 tablespoons nondairy creamer
2 tablespoons confectioners' sugar
6 cups water

Combine all ingredients and place in air tight container. When ready to serve place 3 teaspoons of mix with 7-8 ounces water. Heat at 100% for 2-3 minutes until very hot. Stir before serving. (1 Cup servings.)

```
Nutrition (per serving): 61 calories
    Saturated fat ........................................ 0 g
    Total Fat ............................................. 0 g (5% of calories)
    Protein ............................................... 4 g (27% of calories)
    Carbohydrates .................................... 10 g (68% of calories)
    Cholesterol ......................................... 0 mg
    Sodium ............................................... 43 mg
    Fiber .................................................. 0 g
```

Hot Cranberry Punch

Serves 35

This is an exceptionally good punch and is worth the effort. The cranberry mixture may be made ahead of time and put together with remaining ingredients when ready to use.

4 cups fresh cranberries
12 cups water
3 1/2 cups sugar
1/2 cup red hots candy
10 whole cloves
3 oranges
4 lemons
15 cups hot water

Place cranberries and 8 cups of water in large casserole. Microwave at 100% power for 15-16 minutes until very hot. Reduce heat to 50% power and cook for about 20 minutes or until berries are very soft. Strain through sieve, separating berry meat and skin. Discard skins. Add remaining water, sugar, red hots and cloves to cranberry mixture. Cook at 100% power for 8-12 minutes or until sugar has dissolved. Let mixture cool. Remove cloves. While liquid is cooling, juice oranges and lemons. Add juice to cooled mixture. Serve mixture hot by adding an equal amount of hot water. (1 cup servings.)

```
Nutrition (per serving): 106 calories
   Saturated fat ....................................................... 0 g
   Total Fat ............................................................. 0 g (1% of calories)
   Protein ............................................................... 0 g (1% of calories)
   Carbohydrates .................................................... 26 g (99% of calories)
   Cholesterol ......................................................... 0 mg
   Sodium ............................................................... 1 mg
   Fiber ................................................................... 0 g
```

Cappuccino

Serves 18

Heating times will vary on this as some freezers are colder than others and ice cream will become more firm. Coffee and half and half temperatures may also vary. This is a "special occasion" drink.

> 1/2 gallon lowfat vanilla ice cream
> 1/2 gallon lowfat chocolate ice cream
> 1 cup evaporated skim milk
> 1 1/2 cups strong coffee
> 4 ounces Kahlua
> 4 ounces brandy
> 4 ounces rum

Place ice cream in large casserole. Heat in microwave at 30% power, stirring occasionally until ice cream melts. Add remaining ingredients and continue heating at 50% power until very hot.

```
Nutrition (per serving): 175 calories
   Saturated fat ....................................................... 2 g
   Total Fat ............................................................. 4 g (25% of calories)
   Protein ............................................................... 4 g (7% of calories)
   Carbohydrates .................................................... 22 g (46% of calories)
   Cholesterol ......................................................... 6 mg
   Sodium ............................................................... 79 mg
   Fiber ................................................................... 0 g
```

Banana Punch

Serves 20

7 cups hot water
3 1/2 cups sugar
5 bananas, mashed
1 (6 oz.) can frozen orange juice
1 (6 oz.) can frozen lemonade
1 No. 3 can (46 oz.) pineapple juice
1 quart ginger ale
Vodka, to taste, Optional

Place hot water in casserole along with sugar. Heat at 100% power for 15-20 minutes until sugar is dissolved and water boils. Let cool. Thoroughly mash bananas. Add remaining ingredients except for ginger ale and liquor. Freeze. Remove from freezer 2-3 hours before serving time. Mix in ale and vodka. (1 cup servings.)

Nutrition (per serving): 231 calories
Saturated fat .... 0 g
Total Fat .... 0 g (1% of calories)
Protein .... 1 g (1% of calories)
Carbohydrates .... 57 g (98% of calories)
Cholesterol .... 0 mg
Sodium .... 5 mg
Fiber .... 0 g

notes:

_____
_____
_____
_____
_____
_____
_____
_____
_____
_____
_____
_____
_____
_____
_____
_____
_____
_____
_____
_____
_____

Salads/Soups/Sandwiches

DID YOU KNOW?

♥ Eggs peel more easily if a teaspoon of salt is added while boiling. Plunge immediately into ice water for 10-15 minutes. Gently roll eggs to "shatter" the peeling. Shells will scoot right off.

♥ To seal eggs when they crack during boiling, add a little vinegar to the water.

♥ A teaspoon of salt in the water prevents the eggs from cracking during boiling.

♥ How fresh are your eggs? In a bowl of cool water:

1. A very fresh egg will sink and lie horizontally on bottom. (High yolk and compact white.)
2. A week old egg will lie tilted up. (White will be more liquid.)
3. Two to three week old eggs will stand upright. (Yolk will spread out... watery white will run.)
4. Four weeks or older, egg will float and should be thrown out.

♥ Wet knife to keep egg yolks from crumbling when slicing hard-cooked eggs.

♥ A touch of vinegar in water when poaching eggs helps to set the whites so they will not spread.

♥ Bread crumbs added to scrambled eggs will improve the flavor and also will make larger helpings.

♥ A few drops of lemon juice in beaten eggs improve the taste of an omelette.

♥ To prevent mold, store cheese in a tightly covered container with some sugar cubes.

♥ Cottage cheese stays fresher longer if stored upside down in the refrigerator.

♥ Warm the knife before cutting cheese. It will cut as easily as butter.

♥ Keep packages of blue or Roquefort cheese in the freezer. The cheese will crumble perfectly when scraped with a knife.

♥ Slice a stack of flour tortillas into one-inch strips and add to noodles, stew, etc. Simmer for 5-10 minutes. You will have dumplings that are easy, inexpensive and good enough to fool dumpling experts.

♥ If drained pasta sticks together, boil it another minute or so or run it under boiling water... it will be as good as new.

♥ For perfect pasta, bring salted water to a boil, stir in pasta, cover and turn off heat. Let stand for 15 minutes or until done.

♥ If pasta such as lasagne is to be used in a dish that requires further cooking, reduce pasta cooking time by one-third.

♥ If you are not serving spaghetti immediately when done, you may leave it in hot water if you add enough ice cubes or cold water to stop cooking process. Reheat by running it under hot tap water in strainer while shaking it vigorously.

♥ To keep bread or rolls hot, place aluminum foil under the napkin in your basket.

Salads/Soups/Sandwiches

Salads

Anatole Pasta Salad
Best Ever Shrimp Salad
Fruit Salad
Green And White Salad
Green Bean Salad
Hot Macaroni Salad
Hunters Salad
Name It Yourself Salad
Old Fashioned Cole Slaw
Olé Salad
Oriental Rice Salad
Sinatra Pasta Salad
Sour Cream Potato Salad
Spicy Wine Fruit Salad
Spinach And Apple Salad
Tuna Supreme Salad
Vegetables A´La Grecque

Soups

Avocado Cheese Soup
Bean Soup
Best Chili
Cheesy Corn Soup
Cincinnati Chili
Gazpacho
Onion Soup Picante
Soup Elegant
Vegetable Chili
Vichyssoise

Sandwiches

Cheese Bacon Sandwich
Crab Open Face Sandwich
Ground Beef Sandwiches

Salads

Anatole Pasta Salad

Serves 8

To lower fat grams, use lowfat meats.

1 pound egg noodles or pasta shells
4 ounces pepperoni, julienned
2 ounces dry salami, julienned
1 red bell pepper, seeded and julienned
1 clove garlic, minced
2 mashed anchovy fillets
2 ounces liquid egg substitute
1 teaspoon Dijon mustard
1 cup light olive oil
1/4 cup red wine vinegar
3 tablespoons lemon juice
2 tablespoons parmesan cheese

Cook noodles per directions or in microwave (See Main Dish-Pasta Chart).
Rinse and drain well. Add meat and red pepper. Set aside. Mix garlic,
anchovy fillets, egg and mustard. Set aside. Blend olive oil, wine vinegar,
lemon and cheese. Slowly add olive oil mixture to garlic/anchovy mixture.
Whisk until smooth. Mix into pasta mixture. Chill.

Nutrition (per serving): 599 calories
Saturated fat .... 8 g
Total Fat .... 40 g (60% of calories)
Protein .... 17 g (12% of calories)
Carbohydrates .... 43 g (29% of calories)
Cholesterol .... 81 mg
Sodium .... 898 mg
Fiber .... 0 g

Best Ever Shrimp Salad

Serves 8

2 cups shell or elbow macaroni
1 cup diced celery
1 cup small cooked shrimp
2 tablespoons finely chopped onions
1 cup lowfat sour cream

1/4 cup chili sauce

2 tablespoons creamed horseradish

1 teaspoon Worcestershire sauce

1/2 teaspoon dry mustard

1/2 teaspoon salt

1/8 teaspoon white pepper

1/8 teaspoon dried marjoram

Cook macaroni in the microwave or conventionally. Rinse and drain well. Add celery and shrimp. Combine remaining ingredients and gently mix with macaroni mixture. Chill and serve on greens.

```
Nutrition (per serving): 163 calories
    Saturated fat ....................................................... 1 g
    Total Fat .............................................................. 3 g (15% of calories)
    Protein ................................................................. 10 g (24% of calories)
    Carbohydrates ..................................................... 25 g (61% of calories)
    Cholesterol ......................................................... 39 mg
    Sodium ................................................................ 238 mg
    Fiber .................................................................... 1 g
```

Fruit Salad

Serves 12

3 eggs, slightly beaten

2 tablespoons melted lowfat margarine

2 tablespoons flour

1 cup sugar

1 cup pineapple juice

1 pound miniature marshmallows

1 (16 oz.) can pineapple tidbits in juice, drained

1 (16 oz.) can grapes, drained

1 (16 oz.) can Queen Anne cherries, drained

1 pint evaporated skim milk

1 apple, chopped, optional

2 bananas, sliced, optional

In medium size microwave measure, mix eggs, margarine, flour and sugar. Gradually stir in pineapple juice. Heat at 50% power for 4-6 minutes, stirring once or until mixture thickens. Place marshmallows, pineapple tidbits, grapes and cherries in large mixing bowl. Pour hot egg mixture over fruit and stir thoroughly. Cool for several hours. Whip cream until firm and fold into fruit salad. Add apples and bananas at this time if desired. Refrigerate overnight.

```
Nutrition (per serving): 350 calories
     Saturated fat ....................................................... 1g
     Total Fat ................................................................ 3 g (7% of calories)
     Protein .................................................................. 7 g (8% of calories)
     Carbohydrates ..................................................... 74 g (85% of calories)
     Cholesterol ........................................................... 55 mg
     Sodium .................................................................. 104 mg
     Fiber ..................................................................... 1 g
```

Green And White Salad

Serves 12

For dressing, use remaining part of marinade if you wish. Add only enough " fresh" Italian dressing to make 1 cup.

1 head cauliflower
1 bunch broccoli
4 stalks celery, diagonally sliced
1 large green bell pepper, coarsely chopped
1 1/2 cups small cherry tomatoes
1 1/2 cups low-cal Italian salad dressing, divided
3 tablespoons lemon juice
1 tablespoon half and half
1 1/2 teaspoons freshly ground black pepper

Break cauliflower and broccoli into uniform pieces. Mix with remaining vegetables and marinate in 1-1 1/4 cups Italian dressing for several hours. Mix remaining Italian dressing, lemon juice, half and half and pepper. Set aside. Drain vegetables and add dressing. Chill.

```
Nutrition (per serving): 131 calories
     Saturated fat ....................................................... 1 g
     Total Fat ................................................................ 6 g (40% of calories)
     Protein .................................................................. 4 g (11% of calories)
     Carbohydrates ..................................................... 16 g (50% of calories)
     Cholesterol ........................................................... 0 mg
     Sodium .................................................................. 622 mg
     Fiber ..................................................................... 3 g
```

Green Bean Salad

Serves 6

When onion is strong in flavor, place onion in microwave container, cover and cook (according to size) for 15 seconds - 1 minute at 100% power. This will help the flavor become more mellow.

2 (16 oz.) cans whole green beans
1 onion, chopped

1 teaspoon onion salt
1 pinch black pepper
1/2 cup nonfat sour cream
1/4 cup nonfat mayonnaise
1 teaspoon lemon juice
1/4 teaspoon dry mustard
2 teaspoons chopped fresh chives
1 tablespoon creamed horseradish
1/4 teaspoon onion juice

Drain green beans. Add onion to green beans. Stir in onion, salt and pepper. Let stand in refrigerator for 1 hour. Drain well. Mix dressing ingredients in small mixing bowl. After draining beans, mix dressing into beans. Serve chilled.

Nutrition (per serving): 95 calories
Saturated fat .... 0 g
Total Fat .... 0 g (33% of calories)
Protein .... 5 g (20% of calories)
Carbohydrates .... 18 g (77% of calories)
Cholesterol .... 0 mg
Sodium .... 156 mg
Fiber .... 2 g

Hot Macaroni Salad

Serves 8

This dish with a salad and garlic toast makes a family favorite meal. This is cooked at a temperature that would be comparable to the way it would be cooked conventionally. 70% power is like a 350 degree oven. Also, chicken or turkey may easily be substituted for tuna. For a special treat add 1/2 cup sliced almonds, 1/8 teaspoon thyme and 1/8 teaspoon marjoram.

2 cups cooked drained macaroni
1/4 cup finely chopped green bell peppers
1/4 cup finely chopped green onions including tops
1/2 cup finely chopped celery
1/4 cup chopped pimientos
1 (6 oz.) can sliced mushrooms, drained
1 (4 oz.) can chopped mild green chiles
1 (10 3/4 oz.) can lowfat cond. cream of mushroom soup
2 teaspoons lemon juice
1/2 cup nonfat mayonnaise
1/2 teaspoon salt

1 cup grated longhorn lowfat cheddar cheese
1 (6 oz.) can light tuna in water, drained
1/8 teaspoon paprika
1/3 cup crushed cracker crumbs

Place macaroni in large mixing bowl. Cook onion, green pepper and celery, covered, in microwave casserole for 1-3 minutes at 100% power. Add pimientos, mushrooms and chiles. Mix vegetables and all other remaining ingredients except for paprika and crumbs with macaroni. Put in 8 x 12 inch casserole partially covered. Place in microwave for 20-30 minutes at 70% power until bubbly hot. Sprinkle with cracker crumbs while standing.

Nutrition (per serving): 206 calories
Saturated fat .... 1 g
Total Fat .... 4 g (16% of calories)
Protein .... 16 g (32% of calories)
Carbohydrates .... 27 g (52% of calories)
Cholesterol .... 12 mg
Sodium .... 685 mg
Fiber .... 1 g

Hunters Salad

Serves 12

To cook potatoes, simply peel and cube potatoes, place with about 1/4 cup water in microwave, cover and cook for 4-6 minutes or until potatoes are tender. Drain well. As eggs will be chopped for this salad, microwave hard boil eggs for this salad (See Main Dish-Eggs).

2 cups cooked cubed red potatoes
1 cup frozen lima beans, cooked and drained
1/2 cup chopped green onions including tops
1 cup chopped celery
1 cup shredded carrots
1 (4 oz.) can mushroom stems and pieces, drained
1/3 cup cooked cubed beets
4 hard boiled eggs, chopped
1 cup low-cal French salad dressing
1/2 cup nonfat mayonnaise
1 dash salt
1 dash cayenne pepper

Mix all ingredients except for mayonnaise. Marinate for several hours. Blend in mayonnaise just before serving.

Name It Yourself Salad

Serves 8

Other flavors of gelatin such as lime are good in this salad also.

1 (3 oz.) package lemon gelatin
3 cups hot water
1 (3 oz.) package light cream cheese, softened
8 ounces instant whipped light cream
1 cup diced celery
2 ounces chopped pimientos
1 (14 oz.) can crushed pineapple in juice
1/2 cup chopped pecans or walnuts

Heat water for 6-7 minutes at 100% power until very hot. Dissolve gelatin in hot water. Place gelatin into refrigerator until slightly set. Add softened cream cheese and whip. Mix in whipped topping and remaining ingredients. Refrigerate until firm.

Old Fashioned Cole Slaw

Serves 8

This may be served as a luncheon main dish if chopped turkey, chicken, tuna or ham is added. Other flavors of gelatin such as lemon or lime are also good in this salad.

1 (3 oz.) package vegetable gelatin
1/4 teaspoon salt
1 1/2 cups water, divided

1 tablespoon vinegar

1/2 cup nonfat mayonnaise

1/2 cup nonfat sour cream

1 teaspoon grated onions

1 tablespoon prepared mustard

3 cups shredded cabbage

2 tablespoons chopped pimientos

1 tablespoon chopped fresh parsley

In microwave measure, microwave 1 cup water for about 3 minutes until boiling. Add gelatin and stir until dissolved. Mix vinegar, 1/2 cup cold water, mayonnaise, sour cream and mustard until blended. Blend into gelatin mixture. Stir in onion, cabbage, pimiento and parsley. Turn into mold and refrigerate until firm.

```
Nutrition (per serving): 74 calories
   Saturated fat ..................................................... 0 g
   Total Fat ............................................................ 0 g (2% of calories)
   Protein ............................................................... 3 g (14% of calories)
   Carbohydrates ................................................... 16 g (84% of calories)
   Cholesterol ........................................................ 0 mg
   Sodium ............................................................... 324 mg
   Fiber ................................................................... 0 g
```

Olé Salad

Serves 16

Remember to microwave hard boil eggs in your microwave (See Main Dish-Eggs).

2/3 cup light olive oil

1/3 cup vinegar

1/3 clove garlic, minced

1 teaspoon dried basil

1 teaspoon salt

1/2 teaspoon freshly ground black pepper

3 large tomatoes, peeled and chopped

2 cucumbers, peeled and thinly sliced

10 fresh mushrooms, sliced

1 green bell pepper, seeded and chopped

4 green onions including tops, thinly sliced

4 hard boiled eggs, chopped

1/2 pound lowfat Swiss cheese, cut into strips

Mix oil, vinegar, garlic, basil, salt and pepper. Heat in microwave measure for 1-2 minutes to blend spices. Cool. Mix vegetables in large bowl. Pour oil mixture over vegetables and chill for several hours or overnight. Top with cheese and egg to serve.

```
Nutrition (per serving): 170 calories
        Saturated fat .................................................... 3 g
        Total Fat ........................................................ 14 g (75% of calories)
        Protein .......................................................... 7 g (16% of calories)
        Carbohydrates ................................................ 4 g (10% of calories)
        Cholesterol .................................................... 62 mg
        Sodium .......................................................... 195 mg
        Fiber ............................................................. 0 g
```

Oriental Rice Salad

Serves 12

Remember to cook rice and eggs in the microwave. Rice will be fluffier and will not stick. For eggs there is no need to use conventional methods that take more time and energy when eggs are to be chopped anyway.

2 cups cooked rice
4 hard boiled eggs
1 (16 oz.) can bean sprouts, drained
1/2 cup green bell peppers, julienned
2 green onions including tops, finely minced
1/2 cup thinly sliced black olives
1 clove garlic, finely minced
1/2 cup lowfat mayonnaise
2 teaspoons soy sauce
2 teaspoons cider vinegar
1 teaspoon sugar
1 dash salt
1 dash black pepper

Mix rice and eggs in large mixing bowl. Rinse bean sprouts under cold water and drain well. Add sprouts, green peppers, onions and olives to rice mixture. Chill ingredients. Blend garlic, mayonnaise, soy sauce, vinegar, sugar, salt and pepper. Stir into rice mixture just before serving.

```
Nutrition (per serving): 187 calories
        Saturated fat .................................................... 1 g
        Total Fat ........................................................ 5 g (22% of calories)
        Protein .......................................................... 6 g (12% of calories)
        Carbohydrates ................................................ 31 g (66% of calories)
        Cholesterol .................................................... 73 mg
        Sodium .......................................................... 217 mg
        Fiber ............................................................. 1 g
```

Sinatra Pasta Salad

Serves 12

This is the salad I served to Barbara and Frank Sinatra when they were house guests of friends of ours. Frank liked it so much Barbara asked for the recipe.

12 ounces cooked long spaghetti
1 (16 oz.) can bean sprouts, drained
1 cup frozen peas, defrosted
1/2 cup chopped green bell peppers
1/2 cup chopped onions
1/2 cup sliced celery
1/2 cup drained sliced water chestnuts
1 (4 oz.) can sliced mushrooms, drained
3/4 cup lowfat mayonnaise
1/4 cup soy sauce
1 teaspoon hot Chinese mustard
1/2 teaspoon garlic powder
1 teaspoon salt
1/4 teaspoon white pepper

Break spaghetti into 3 inch lengths and cook as directed. Drain and rinse several times in cold water. Stir together spaghetti and remaining vegetables. Mix mayonnaise, soy sauce, Chinese mustard, garlic powder, salt and pepper. Stir into spaghetti mixture. Chill overnight.

```
Nutrition (per serving): 178 calories
    Saturated fat ...................................................... 1 g
    Total Fat ............................................................ 3 g (18% of calories)
    Protein ............................................................... 6 g (14% of calories)
    Carbohydrates .................................................... 30 g (68% of calories)
    Cholesterol ........................................................ 4 mg
    Sodium ............................................................... 621 mg
    Fiber .................................................................. 1 g
```

Sour Cream Potato Salad

Serves 12

Remember, eggs may be microwave hard boiled (See Main Dish– Eggs).

8 red potatoes, cubed and cooked
6 hard boiled eggs, chopped
3/4 cup finely diced celery

1/2 cup finely chopped green onions including tops
1/3 cup finely chopped cucumbers
1/2 cup clear lite Italian salad dressing
3/4 cup nonfat mayonnaise
1/2 cup nonfat sour cream
1 1/2 teaspoons celery seed
1 teaspoon prepared mustard
1/2 teaspoon creamed horseradish
1 dash tabasco sauce
1/8 teaspoon garlic powder
1 dash salt
1 dash black pepper

Peel and cube potatoes. Place potatoes with 1/2 cup water in microwave casserole. Cover and cook for 6 minutes per pound, stirring occasionally or until potatoes are done. Drain and let potatoes cool slightly. After eggs are hard boiled, cool and chop, reserving one yolk for garnish. Mix in remaining vegetables and Italian dressing. Let vegetables marinate in refrigerator for several hours. Mix mayonnaise, sour cream and remaining ingredients. Blend into potato mixture and chill covered overnight. Garnish with crumbled egg yolk before serving.

Nutrition (per serving): 217 calories
Saturated fat .... 1 g
Total Fat .... 4 g (16% of calories)
Protein .... 7 g (14% of calories)
Carbohydrates .... 38 g (70% of calories)
Cholesterol .... 107 mg
Sodium .... 350 mg
Fiber .... 1 g

Spicy Wine Fruit Salad

Serves 6

1 (16 oz.) can apricot halves in syrup
1/2 cup port wine
4 tablespoons lemon juice
1 stick cinnamon
2 tablespoons frozen orange juice concentrate
2 fresh pears, pared and quartered
2 bananas, sliced
4 lettuce leaves

Drain apricots and reserve 1/2 cup syrup. Mix syrup, wine, lemon juice, cinnamon and orange juice in medium sized microwave measure. Heat at 100% power for 2-3 minutes. Cool. Place apricots and pears in bowl and add wine mixture. Toss and chill thoroughly. Add bananas before serving. Serve on lettuce leaves.

```
Nutrition (per serving): 189 calories
  Saturated fat ........................................................ 0 g
  Total Fat ............................................................. 1 g (2% of calories)
  Protein ................................................................ 1 g (3% of calories)
  Carbohydrates .................................................... 39 g (83% of calories)
  Cholesterol ......................................................... 0 mg
  Sodium ................................................................ 7 mg
  Fiber ................................................................... 1 g
```

Spinach And Apple Salad

Serves 8

Dressing may be prepared ahead and refrigerated. Reheat before serving. May be stored for up to 1 week. Also, for a sweeter dressing add a bit more sugar. .

1 1/2 pounds fresh spinach
1 red delicious apple, coarsely chopped
1/4 cup salted peanuts
1 cup liquid egg substitute, well beaten
1/2 cup sugar
1/4 cup dry mustard
1 teaspoons salt
2 cups evaporated skim milk
2/3 cup white vinegar

Wash, stem and dry spinach. Tear leaves into large bowl and sprinkle with apple and peanuts. Blend eggs, sugar, mustard and salt. Mix well. Slowly stir in 1 cup cream and vinegar. Heat at 70% power for 6-10 minutes, stirring occasionally until mixture thickens. Whisk in remaining cream. Pour over spinach. Toss and serve.

```
Nutrition (per serving): 226 calories
  Saturated fat ........................................................ 1 g
  Total Fat ............................................................. 6 g (24% of calories)
  Protein ................................................................ 14 g (25% of calories)
  Carbohydrates .................................................... 29 g (52% of calories)
  Cholesterol ......................................................... 3 mg
  Sodium ................................................................ 510 mg
  Fiber ................................................................... 1 g
```

Tuna Supreme Salad

Serves 8

Noodles may be served separately for each person to sprinkle on salad if desired.

2 (6 oz.) cans solid white tuna in water, drained
1 cup chopped celery
1/2 cup diced green bell peppers
1 (6 oz.) can sliced water chestnuts, drained
1/3 cup sliced green onions including tops
1/4 cup chopped pimientos
1/2 cup sliced pitted black olives, drained
1/2 cup non fat mayonnaise
1 tablespoon cider vinegar
2 tablespoons light cream
1/2 clove garlic, crushed
1 (4 oz.) can chow mein noodles

Place tuna and vegetables in large mixing bowl. Mix mayonnaise, vinegar, cream and garlic and stir into tuna/vegetable mixture. Chill. Just before serving add Chinese noodles. Serve immediately on salad greens.

Nutrition (per serving): 178 calories
Saturated fat .... 2 g
Total Fat .... 6 g (33% of calories)
Protein .... 13 g (30% of calories)
Carbohydrates .... 17 g (37% of calories)
Cholesterol .... 21 mg
Sodium .... 598 mg
Fiber .... 1 g

Vegetables Á La Grecque

Greek Vegetables

Serves 24

I use this colorful, easy to serve salad when catering large groups. Green beans may be substituted for artichoke hearts if desired.

1 head cauliflower
6 stalks celery, sliced into 1 inch pieces
4 large carrots, julienned
2 green bell peppers, seeded and chopped into bite size pieces

1 onion, sliced into thin rings
1/2 pound fresh mushrooms, halved
2 (10 oz.) packages frozen artichoke hearts, defrosted
1 (16 oz.) can pitted black olives, drained
4 ounces chopped pimientos
2 3/4 cups water
3/4 cup light olive oil
1/4 cup lemon juice
1 tablespoon sugar
2 tablespoons red wine vinegar
3/4 teaspoon salt
1 1/2 teaspoons dried thyme
1 teaspoon dried sage
1 teaspoon fennel seeds
1/2 teaspoon cracked black pepper
2 teaspoons seasoned salt
1/2 teaspoon tabasco sauce
Boston lettuce leaves

Break cauliflower into florets. Place in large 5 quart casserole with celery, carrots, green peppers and onion rings. Microwave, covered, for approximately 4 minutes per pound. Add mushrooms and remaining vegetables except for lettuce. Mix remaining ingredients in a separate microwave casserole and heat for 3-12 minutes at 100% power until boiling. Pour over vegetables and let marinate for at least 12 hours in refrigerator before serving. Serve on lettuce leaves in chilled salad bowl.

Nutrition (per serving): 162 calories
Saturated fat .... 1 g
Total Fat .... 9 g (52% of calories)
Protein .... 3 g (8% of calories)
Carbohydrates .... 16 g (40% of calories)
Cholesterol .... 0 mg
Sodium .... 806 mg
Fiber .... 3 g

Soups

Avocado Cheese Soup

Serves 12

This is a very thick rich soup. If you like a bit thinner consistency, thin with milk. Remember to soften cream cheese at 30% power in the microwave so it will not curdle.

2 (8 oz.) packages light cream cheese, softened
12 ounces prepared guacamole
4 cups chicken broth
8 ounces nonfat sour cream
1 teaspoon curry powder
1 teaspoon reduced calorie ranch salad dressing mix
1/2 teaspoon white pepper
3 tablespoons rum, optional
1/4 teaspoon dried dill weed
2 dashes tabasco sauce
Toasted slivered almonds

Place softened cream cheese with guacamole in blender or food processor. Add remaining ingredients except for almonds and blend well. Chill before serving. Garnish with almonds.

Nutrition (per serving): 171 calories
Saturated fat	6 g
Total Fat	14 g (73% of calories)
Protein	6 g (14% of calories)
Carbohydrates	5 g (13% of calories)
Cholesterol	30 mg
Sodium	690 mg
Fiber	0 g

Bean Soup

Serves 4

1 (10 3/4 oz.) can cond. bean and bacon soup
2 1/2 cups skim milk
1 (10 oz.) can tomatoes and green chiles
2 teaspoons curry powder
1 dash salt
1 dash black pepper

Mix all ingredients and heat at 70% power for 15-20 minutes until mixture is very hot.

Nutrition (per serving): 171 calories
Saturated fat	1 g
Total Fat	4 g (20% of calories)
Protein	10 g (24% of calories)
Carbohydrates	24 g (55% of calories)
Cholesterol	4 mg
Sodium	1000 mg
Fiber	1 g

Best Chili

Serves 12

Notice that we are using conventional methods to cook this recipe—brown meat, saute vegetables and then slow cook to blend flavors. Use your microwave as you would your stove. Ground turkey may also be used in this recipe.

2 pounds lean ground beef
1 large green bell pepper, chopped
1 large onion, chopped
4 stalks celery, chopped
1 (10 oz.) can tomatoes and green chiles
2 cups beef broth
1 1/2 cups beer or water
1 (6 oz.) can tomato paste
2 (4 oz.) cans mild green chiles
3 tablespoons chili powder
2 tablespoons cocoa
2 teaspoons sugar
2 tablespoons vinegar
1 1/4 teaspoons dried oregano
1 bay leaf
1/2 teaspoon ground allspice
1/2 teaspoon garlic powder
1/2 teaspoon dried basil
1/2 teaspoon ground cumin
1/2 teaspoon crushed red pepper
4 jalapeño peppers, seeded, optional
2 (16 oz.) cans chili beans

Place ground beef, onion, green pepper and celery in microwave colander. Cook 6 minutes at 100% power, stirring once to break apart. Cook an additional 6-9 minutes until meat is no longer pink. Place beef, onion, green pepper and celery in large microwave casserole. Add remaining ingredients except for beans. Continue to cook approximately 15-20 minutes at 100% power until mixture is boiling. Reduce power to 50% and simmer for 30 minutes to 1 hour, stirring once or twice, so flavors will blend. Add beans and continue to heat until very hot.

```
Nutrition (per serving): 464 calories
    Saturated fat .......................................................... 7 g
    Total Fat ................................................................. 17 g (34% of calories)
    Protein .................................................................... 27 g (24% of calories)
    Carbohydrates ........................................................ 48 g (41% of calories)
    Cholesterol ............................................................. 57 mg
    Sodium .................................................................... 1057 mg
    Fiber ........................................................................ 6 g
```

Cheesy Corn Soup

Serves 4

This is a very hearty soup and needs only garlic bread and perhaps a salad to complete the meal.

> 1/3 cup chopped green bell peppers
> 1/4 cup chopped onions
> 8 ounces light cream cheese, cubed
> 1 cup skim milk
> 1 cube chicken bouillon
> 1 cup boiling water
> 1 (8 oz.) can cream-style corn
> 1/2 teaspoon salt
> 1/8 teaspoon black pepper

Place pepper and onion in microwave casserole. Cover and cook for 1-2 minutes until vegetables soften. Add cream cheese and milk. Heat at 70% power for 3-6 minutes, stirring once or twice until cheese is melted and mixture is smooth. Dissolve bouillon cube in boiling water. Stir into cream cheese mixture. Add remaining ingredients and continue to heat at 70% power, stirring occasionally for 5-10 minutes or until soup is very hot.

```
Nutrition (per serving): 228 calories
    Saturated fat .......................................................... 9 g
    Total Fat ................................................................. 14 g (55% of calories)
    Protein .................................................................... 9 g (16% of calories)
    Carbohydrates ........................................................ 17 g (29% of calories)
    Cholesterol ............................................................. 44 mg
    Sodium .................................................................... 992 mg
    Fiber ........................................................................ 0 g
```

Cincinnati Chili

Serves 8

This is the chili made famous in Cincinnati, Ohio. Spices may be adjusted to taste. Toppings may be added or left off. If two ingredients are added it is called 3 way chili... if all three are added it is called 4 way chili. This is fun to serve to guests as it is different from the chili known by most people.

  1 pound extra lean ground beef
  2 onions, finely chopped
  3 cloves garlic, minced
  1 cup tomato sauce
  2 tablespoons catsup
  3/4 cup water
  1 tablespoon red wine vinegar
  1 tablespoon paprika
  1/2 teaspoon salt
  1/2 teaspoon freshly ground black pepper
  1/2 teaspoon crushed red pepper
  1/2 teaspoon ground cumin
  1/2 teaspoon ground turmeric
  1/2 teaspoon dried marjoram
  1/2 teaspoon ground allspice
  1/2 teaspoon ground cinnamon
  1/4 teaspoon ground cloves
  1/4 teaspoon ground nutmeg
  1/4 teaspoon ground mace, optional
  1/4 teaspoon ground cardamom, optional
  1/4 teaspoon ground coriander
  1 whole bay leaf
  1 tablespoon chili powder
  1 teaspoon honey
  1 tablespoon cocoa
  1 cup tomato juice, optional
  9 ounces cooked spaghetti
  1 (16 oz.) can kidney beans, heated
  2 sweet onions, chopped
  1 1/2 cups grated lowfat cheddar cheese

Place beef, onion and garlic in casserole dish. Cook for 6-10 minutes at 100% power, stirring occasionally, until meat is no longer pink and vegetables are tender. Drain thoroughly. Add tomato sauce, catsup and water. Cook at 100% power for 4-7 minutes until mixture boils. Add spices, honey and cocoa. Cover. Lower power to 50% and simmer for 15 minutes. Add tomato juice if mixture is dry. Remember, however, that this should be a thick sauce. Discard bay leaf. Place a portion of spaghetti in bowl. Top with chili, beans, onion and cheese to taste.

```
Nutrition (per serving): 514 calories
    Saturated fat ....................................................... 6 g
    Total Fat ............................................................. 15 g (26% of calories)
    Protein ................................................................ 36 g (28% of calories)
    Carbohydrates .................................................... 60 g (46% of calories)
    Cholesterol ........................................................ 51 mg
    Sodium ............................................................... 559 mg
    Fiber .................................................................. 5 g
```

Gazpacho

Serves 12

Heat a cup of water for 1-2 minutes in your microwave. Add bouillon granules to dissolve.

4 large tomatoes, chopped
2 cucumbers, peeled and sliced
2 sweet onions, chopped
24 ounces V8 type vegetable juice
1 teaspoon beef bouillon granules
3 cups water
3 tablespoons vinegar
1 tablespoon olive oil
2 cloves garlic, minced
1/4 teaspoon ground cumin
1/2 teaspoon seasoned salt
1/2 cup Picante sauce, mild to hot, optional
2 tablespoons Worcestershire sauce
2 tablespoons lemon juice
1/2 teaspoon sugar

Puree tomatoes, cucumbers and onion in food processor. In large mixing bowl, blend in vegetable juice and bouillon which has been dissolved in a small amount of water. Mix in all remaining ingredients and chill thoroughly before serving.

```
Nutrition (per serving): 64 calories
    Saturated fat ....................................................... 0 g
    Total Fat ............................................................. 2 g (21% of calories)
    Protein ................................................................ 2 g (10% of calories)
    Carbohydrates .................................................... 11 g (69% of calories)
    Cholesterol ........................................................ 0 mg
    Sodium ............................................................... 412 mg
    Fiber .................................................................. 1 g
```

Onion Soup Picante

Serves 8

3 cups thinly sliced onions
2 drops microwave browning sauce, optional

2 cloves garlic, minced

1/4 cup melted lowfat margarine

2 2/3 cups beef broth

2 cups tomato juice

1/2 cup Picante sauce, mild to hot

1 cup shredded light Monterey Jack cheese

1 cup croutons

Place onions and garlic into melted margarine and browning drops. Cook uncovered, for 4-5 minutes at 100% power stirring once or until onions are golden. Stir in remaining ingredients except for croutons and cheese. Microwave at 50% power for 5-10 minutes or until very hot. Ladle into bowls. Sprinkle with cheese and croutons.

Nutrition (per serving): 156 calories
Saturated fat .... 3 g
Total Fat .... 8 g (48% of calories)
Protein .... 8 g (20% of calories)
Carbohydrates .... 12 g (32% of calories)
Cholesterol .... 0 mg
Sodium .... 784 mg
Fiber .... 1 g

Soup Elegant

Serves 8

This soup is easy to make but your guests will think you have worked all day to present such an elegant dish. Try substituting lobster meat or shrimp for a change.

1 (10 3/4 oz.) can lowfat cond. cream of mushroom soup

1 (10 3/4 oz.) can cond. cream of asparagus soup

1 1/2 cups skim milk

3/4 cup nonfat sour cream

1/4 cup dry sherry

1 (8 oz.) can lump crabmeat, drained

Mix soups and milk in 2 quart microwave casserole. Microwave at 100% power for 10 minutes, stirring once. Stir in remaining ingredients. Continue to heat at 50% power for another 10-15 minutes or until mixture is very hot but not boiling.

Nutrition (per serving): 119 calories
Saturated fat .... 1 g
Total Fat .... 4 g (29% of calories)
Protein .... 8 g (28% of calories)
Carbohydrates .... 11 g (37% of calories)
Cholesterol .... 43 mg
Sodium .... 626 mg
Fiber .... 0 g

Vegetable Chili

Serves 14

Other vegetables may be substituted in this recipe if desired. Slow cooking in the microwave blends flavors and may be used instead of time consuming conventional cooking methods.

1 zucchini squash, chopped
2 onions, diced
4 cloves garlic, minced
2 large green bell peppers, seeded and diced
4 stalks celery, sliced
2 whole fresh or canned jalapeño peppers, seeded and minced
3 tomatoes, chopped
1 (8 oz.) can tomato sauce
1 cup low sodium chicken broth
2 tablespoons chili powder
1 tablespoon ground cumin
1 tablespoon dried parsley
1 tablespoon dried oregano
1 tablespoon dried basil
1 teaspoon fennel seeds
1 teaspoon black pepper
1 teaspoon seasoned salt
1 tablespoon sugar
1 cup cooked red kidney beans
1 cup cooked garbanzo beans
2 teaspoons dried dill weed
2 tablespoons lemon juice
1 dash Tabasco sauce
2 cups cooked rice
1 cup grated lowfat cheddar cheese

Place zucchini, onion, garlic, green pepper and celery in large microwave casserole. Cover and cook for 6-8 minutes until vegetables soften. Add tomatoes, tomato sauce, jalapeño peppers, seasonings except for dill and sugar. Microwave for 5-10 minutes at 100% power until mixture begins to boil. Reduce power to 30-50% power and slow cook, covered for 1-2 hours so flavors will blend. Add beans, lemon juice and dill. Cook 15-20 minutes, uncovered, until beans are hot. Serve with rice and cheese.

Nutrition (per serving): 194 calories
Saturated fat .... 1 g
Total Fat .... 3 g (14% of calories)
Protein .... 9 g (18% of calories)
Carbohydrates .... 33 g (68% of calories)
Cholesterol .... 4 mg
Sodium .... 748 mg
Fiber .... 4 g

Vichyssoise

Serves 10

For a recipe which contains less fat, substitute evaporated skim milk for heavy cream.

3 cups peeled and cubed red potatoes

2 1/2 cups sliced leeks

5 cups chicken broth

1 1/2 cups heavy cream

1/8 teaspoon white pepper

1/2 teaspoon Worcestershire sauce

1 dash cayenne pepper

2 tablespoons chopped fresh chives

Place potatoes and leeks in 3 quart microwave casserole. Cook for 6 minutes per pound at 100% power or until vegetables are tender. Add broth to vegetables and cook for another 10-15 minutes until mixture is hot and vegetables are very tender. Stir in remaining ingredients except for chives. Puree mixture in food processor. Chill thoroughly. Garnish with chives to serve.

Nutrition (per serving): 160 calories
Saturated fat .... 6 g
Total Fat .... 10 g (54% of calories)
Protein .... 3 g (7% of calories)
Carbohydrates .... 15 g (38% of calories)
Cholesterol .... 31 mg
Sodium .... 752 mg
Fiber .... 1 g

Sandwiches

Cheese Bacon Sandwich

Serves 6

Do not overcook sandwiches or bread will become tough.

1/2 pound bacon, cooked and crumbled
1/2 pound light Velveeta cheese, softened
1/2 cup finely minced sweet onions
1/2 teaspoon Worcestershire sauce
1/2 teaspoon paprika
1/4 teaspoon dry mustard
6 hamburger buns

Cut cheese into chunks and soften at 30% power for 1-2 minutes. Add onion and remaining ingredients. Stir until mixture is smooth. Spread mixture on buns and sprinkle with bacon. Top with other half of bun, wrap buns in napkin and heat for about 20-30 seconds until sandwiches are hot.

Nutrition (per serving): 427 calories
Saturated fat	.11 g
Total Fat	29 g (62% of calories)
Protein	14 g (13% of calories)
Carbohydrates	27 g (25% of calories)
Cholesterol	48 mg
Sodium	1086 mg
Fiber	0 g

Crab Open Face Sandwich

Serves 6

If desired, heat two sandwiches at a time for 20-30 seconds.

1 (8 oz.) can lump crabmeat, drained and flaked
1/4 cup nonfat mayonnaise
1 teaspoon finely chopped onions
1/4 teaspoon prepared mustard
1/2 teaspoon Worcestershire sauce
1 dash Tabasco sauce
3 English muffins, split
2 tablespoons lowfat margarine, softened
Chopped fresh parsley
1 dash paprika

Stir together crabmeat and mayonnaise and set aside. Mix onion, mustard, Worcestershire sauce and Tabasco. Mix this with crabmeat. Spread muffins with margarine and toast conventionally. Spread muffins with crabmeat mixture and sprinkle with parsley and paprika. Cover a large microwave tray with paper towel and arrange muffin halves on tray in a circle. Microwave for 1-1 1/2 minutes at 100% power until mixture is bubbly.

Ground Beef Sandwiches

Serves 8

For a change, serve this recipe on English muffins.

1 pound lean ground beef
1 onion, chopped
1 cup pitted black olives, chopped
1 pound grated lowfat cheddar cheese
1 (10 3/4 oz.) can cond. reduced-sodium tomato soup
2 teaspoons taco seasoning mix
1/4 teaspoon dried oregano
1/4 cup barbecue sauce
1 dash salt, optional
1 dash black pepper
8 hamburger buns

Place ground beef and onions in microwave colander if available or in 1 1/2 quart casserole. Microwave at 100% power, covered for 5-7 minutes, stirring once until meat is no longer pink. Drain well. Cool a few minutes and then stir in olives, cheese, soup and seasonings. Heat mixture at 50% power, stirring occasionally until cheese melts. Serve on buns or muffins.

notes:

_____
_____
_____
_____
_____
_____
_____
_____
_____
_____
_____
_____
_____
_____
_____
_____
_____
_____
_____
_____
_____

Side Dishes—Fruit/Vegetables/Grains

BUY GOOD FOOD.
WHAT YOU SHOULD KNOW!

Fruits and Vegetables

1. Choose beautiful vegetables and fruits, bright in color, firm in texture.
2. Before purchasing berries, check bottom of container. If badly stained, you will find the berries mushy and moldy.
3. Bruises, spots, cuts cause rapid decay so avoid damaged vegetables and fruits. A trace of sweet scent is a sure sign of good quality in fruit.
4. Many vegetables toughen as they mature so choose smaller vegetables to get the youngest and most tender.
5. Enzymes alter vegetable flavors as well as texture. Vegetables will have less sugar and more starch as they age, therefore less intense flavor. They become bland during storage.

Storing Fruits and Vegetables

♥ Most vegetables, such as asparagus, celery, peas, spinach do well when put fresh and unwashed in plastic bag or container. This creates a small damp environment, humidified by the vegetables own moisture. A vegetable that is actually wet is receptive to bacterial growth and spoilage.

♥ Store mushrooms, unwashed, in a single layer in a paper bag.

♥ A number of vegetables, like potatoes and onions, don't like refrigeration. They thrive on higher temperature and lower humidity. Potatoes and onions should not be stored next to one another as each exudes a different gas that shortens the storage life of the other. For longer life, potatoes can be stored in refrigerator, which converts starch to sugar, changing the flavor. If you remember to leave at room temperature for a day or two, sugar will convert back to starch.

♥ Most fruits can be washed and dried before they are put away. However, wash berries and cherries right before serving as too much moisture will hasten decay.

♥ Ripen fruits quickly by placing the unripe fruit in a brown bag with the end closed loosely or the bag poked full of small holes. Set on cool shelf and check fruit every day.

♥ Bananas, after reaching desired stage of ripeness, may be stored in the refrigerator for several days. The skin will turn black, but the flesh will remain ivory.

♥ Store lemons and limes in an air tight container. They will keep for weeks.

♥ Tomatoes should be stored at room temperature for maximum flavor.

♥ Keep putting all leftover vegetables in a container in your freezer. When you have enough, blend and freeze in ice-cube trays. Thaw just the amount needed. Good for adding extra flavor and nutrition to cooking.

♥ Once an onion has been cut in half, rub the leftover side with butter and it will keep fresh longer.

Side Dishes—Fruits/Vegetables/Grains

Asparagus Casserole
Baked Mushrooms
Bar B Q Green Beans
Broccoli Rice Casserole
Celery Bake
Cheese Polenta
Cheesy Mixed Vegetables
Chili Stuffing
Corn and Macaroni Casserole
Corn On The Cob
Creamed Cabbage
Deluxe Potato Casserole
Fideo
Green Beans and New Potatoes
Herbed Spaghetti
Hominy Delight
Hot Pineapple
Italian Brussels Sprouts
Jalapeño Spinach
Micro Fried Eggplant
Oriental Peas
Party Broccoli
Perfect Sweet Potatoes
Pineapple Acorn Squash
Polenta
Rice Dressing
Scalloped Potatoes
Tangy Rice Casserole
Texas Rice
Zucchini Custard

Asparagus Casserole

Serves 8

3 hard boiled eggs, chopped
2 (16 oz.) cans canned asparagus spears, drained
2 ounces chopped pimientos
1 (10 3/4 oz.) can lowfat cond. cream of mushroom soup
1/2 cup crushed yellow crackers
1/2 cup grated mild lowfat cheddar cheese
1/4 cup melted lowfat margarine, optional
1 dash salt
1 dash pepper

Place drained asparagus in 8 x 12 inch casserole. Top with eggs and pimientos. Spread with soup. Sprinkle with cracker crumbs and cheese. Drizzle with margarine, salt and pepper. Microwave for 8-15 minutes for 70% power until bubbly hot.

Nutrition (per serving): 114 calories
Saturated fat .... 2 g
Total Fat .... 5 g (40% of calories)
Protein .... 8 g (28% of calories)
Carbohydrates .... 9 g (32% of calories)
Cholesterol .... 84 mg
Sodium .... 686 mg
Fiber .... 1 g

Baked Mushrooms

Serves 4

This is extremely rich, but delicious as a side dish or appetizer. If you wish to eat lighter, use evaporated skim milk in place of cream and use lowfat margarine. On occasion, however, you may want to splurge.

1/2 pound fresh mushrooms, sliced
2 tablespoons lemon juice
1/4 cup melted butter or margarine
1/4 teaspoon salt
1/8 teaspoon black pepper
1 tablespoon flour
2 tablespoons grated parmesan cheese
1 cup whipping cream
2 egg yolks, slightly beaten
2 tablespoons crisp dried bread crumbs
1 dash paprika

Place mushrooms in 2 quart microwave casserole. Mix remaining ingredients except for crumbs in 2 cup measure. Heat for 2-3 minutes at 70% power until liquid is quite hot, but not boiling. Pour over mushrooms and heat for 2-3 minute at 70% power. Sprinkle with crumbs and paprika to serve.

```
Nutrition (per serving): 394 calories
    Saturated fat ................................................. 22 g
    Total Fat ........................................................ 37 g (48% of calories)
    Protein ........................................................... 6 g (6% of calories)
    Carbohydrates ................................................ 9 g (9% of calories)
    Cholesterol ..................................................... 217 mg
    Sodium ........................................................... 362 mg
    Fiber ............................................................... 1 g
```

Bar B Q Green Beans

Serves 8

This is a very good dish to double in quantity. This seems to be everyone's favorite at family cookouts. For a change, use chili sauce or barbecue sauce instead of catsup.

2 (16 oz.) cans French style green beans, drained
2 slices bacon, cooked and crumbled
1 small onion, finely minced
1/2 cup catsup
1/3 cup packed brown sugar
1/2 teaspoon dry mustard
1 pinch salt
1 dash black pepper

Drain green beans and combine with all other ingredients. Place in 3 quart casserole and cook, partially covered, for 8-12 minutes at 100% power.

```
Nutrition (per serving): 112 calories
    Saturated fat ................................................. 1 g
    Total Fat ........................................................ 4 g (30% of calories)
    Protein ........................................................... 2 g (7% of calories)
    Carbohydrates ................................................ 18 g (63% of calories)
    Cholesterol ..................................................... 1 mg
    Sodium............................................................ 273 mg
    Fiber ............................................................... 1 g
```

Broccoli Rice Casserole

Serves 10

By heating the liquid ingredients before assembling, the casserole cooking time is shortened considerably.

1/2 cup diced celery
1 onion, chopped
2 cups cooked rice
1 (10 oz.) package frozen chopped broccoli
1 (6 oz.) jar cheddar cheese
1 (10 3/4 oz.) can lowfat cond. cream of chicken soup
1/2 cup skim milk
1 teaspoon Worcestershire sauce
1/4 teaspoon Greek seasoning
1/8 teaspoon garlic salt
1 dash tabasco sauce

Place celery and onion in microwave casserole. Cover and cook for 1-2 minutes until vegetables begin to soften. Stir in rice and broccoli. Mix in all remaining ingredients. Heat for 4-5 minutes at 100% power, stirring occasionally until cheese melts. Stir into rice/broccoli mixture. Smooth ingredients. Place in microwave casserole and cook at 70% power, partially covered, for 12-15 minutes until hot and bubbly.

```
Nutrition (per serving): 196 calories
    Saturated fat ........................................... 3 g
    Total Fat ................................................. 5 g (24% of calories)
    Protein ................................................... 7 g (14% of calories)
    Carbohydrates ......................................... 30 g (62% of calories)
    Cholesterol ............................................. 16 mg
    Sodium ................................................... 247 mg
    Fiber ..................................................... 0 g
```

Celery Bake

Serves 8

For a lighter version of this dish substitute light cream cheese and evaporated skim milk.

1 bunch celery
1 onion, chopped
1 green bell pepper, seeded and chopped
3 ounces cream cheese
3 ounces crumbled blue cheese
3/4 cup heavy cream
2 tablespoons dry sherry
1 dash salt
1 dash black pepper

Wash celery and trim off bottom end of stalk. Cut ribs into 1 inch pieces. Place celery, onion and green pepper in large microwave casserole. Cover and cook 5 minutes per pound at 100% power until crisp tender. Drain off excess liquid. Into 2 cup microwave measure, mix softened cream cheese, crumbled blue cheese, heavy cream, sherry, salt and pepper. Heat for 1-2 minutes until mixture blends smoothly. Pour sauce over celery and stir into vegetables. Spread mixture into 8 x 12 inch microwave casserole. Microwave for 20-35 minutes at 70% power or until vegetables are tender.

```
Nutrition (per serving): 190 calories
    Saturated fat ....................................................... 10 g
    Total Fat ............................................................. 15 g (72% of calories)
    Protein ................................................................   5 g (10% of calories)
    Carbohydrates .....................................................   8 g (17% of calories)
    Cholesterol ......................................................... 50 mg
    Sodium ................................................................ 337 mg
    Fiber ...................................................................  1 g
```

Cheese Polenta

Serves 4

1/2 cup yellow corn meal

1 3/4 cups skim milk

2 tablespoons plain lowfat yogurt

2 tablespoons grated parmesan cheese

1/4 teaspoon freshly ground black pepper

1/8 teaspoon ground nutmeg

1 dash cayenne

Place cornmeal in a 2 quart microwave casserole. Stir in the milk. Cover and cook for 1 minute at 100% power. Stir thoroughly. Cover and cook an additional 4-5 minutes, stirring every minute until liquid is absorbed. Stir in remaining ingredients. Divide mixture into four 6 ounce custard cups. Cover and set aside until serving time. Reheat a minute or two at 50% power if needed. To serve, invert onto plates.

```
Nutrition (per serving): 117 calories
    Saturated fat ....................................................... .1 g
    Total Fat . ........................................................... ..2 g (12% of calories)
    Protein ................................................................ ..6 g (22% of calories)
    Carbohydrates ..................................................... 19 g (66% of calories)
    Cholesterol ......................................................... 5 mg
    Sodium ................................................................ 105 mg
    Fiber ................................................................... ..0 g
```

Cheesy Mixed Vegetables

Serves 4

16 ounces frozen mixed vegetables, defrosted
1 teaspoon prepared horseradish
1 (3 oz.) package light cream cheese
2 tablespoons skim milk
1/4 teaspoon dried dill weed
1/4 teaspoon salt

Drain any excess moisture from defrosted vegetables and place in 1 quart microwave casserole. Soften cream cheese in 1 cup measure for 1 minute at 30% power. Stir in milk, horseradish, dill and salt. Blend through vegetables. Cover and microwave at 70% power for 5-10 minutes until mixture is very hot. Stir and let stand a minute before serving to distribute heat evenly.

```
Nutrition (per serving): 100 calories
  Saturated fat .......................................................... ..3 g
  Total Fat ................................................................ ..5 g (48% of calories)
  Protein .................................................................. 4 g (16% of calories)
  Carbohydrates ....................................................... 9 g (36% of calories)
  Cholesterol ........................................................... 16 mg
  Sodium .................................................................. 490 mg
  Fiber ..................................................................... .1 g
```

Chili Stuffing

Serves 8

Bouillon amounts may vary depending on desired moistness.
1 cup chopped celery
1 cup chopped onions
1/4 cup lowfat margarine, optional
1 (4 oz.) can chopped mild green chiles
1 (8 oz.) package dried herb seasoned stuffing
1 (8 oz.) package dried corn bread stuffing
1/2 teaspoon poultry seasoning
1/2 pound cooked pork sausages, optional
1 1/4 cups low sodium chicken bouillon

Place celery and onion in 3 quart casserole with melted margarine. Microwave at 100% power for 2-3 minutes, stirring once, or until vegetables begin to soften. Mix all remaining ingredients and smooth stuffing into casserole. Microwave at 70% power for 20-30 minutes until very hot and cooked through.

Corn and Macaroni Casserole

Serves 8

Pasta may be cooked in the microwave (See Side Dish-Pasta).

2 cups elbow macaroni
1 (16 oz.) can cream-style corn
8 ounces American cheese, grated
1 small green bell pepper, finely chopped
1 (4 oz.) can sliced mushrooms, drained
1/2 teaspoon salt
3 tablespoons melted lowfat margarine
1/2 cup dried bread crumbs

Cook and drain macaroni. Mix macaroni, corn, cheese, bell pepper, mushrooms and salt. Place in 2 quart casserole. Toss crumbs and melted margarine. Sprinkle over casserole. Microwave at 70% power for 12-14 minutes, uncovered, until bubbly hot throughout.

Corn On The Cob

Serves 4

The 6 Minute Per Pound Rule is not accurate when cooking corn on the cob. We cannot count the weight of the cob. Instead figure 2-3 minutes per ear for corn. The variation in time is due to the size of corn niblets. Smaller niblets will take only 2 minutes per ear whereas larger ones may take 3 minutes. Refer to Dealing with Multiples *if cooking a larger quantity of corn.*

4 whole fresh corn on the cob
4 tablespoons lowfat margarine

VARIATION 1: corn on the cob
4 tablespoons butter or margarine
1 tablespoon curry powder
VARIATION 2: corn on the cob
2 tablespoons butter or margarine
2 tablespoons Italian salad dressing
1 tablespoon chili powder
VARIATION 3: corn on the cob
4 tablespoons butter or margarine
1 finely minced seeded jalapeño pepper
1/4 teaspoon ground cumin

Remove husks and silks from corn. Trim ends and wash. Do not shake water off ears. Place in microwave casserole, alternating ends (one large end, one small end, etc.). Spread with desired spice variation before cooking. Cover and cook 2-3 minutes per ear at 100% power. Let stand a minute or two before serving.

```
Nutrition (per serving): 194 calories
    Saturated fat ....................................................... 1 g
    Total Fat ............................................................. 7 g (31% of calories)
    Protein ............................................................... 4 g (9% of calories)
    Carbohydrates .................................................... 29 g (61% of calories)
    Cholesterol ........................................................ 0 mg
    Sodium .............................................................. 145 mg
    Fiber .................................................................. 1 g
```

Creamed Cabbage

Serves 6

When cooking foods by the 6 Minute Per Pound Rule, make certain you use the weight of the food only... not that of the food and container combined... for calculating cooking time.

1 head cabbage
2 tablespoons light margarine, stick form
3 tablespoons flour
1 cup skim milk
1 1/2 cups cubed light Velveeta cheese
1/2 cup nonfat mayonnaise
1 teaspoon Worcestershire sauce

1/4 teaspoon Greek seasoning, optional
2 ounces chopped pimientos
1/3 cup toasted bread crumbs

Cut cabbage into thin wedges. Place in 3 quart casserole. Cover tightly and microwave 6 minutes per pound. Melt margarine in small microwave measure. Stir flour into margarine. Microwave for 30-45 seconds at 100% power. Gradually whisk in milk. Cook for 2-4 minutes at 100% power until thickened. Whisk well. Add cheese. Stir until melted. Mix in mayonnaise, Worcestershire sauce, spices and pimientos. Pour cheese sauce over cabbage and microwave for 8-12 minutes at 70% power until bubbly hot and cabbage is tender.

Nutrition (per serving): 262 calories
Saturated fat ....5 g
Total Fat .... .11 g (36% of calories)
Protein .... .14 g (22% of calories)
Carbohydrates .... 27 g (42% of calories)
Cholesterol .... 31 mg
Sodium .... 1272 mg
Fiber ....1 g

Deluxe Potato Casserole

Serves 12

You may fix half of this recipe if desired and cook a shorter time. Freeze the other half. The large difference in cooking times depends on the temperature of potatoes when placed in the microwave. If made early in the day and refrigerated, they will take longer to heat than if fixed right before serving time. For an added touch, use 1 teaspoon of caraway seeds .

6 cups hot water
6 cups dehydrated mashed potato flakes
3/4 cup skim milk
1/2 cup lowfat margarine, cubed
4 ounces light cream cheese, cubed
3/4 cup lowfat sour cream
3/4 cup grated lowfat cheddar cheese
1/2 cup grated parmesan cheese
1 small green bell pepper, finely minced
1/2 cup finely minced onions
2 ounces chopped pimientos
1 (4 oz.) can sliced mushrooms, drained
1 teaspoon seasoned salt

1/2 teaspoon seasoned pepper
1 dash paprika

Place water in 3 quart casserole. Cover and heat at 100% power for 10-15 minutes until boiling, or use boiling water from stove top. Add milk and potato flakes. Stir in margarine and cream cheese. Mix until melted. Blend in sour cream, cream cheese, 1/2 cup cheddar cheese and 1/4 cup parmesan cheese. Thoroughly mix all ingredients until cheese begins to melt. Stir in remaining ingredients and place in 9 x 13 inch casserole. Sprinkle with remaining cheese and paprika. Place in microwave oven and heat at 70% power for 15-30 minutes until bubbly hot.

```
Nutrition (per serving): 351 calories
    Saturated fat ........................................................ ..4 g
    Total Fat ............................................................... ...9 g (25% of calories)
    Protein .................................................................. 12 g (14% of calories)
    Carbohydrates ...................................................... .54 g (62% of calories)
    Cholesterol ........................................................... 16 mg
    Sodium ................................................................. 733 mg
    Fiber ..................................................................... ..1 g
```

Fideo

Serves 4

1 (8 oz.) package thin spaghetti
3 tablespoons vegetable oil
1 onion, finely chopped
1 clove garlic, minced
1 (16 oz.) can stewed tomatoes
1 dash salt
1 dash black pepper
1 tablespoon ground cumin

Place vegetable oil into 3 quart microwave casserole. Break spaghetti into 4 inch pieces. Put spaghetti and oil in 2 quart microwave casserole. Stir to coat. Microwave at 100% power for 2 minutes at 100% power. Stir and repeat procedure until spaghetti turns light brown in color. Drain on paper towel. Saute onion and garlic for a 1-3 minutes in microwave casserole. Add tomatoes, broth and spices. Microwave for 3-4 minutes until mixture is hot. Add spaghetti, cover and cook for 8-10 minutes at 100% power until spaghetti is tender.

Green Beans and New Potatoes

Serves 6

I like fresh green beans cooked soft. If a more crisp bean is desired, simply put beans and potatoes in at the same time, cook for 12 minutes at 100% power. Lower to 50% power and cook for an additional 10-20 minutes until vegetables are to your liking.

1 1/2 pounds fresh green beans

1 tablespoon bacon grease, optional

1/ 4 cup water

1 cube beef flavored bouillon

1 clove garlic, mashed

1 1/2 pounds small new potatoes

1 dash salt

1 dash pepper

Place beans, water, bacon grease, bouillon and garlic in microwave 2-3 quart casserole. Cook, covered, 9 minutes at 100% power. Stir and cook 5-10 minutes at 50% power. Add potatoes, circle fashion, on top of beans. Cook for 6 minutes at 100% power. Salt and pepper. Cover and cook an additional 15 minutes at 50% power. Stir gently before serving.

Herbed Spaghetti

Serves 8

6 cloves garlic, mashed
2 tablespoons light olive oil
1/2 cup lowfat margarine
1/4 cup minced fresh chives
1/4 cup minced fresh dill weed
1/4 cup minced fresh basil
1/4 cup minced fresh parsley
1 pound thin spaghetti, cooked and drained
1 dash salt
1/4 teaspoon freshly ground black pepper

Place garlic in oil. Microwave uncovered for 4-5 minutes at 100% power until garlic begins to brown. Add margarine and herbs. Microwave at 30% power until mixture is very hot. Toss with cooked, drained spaghetti, salt and pepper.

Nutrition (per serving): 295 calories
Saturated fat .... 2 g
Total Fat .... 10 g (30% of calories)
Protein .... .8 g (10% of calories)
Carbohydrates .... 44 g (59% of calories)
Cholesterol .... 0 mg
Sodium .... 193 mg
Fiber ....0 g

Hominy Delight

Serves 4

If food is taken from the warm oven for standing time, it is important to cover, as it continues to cook 25% after the microwave shuts off. This is the time it takes the vibrating water molecules inside the food to stop. If food is not covered, it would be like cooking conventionally for the last 1/4 of the cooking time with the oven door open. For a change, substitute 2 teaspoons of chili powder for the mustard and garlic.

1 (16 oz.) can white hominy
2 tablespoons skim milk
3/4 cup nonfat sour cream
1 (4 oz.) can chopped green chiles
1 cup grated lowfat cheddar cheese
1/2 teaspoon dry mustard

1/4 teaspoon garlic powder

1/4 teaspoon paprika

Drain hominy and mix with remaining ingredients except for paprika. Place mixture in 1 quart casserole. Sprinkle with paprika. Cook, partially covered, for 10-16 minutes at 70% power until hot and bubbly.

```
Nutrition (per serving): 221 calories
    Saturated fat ...................................................... .3 g
    Total Fat ............................................................ ..7 g (28% of calories)
    Protein .............................................................. 16 g (28% of calories)
    Carbohydrates ................................................... 24 g (44% of calories)
    Cholesterol ....................................................... 16 mg
    Sodium ............................................................. 815 mg
    Fiber ................................................................. ..1 g
```

Hot Pineapple

Serves 8

1/2 cup flour

1/2 cup sugar

1 dash salt, optional

1 (16 oz.) can crushed pineapple in juice

1(16 oz.) can pineapple chunks

1 pound light Velveeta cheese, cubed

1/4 cup dried bread crumbs

Mix flour, sugar and salt in 2 quart casserole. Add undrained pineapple and cheese, stirring well. Microwave, partially covered, at 70% power for 12-18 minutes, stirring once, until sauce is thickened and cheese is melted. Sprinkle with crumbs before serving.

```
Nutrition (per serving): 296 calories
    Saturated fat ...................................................... ..4 g
    Total Fat ............................................................ ..8 g (26% of calories)
    Protein .............................................................. 12 g (16% of calories)
    Carbohydrates ................................................... 43 g (58% of calories)
    Cholesterol ....................................................... 31 mg
    Sodium ............................................................. 936 mg
    Fiber ................................................................. ..0 g
```

Italian Brussels Sprouts

Serves 4

1 onion

1 (10 oz.) package frozen Brussels sprouts

2 tablespoons no fat Italian salad dressing

1/2 cup cherry tomatoes, halved

Hold frozen sprouts under cold running water to separate. Cut large sprouts in half and place in 1 quart casserole. Cut onion into 12 wedges. Add onion and salad dressing to sprouts. Cover and cook at 100% power for 8-10 minutes or until tender. Stir in tomato halves. Cook, covered for 30-60 seconds at 100% power until heated through.

```
Nutrition (per serving): 65 calories
    Saturated fat ..................................................... .0 g
    Total Fat ........................................................... .0 g (5% of calories)
    Protein .............................................................. ..3 g (20% of calories)
    Carbohydrates ................................................... 12 g (75% of calories)
    Cholesterol ....................................................... 0 mg
    Sodium ............................................................. 127 mg
    Fiber ................................................................. .2 g
```

Jalapeño Spinach

Serves 6

Broccoli is a good substitute in this dish. Also, try different types of cheese.

2 (10 oz.) packages frozen chopped spinach
3 tablespoons lowfat margarine
2 tablespoons flour
2 tablespoons minced onions
1/3 cup evaporated skim milk
2 tablespoons water or spinach liquid
1/2 teaspoon black pepper
1 teaspoon garlic salt
1 1/2 cups cubed jalapeño pepper cheese
1 teaspoon Worcestershire sauce
1 pinch crushed red pepper
1/4 cup seasoned dry bread crumbs

Defrost and cook vegetables. Drain and save vegetable liquid. Melt margarine. Stir in flour, onions, milk, 2 tablespoons vegetable liquid, pepper and garlic salt. Cook at 100% power for 1-2 minutes at 100% power until mixture is thickened. Whisk until smooth. Add cheese, worcestershire and red pepper, stirring until melted. Stir mixture through vegetables. Place in 1 quart microwave casserole. Top with crumbs and cook, uncovered, for 5-10 minutes at 50% power or until mixture is bubbly hot.

Nutrition (per serving): 199 calories
Saturated fat ....6 g
Total Fat .... 12 g (54% of calories)
Protein .... .5 g (10% of calories)
Carbohydrates .... 18 g (36% of calories)
Cholesterol .... 26 mg
Sodium .... 352 mg
Fiber ....1 g

Micro Fried Eggplant

Serves 4

The cooking time for this recipe is based on the 6 Minute Per Pound Rule. Check to make certain eggplant is cooking evenly. If not, rearrange half way through the cooking time.

1/4 cup seasoned dry bread crumbs
1/3 cup grated parmesan cheese, divided
1 whole eggplant, peeled and sliced
1/4 cup light salad oil, optional

Mix bread crumbs and 1/4 cup parmesan. Cut eggplant into 1"x4" strips. Toss eggplant strips in oil and roll in breadcrumbs. Place a single layer of eggplant in microwave casserole making certain not to crowd. Cover with a paper towel and microwave for 4-8 minutes. Sprinkle with remaining parmesan before serving.

Nutrition (per serving): 59 calories
Saturated fat .... 1 g
Total Fat .... 2 g (32% of calories)
Protein .... 4 g (24% of calories)
Carbohydrates .... 6 g (43% of calories)
Cholesterol .... 5 mg
Sodium .... 160 mg
Fiber .... 0 g

Oriental Peas

Serves 8

Fresh mushrooms and bean sprouts may be used in this casserole if desired.

1/2 cup thinly sliced onions
1 (6 oz.) can sliced mushrooms, drained
1 (10 oz.) package frozen peas, defrosted
1 (16 oz.) can bean sprouts, drained
1 (8 oz.) can sliced water chestnuts, drained
1 (10 3/4 oz.) can lowfat cond. cream of mushroom soup

1/4 cup milk
1/2 teaspoon salt, optional
1/4 teaspoon black pepper
1 cup chow mein noodles

Place onions in 2 quart microwave casserole. Cover and cook for 1-2 minutes until onions begin to soften. Add mushrooms, peas, bean sprouts and water chestnuts. Blend soup, milk, salt and pepper. Pour over vegetables and mix gently. Microwave covered for 10 minutes at 70% power. Remove, sprinkle with chow mein noodles and let stand a few minutes before serving.

Nutrition (per serving): 229 calories
Saturated fat ....2 g
Total Fat ....8 g (30% of calories)
Protein ....8 g (14% of calories)
Carbohydrates .... 33 g (57 % of calories)
Cholesterol .... 2 mg
Sodium .... 534 mg
Fiber ....1 g

Party Broccoli

Serves 8

This is a rich dish, but very elegant. If you wish to cut down on nuts and margarine you may do so.

2 (10 oz.) packages frozen chopped broccoli
1/2 cup melted lowfat margarine
1/2 (3 oz.) package dehydrated onion soup mix
1 cup chopped pecans
1 (8 oz.) can water chestnuts, drained and chopped
1/4 cup seasoned dry bread crumbs

Defrost and drain broccoli. Mix margarine, soup mix, pecans and water chestnuts. Stir gently through broccoli. Pour into flat 8 x 12 inch microwave casserole. Cook for 4-10 minutes at 100% power. Sprinkle with crumbs before serving.

Nutrition (per serving): 219 calories
Saturated fat ....2 g
Total Fat .... 16 g (66% of calories)
Protein ....4 g (8% of calories)
Carbohydrates .... 14 g (26% of calories)
Cholesterol .... 0 mg
Sodium .... 658 mg
Fiber ....1 g

Perfect Sweet Potatoes

Serves 6

Drained canned sweet potatoes may be substituted for this recipe if fresh potatoes are not available.

6 sweet potatoes, approximately 2 pounds
1/2 cup packed brown sugar
1/3 cup broken cashews
1/4 teaspoon ground ginger
1/2 teaspoon salt
1 (8 oz.) can sliced peaches in juice
3 tablespoons lowfat margarine
1/2 cup flaked coconut, optional

Cook potatoes 6 minutes per pound. Cool, peel and slice. Mix sugar, nuts and spices. Drain peaches. Layer 1/2 potatoes, peaches and sugar mixture. Repeat layers and dot with margarine. Cook covered for 10-15 minutes at 70% power. Sprinkle with coconut and heat uncovered for another 1-2 minutes.

```
Nutrition (per serving): 266 calories
    Saturated fat ...................................................... ..1 g
    Total Fat ............................................................... ..7 g (23% of calories)
    Protein ................................................................. .4 g (5% of calories)
    Carbohydrates ................................................... 48 g (72% of calories)
    Cholesterol ......................................................... 0 mg
    Sodium ................................................................ 288 mg
    Fiber ................................................................... ..1 g
```

Pineapple Acorn Squash

Serves 4

Cooking time of this dish is determined by the 6 Minutes Per Pound Rule.

2 whole acorn squash
1 cup whole berry cranberry sauce
1/4 cup crushed pineapple in juice, drained
1/4 cup brown sugar
3 tablespoons softened butter
1/2 teaspoon ground cinnamon
1/8 teaspoon ground nutmeg

Pierce squash. Elevate squash off bottom of microwave. Cook at 100% power for 7-8 minutes, turning squash over after half of cooking time. Cut squash in half and discard seeds. Mix all remaining ingredients. Place squash halves in microwave casserole, cut side up. Fill with fruit mixture. Microwave for 4-6 minutes at 100% power until squash and filling are soft and bubbly hot.

```
Nutrition (per serving): 326 calories
   Saturated fat ..................................................... 5 g
   Total Fat ........................................................... 9 g (25% of calories)
   Protein ............................................................. 2 g (2% of calories)
   Carbohydrates .................................................. 59 g (73% of calories)
   Cholesterol ...................................................... 23 mg
   Sodium ............................................................ 117 mg
   Fiber ................................................................ 3 g
```

Polenta

Serves 12

Microwave polenta is half done in the time it takes the water to boil the traditional stove top way. This recipe may be used in variations of recipes using polenta. For example, pour on an oiled work surface and spread 1/4 inch thick. Let cool completely until firm. Cut into 3 inch squares. Bake and serve with sauce. Or, pour polenta into a shallow serving bowl and make a large well in the center of the polenta with the back of large spoon that has been dipped in hot water. Serve with sauce.

2 cups coarse yellow corn meal
1 tablespoon salt
7 cups water

Place cornmeal, salt and water in 4 or 5 quart microwave container. Cover and cook at 100% power for 24 minutes, stirring every 6 minutes.

```
Nutrition (per serving): 83 calories
   Saturated fat ..................................................... .0 g
   Total Fat ........................................................... .0 g (4% of calories)
   Protein ............................................................. .2 g (9% of calories)
   Carbohydrates .................................................. 18 g (86% of calories)
   Cholesterol ...................................................... 0 mg
   Sodium ............................................................ 586 mg
   Fiber ................................................................ .0 g
```

Rice Dressing

Serves 10

This is an excellent stuffing for cornish game hens.

6 slices bacon, minced
4 tablespoons chopped onions

1 cup chopped celery

4 cups cooked brown rice

1 teaspoon salt

1/2 teaspoon black pepper

1/4 teaspoon ground sage

1/2 cup skim milk

Place bacon and onion in microwave casserole. Microwave for 3-4 minutes until bacon is beginning to brown. Drain all but 1 or 2 tablespoons of bacon grease. Add celery and microwave another 2-3 minutes until celery begins to soften. Mix in remaining ingredients. Place in microwave casserole and microwave at 70% power for 12-18 minutes until mixture is hot and cooked throughout.

```
Nutrition (per serving): 357 calories
    Saturated fat ........................................................ ..3 g
    Total Fat .............................................................. .8 g (21% of calories)
    Protein ................................................................. ..7 g (8% of calories)
    Carbohydrates .................................................... 63 g (71% of calories)
    Cholesterol .......................................................... 9 mg
    Sodium ................................................................. 353 mg
    Fiber ..................................................................... ..0 g
```

Scalloped Potatoes

Serves 10

More cheddar cheese or Swiss cheese may be substituted for cream cheese if desired. Minced green pepper and onion are good in these also. This freezes well so eat half and freeze the other half. You may also use low fat versions of butter, soups, cheese and creams if you wish.

2 pounds frozen hash brown potatoes

1 teaspoon seasoned salt

1/4 teaspoon black pepper

1 (10 3/4 oz.) can lowfat cond. cream of mushroom soup

3/4 cup grated lowfat cheddar cheese

2 cups nonfat sour cream

1 (8 oz.) package light cream cheese

1 dash Worcestershire sauce

1 cup crushed Total cereal

1 dash paprika

Thaw potatoes and drain liquid if necessary. Mix remaining ingredients other than cornflakes. Stir into potatoes. Place in 3 quart microwave casserole or large rectangular casserole. Potatoes should be only 1 1/2 to 2 inches deep if cooking in rectangular casserole. Sprinkle cereal and paprika over potatoes. Microwave uncovered for 15-20 minutes at 70% power or until potatoes are hot and bubbly throughout.

```
Nutrition (per serving): 283 calories
        Saturated fat ........................................................ ..8 g
        Total Fat ............................................................... 16 g (50% of calories)
        Protein ................................................................. 10 g (14% of calories)
        Carbohydrates .................................................... 26 g (36% of calories)
        Cholesterol .......................................................... 29 mg
        Sodium ................................................................. 698 mg
        Fiber .................................................................... 0 g
```

Tangy Rice Casserole

Serves 10

As this is not a typical rice casserole, 1/2 cup represents a serving. Rich and delicious! Larger portions could be used as a main dish.

1 pound light Monterey Jack cheese

2 1/2 cups nonfat sour cream

2 (4 oz.) cans chopped green chiles

3 1/2 cups cooked rice

1/4 teaspoon salt

1/8 teaspoon black pepper

3/4 cup grated lowfat cheddar cheese

Cut Jack cheese into 1/2 inch strips. Mix sour cream and green chiles. Season rice with salt and pepper. In 2 quart casserole layer rice, sour cream mixture and cheese strips. Finish with rice on top. Microwave partially covered for 10-12 minutes at 70% power. Sprinkle with grated cheddar cheese. Cook uncovered for an additional 2-4 minutes until cheese is melted and mixture is hot.

```
Nutrition (per serving): 454 calories
        Saturated fat ........................................................ ..6 g
        Total Fat ............................................................... 12 g (23% of calories)
        Protein ................................................................. 25 g (22% of calories)
        Carbohydrates .................................................... 62 g (55% of calories)
        Cholesterol .......................................................... 5 mg
        Sodium ................................................................. 624 mg
        Fiber .................................................................... 1 g
```

Texas Rice

Serves 6

As more headroom is needed when boiling rice or pasta in the microwave, use a larger container than when cooking conventionally.

1 cup long grain rice
1 (4 oz.) can mushrooms, drained
1 teaspoon chicken bouillon granules
1 (10 3/4 oz.) can cond. onion soup
3/4 cup hot water

Place rice and mushrooms in 3 quart casserole. Stir in onion soup, hot water and bouillon. Microwave for 5 minutes at 100% power until boiling. Stir, reduce power to 50% and continue to cook for 15 minutes. Fluff with fork and let stand another few minutes.

```
Nutrition (per serving): 146 calories
    Saturated fat .......................................................... ..0 g
    Total Fat ................................................................ ..1 g (6% of calories)
    Protein .................................................................. ..4 g (11% of calories)
    Carbohydrates ...................................................... 30 g (83% of calories)
    Cholesterol ........................................................... 0 mg
    Sodium .................................................................. 490 mg
    Fiber ..................................................................... ..0 g
```

Zucchini Custard

Serves 8

Egg substitute may be used for lower fat content.

3 medium zucchini
3/4 teaspoon salt
1/4 cup chopped onions
6 eggs, well beaten
1 cup skim milk
1/2 teaspoon crushed dried basil
1/2 teaspoon dried oregano
2 tablespoons flour
2 cups shredded lowfat cheddar cheese

Wash zucchini. Cut off ends. Cut crosswise into 1/4 inch slices, then quarter slices. Sprinkle with salt and let stand 10 minutes. Place in microwave casserole with onion. Cook at 100% power for 6 minutes, covered, or until vegetables are crisp tender. Drain off liquid. Mix eggs, milk and seasonings until well blended. Sprinkle flour over zucchini, tossing lightly. Pour on egg mixture. Add 1 1/2 cup cheese and stir to mix. Cover tightly and microwave for 7-9 minutes at 70% power, stirring once. Top with remaining cheese. Replace cover and let stand until cheese is melted.

Nutrition (per serving): 178 calories
Saturated fat .... .4 g
Total Fat ....9 g (48% of calories)
Protein .... 17 g (37% of calories)
Carbohydrates .... .7 g (15% of calories)
Cholesterol .... 175 mg
Sodium .... 410 mg
Fiber ....0 g

CHART FOR COOKING CEREAL

Item	Container	Amount of Water	Cereal	Salt	Time
Oatmeal (Old Fashioned)	1 quart	3/4 cup	1/3 Cup	Dash	3-5 min.
Oatmeal (Quick)	1 pint.	3/4 cup	1/3 Cup	Dash	1-2 min.
Cream of Wheat	1 quart	1 cup	21/2 Tbs.	Dash	3-4 min.
Cream of Wheat (instant)	per pkg.	per pkg.	per pkg.	Dash	1/2-1 min.

Mix cereal with hottest tap water. You will notice large bowls are used in proportion to amounts of cereal. This prevents boil over. Cook at 100% power, uncovered and stir halfway through the cooking time. Tip: You might like to add a dip of ice cream instead of cream and sugar sometime.

CHART FOR COOKING RICE AND OTHER GRAINS

Item	Container	Amount of Hot Water	Approx. Time To Boil Water 100 % Power	Cook Time 30 % Power	Stand Time
Brown Rice 1 cup	2 qt. bowl	3 cups	5-6 min.	40-50 min.	15 min.
Mixed Rice (6 oz.)	2 qt. bowl	2 c. or per pkg. direct.	4 -5 min.	20-25 min.	5-10 min.
Long Grain Rice- 1 c.	2 qt. bowl	2 cups	4-5 min.	14-16 min.	10 min.
Quick Rice 1 cup	1 qt. bowl	1 cup	2-3 min.	5 min.	5 min.
Short Grain Rice- 1 c.	2 qt. bowl	2 cup	4-5 min.	10-12 min.	10 min.
Instant Rice 1 cup	2 qt. bowl	1 cup	2-3 min.	1 min. (optional)	5-10 min.
Grits 2/3 Cup	3 qt. bowl	31/2 c.	5-6 min.	10 min.	10 min.

Always cook rice covered well. Also, larger amounts should be stirred once to separate the grains before the long cooking time takes place. You may add bouillon cubes and desired spices to water before boiling, if you wish. You will also notice that cooking rice and grains in the microwave does not save time, but it will give you a good product.

COOKING PASTA

Basic Pasta

Serves 6

6 cups hottest tap water
1 tablespoon oil
1 teaspoon salt
8 ounces pasta

Place water in 4 quart casserole. cover and Microwave at 100% power for 8 minutes or until water boils. Add oil, salt and pasta; stir to prevent strands from sticking together. Cover. Cook at 100% power for 6-8 minutes, or until pasta tests "al dente", stirring half way through cooking. Drain and rinse in colander. Tip: After cooking toss with olive oil or magarine to prevent pasta from sticking together.

Lasagna

Serves 6

6 cups hottest tap water
1 tablespoon oil
1 teaspoon salt
8 ounces lasagne noodles

Place noodles in 12 x 8 inch rectangular baking dish. Pour boiling water over noodles. Add oil and salt and stir. Cook, uncovered, for 8-10 minutes at 100% power or until noodles tests "al dente". Stir half way through cooking time.

General Information:

When cooking pasta, the same method is used in the microwave as stove top. Microwaving produces wonderful pasta. It is "al dente"—soft, but slightly resistant to the bite. Also remember, leftover pasta may be frozen and rejuvenated in the microwave oven on a busy day. Place cooked pasta in freezer-weight zip-locking bag. Spread out in an even flat layer. Freeze. To reheat, unzip bag part way and microwave at 100% power for approximately 2 minutes per cup, redistributing the pasta as it defrosts.

notes:

_____

_____

_____

_____

_____

_____

_____

_____

_____

_____

_____

_____

_____

_____

_____

_____

_____

_____

Main Dish/Brunch

DID YOU KNOW?

♥ Leaf lettuce dipped into soup will remove excess fat. Or... drop in ice cubes. The fat clings to the cubes. Remove and discard.

♥ Add two or three slices of raw potato and boil a few minutes to remove excess salt.

♥ Too sweet... add a touch of salt.

♥ A stiffly beaten egg white for each pound of ground beef makes juicier burgers. (Especially good with very lean beef that tends to be dry.

♥ Instead of a roasting rack, make a grid or rack of carrot and celery sticks to place meat, or poultry on. The vegetables flavor the drippings and keep the meats out of grease.

♥ You may tenderize "tough" meat by rubbing all sides with a mixture of vinegar and olive oil. Let stand for two hours before cooking. You may also tenderize very tough meat by rubbing it thoroughly with baking soda and letting it stand for a few hours. Rinse thoroughly before cooking.

♥ Bake fish on a bed of chopped onion, celery and parsley... fish tastes wonderful.

♥ Try soaking fish in 1/4 cup of vinegar, wine or lemon and water before cooking to make it sweet and tender.

♥ Use stuffing cubes as breadcrumbs for meatloaf and meatballs for less mess.

♥ Drop carrots in boiling water and let stand for 5 minutes. Place immediately into cold water. The skins will slip right off.

♥ To peel lots of tomatoes at once, place them in an old pillow case or onion netting and plunge them in a pot of boiling water for a minute. Skins slide right off. You may also do a few at a time by dropping them individually in boiling water for a minute. Remove and slip skins off.

♥ Butter and margarine can be kept firm without ice by wrapping in cloth wrung out in salt water.

♥ Children can handle tacos, gooey sandwiches and fruit easily if they use a coffee filter instead of a napkin.

♥ Place heel of bread on top of cabbage, broccoli or Brussels sprouts to absorb cooking odor.

♥ Mask cabbage odor by adding a few cloves to the container in which you cook it.

♥ Don't throw away steak, roast or chicken bones. Wrap and freeze until needed for soup stock... always start cooking bones in cold salted water for stock.

♥ For a juicier bird, fill a basting needle with a mixture of butter and wine (bouillon and wine for low fat) and inject into the raw turkey around the breast and thigh in several spots.

Main Dish/Brunch

Beef/Veal

Avocado Tostadas
Barbecued Brisket
Beef Casserole
Beef Paprika
Beef Stroganoff
Corned Beef And Cabbage
Enchilada Casserole
Fajitas
Lazy Day Stew
Liver Superb
Meatloaf
Party Meat Loaf
Pepper Steak
Pot Roast Supreme
Roast Beef
Stuffed Hamburgers
Tamale Casserole
Veal Marsala
White Lasagne

Egg/Cheese/Meatless

Breakfast Crepes
Brunch Egg Casserole
Casserole Relleno
Cheese and Mushroom Rarebit
Cheese Enchiladas
Easy Souffle
Egg And Potato Casserole
Eggs Rockefeller
Eggs Sunny Side Up
Fettuccine Sour Cream
Frittata
Happy Day Potatoes
Hard Boiled Eggs
Lone Star Eggs
Mexican Scrambled Eggs
Pasta With Green Sauce
Penne With Spicy Sauce
Puffy Cheese Omelet
Shirred Eggs
Sour Cream Enchiladas
Southwestern Eggs
Zucchini Lasagne

Fish and Seafood

Cajun Baked Fish
Florentine Flounder
Golden Fish Fillets
Non-fishlovers Bake
Scallops Exceptional
Seafood Au Gratin
Seafood Gumbo
Seafood Imperial
Shrimp Chafing Dish
Shrimp Curry Au Gratin
Spanish Shrimp

Pork and Lamb

Bacon Bits
Barbecued Pork Chops
Barbecued Ribs
Cajun Pork Roast
Cheese And Sausage Grits
Cranberry Ham
Ham Loaf
Maple Pork Chops
Pineapple Lamb Chops
Plan Over Casserole
Pork With Mustard Sauce
Sportsman's Sausage
Stuffed Pork Cutlets

Poultry/Game

Apricot Chicken
Chestnut Chicken
Chicken Alfredo
Chicken Asparagus
Chicken Divan
Chicken Risotto
Chicken Tetrazzini
Chicken Tostadas
Chicken With Lobster
Dirigibles
Duck A La Orange
Fiery Chicken
Garden Turkey Breast
Mexican Casserole
Pheasant With Sauerkraut
Picante Chicken
Raspberry Praline Hens
Roquefort Chicken
Sherried Chicken
Tarragon Cream Chicken
Turkey A La Orange

Avocado Tostadas

Serves 12

These tostadas may be made without meat or substitute chicken for beef if you are watching your fat intake.

12 tostada shells
1 (16 oz) can fat free refried beans
2 pounds extra lean ground beef
2 3/4 cups prepared guacamole
1/2 cup sliced pitted black olives
4 cups shredded lettuce
1 cup grated lowfat cheddar cheese
1/2 cup nonfat sour cream
Hot to mild Picante sauce

Brown ground beef, 6 minutes per pound at 100% power, drain and set aside. Prepare remaining ingredients and assemble as follows: Spread tostada shell with refried beans; top with ground beef, guacamole, olives, lettuce, cheese and sour cream. Garnish with guacamole and Picante sauce if desired.

```
Nutrition (per serving): 342 calories
       Saturated fat .......................................................... ..6 g
       Total Fat ............................................................... 24 g (62% of calories)
       Protein .................................................................. 21 g (25% of calories)
       Carbohydrates ...................................................... 11 g (13% of calories)
       Cholesterol ........................................................... 60 mg
       Sodium ................................................................. 346 mg
       Fiber .................................................................... ..0 g
```

Barbecued Brisket

Serves 12

This marinade makes an excellent sauce or may be thickened for gravy. Make certain that the roast is uniform is shape so that it will cook evenly.

4 pounds beef brisket
2 tablespoons catsup
1 teaspoon chili powder

2 tablespoons liquid woodsmoke flavoring

2 teaspoons Worcestershire sauce

2 teaspoons celery seed

1 teaspoon garlic salt

1 teaspoon seasoned salt

1 teaspoon soy sauce

1 teaspoon onion salt

1 1/2 teaspoons seasoned pepper

1/4 teaspoon dried parsley

1/2 cup lite Italian salad dressing

1/2 cup barbecue sauce

Trim all fat, score meat and pierce well. Mix all ingredients. Pour over meat and let marinate for 12-24 hours. When ready to cook, place meat in microwave roaster, pour on marinade. Cover and cook for 8-12 minutes at 100% power until mixture is boiling. Reduce power to 30% power and cook for 45 minutes. Turn brisket over and cook for an additional 1 hour or until meat is tender. Let stand 5-10 minutes before serving. Allow meat to cool before slicing.

```
Nutrition (per serving): 493 calories
    Saturated fat ..................................................... 16 g
    Total Fat ............................................................ 41 g (76% of calories)
    Protein ............................................................... 26 g (21% of calories)
    Carbohydrates .................................................. ..4 g (3% of calories)
    Cholesterol ...................................................... 111 mg
    Sodium ............................................................. 758 mg
    Fiber ................................................................. .0 g
```

Beef Casserole

Serves 12

Don't forget you can cook your noodles in the microwave.

1 (8 oz.) package thin egg noodles

1 clove garlic, minced

1 1/2 pounds extra lean ground beef

3 (8 oz.) cans tomato sauce

1/4 teaspoon salt

1/4 teaspoon black pepper

1 tablespoon sugar

1 cup lowfat creamed cottage cheese

1 (8 oz.) package light cream cheese

1/4 cup nonfat sour cream

1/3 cup chopped onions

1/4 cup finely chopped green bell peppers
1 cup grated lowfat cheddar cheese

Cook and drain noodles according to directions. Place garlic and beef in colander or microwave casserole. Microwave at 100% power for 5 minutes or until no longer pink, stirring once. Place drained beef in casserole and add tomato sauce, salt, pepper and sugar. Blend in cottage cheese, cream cheese, onion and green pepper. Place 1/2 of noodles in 9 x 13 inch casserole. Top with 1/2 cheese mixture. Add remaining noodles and cover with cheddar cheese and beef. Microwave at 70% power for 10-15 minutes until very hot and bubbly.

```
Nutrition (per serving): 329 calories
    Saturated fat ............................................ ..8 g
    Total Fat .................................................. 17 g (47% of calories)
    Protein .................................................... 22 g (27% of calories)
    Carbohydrates ......................................... 21 g (26% of calories)
    Cholesterol ............................................. 78 mg
    Sodium .................................................... 631 mg
    Fiber ....................................................... 1 g
```

Beef Paprika

Serves 8

1 3/4 pounds boneless beef sirloin, trimmed and cut into 1" cubes
1 whole onion, sliced
2 cloves garlic, minced
1/2 teaspoon browning powder, optional
2/3 cup catsup
1/4 cup beef flavored bouillon
2 tablespoons Worcestershire sauce
1 tablespoon packed brown sugar
1 teaspoon paprika
1/2 teaspoon dry mustard
1/8 teaspoon ground cayenne pepper
2 tablespoons flour
1/4 cup water

Place meat, onion and garlic in 2 quart casserole in circle fashion. Dampen and sprinkle with browning powder. Cover and cook at 100% power for 4-6 minutes. Rearrange once, sprinkle with more browning powder and cook additional 4-5 minutes until meat is nearly done. Add catsup, bouillon, Worcestershire sauce, sugar and spices. Heat at 100% power for 4-6 minutes until bubbling. Whisk flour and water thoroughly and stir through meat mixture. Stir and reduce power to 50% power for 10-15 minutes until very hot throughout. Serve over buttered noodles.

Nutrition (per serving): 255 calories
Saturated fat .... 5 g
Total Fat .... 10 g (36% of calories)
Protein .... 30 g (47% of calories)
Carbohydrates .... 11 g (17% of calories)
Cholesterol .... 88 mg
Sodium .... 595 mg
Fiber .... 0 g

Beef Stroganoff

Serves 8

This is an elegant sauce which may be served over noodles or wild rice. When cooking conventionally, the same techniques are followed: sear meat, saute vegetables, thicken sauce and gradually warm sour cream sauce until it is hot. Learn to use your microwave as you would your stove top whether preparing entire dishes or as a helping hand for conventional preparation.

2 pounds beef tenderloin
1/2 teaspoon browning powder, optional
3 tablespoons lowfat margarine
1 cup chopped onions
1/2 pound fresh mushrooms, 1/4" slice
2 cloves garlic, minced
4 tablespoons flour
2 teaspoons beef base concentrate
1 teaspoon Greek seasoning, or seasoned salt
1 tablespoon catsup
1/8 teaspoon black pepper
10 ounces low sodium beef broth
1/4 cup dry white wine
1 1/2 tablespoons fresh dill weed
1 1/2 cups nonfat sour cream

Trim all fat and silver from beef. Cut crosswise into 1/2 inch thick slices. Cut each slice across grain into 1/2 inch wide strips. Place beef in colander, circle fashion (3/4 pound at a time). Dampen meat and sprinkle with browning powder. Cover and cook 3-5 minutes at 100% power, rearranging once, if necessary. This step "sears" in meat juices, but meat is rare. Remove and set aside. Place margarine in 3 quart casserole. Heat 2-3 minutes at 100% power until melted. Add onion, garlic and mushrooms. Cover and microwave at

100% power for 3-4 minutes, stirring once until onions begin to soften. Stir in flour, beef base, catsup, and pepper until smooth. Gradually add bouillon. Microwave at 100% power for 4-8 minutes, stirring once until liquid begins to thicken. Add meat, wine, dill and sour cream. Heat at 50% power for 10-15 minutes until very hot, but not boiling.

Nutrition (per serving): 401 calories	
Saturated fat	9 g
Total Fat	23 g (52% of calories)
Protein	35 g (35% of calories)
Carbohydrates	13 g (12% of calories)
Cholesterol	97 mg
Sodium	718 mg
Fiber	0 g

Corned Beef And Cabbage

Serves 8

Brisket may be cooked at 50% power, but it is very muscular and does better at 30% power. Start muscular roasts at 100% power until liquid is boiling, then reduce power. Because it is the liquid that tenderizes muscular meat, the liquid around the roast must be heated to nearly boiling before reducing heat. If this is not done, it takes so long at the lower power setting to heat the liquid that the meat will not have time to tenderize.

3 pounds corned beef brisket
1 onion, quartered
1 clove garlic, minced
1 1/2 cups water
4 whole small carrots, cut into 2" pieces
1 small head cabbage, cut into wedges

Place brisket including seasoning pack, onion and garlic in 3 quart covered casserole. Pour water over all. Microwave, covered, at 100% power for 10-15 minute until liquid is boiling. Reduce heat to 30% power and cook for 45 minutes. Turn brisket over and add vegetables. Cover and cook an additional 1 hour at 30% power or until meat and vegetables are tender. Let stand for 5-10 minutes before serving. Allow meat to cool a bit before slicing.

Nutrition (per serving): 563 calories	
Saturated fat	18 g
Total Fat	45 g (73% of calories)
Protein	30 g (22% of calories)
Carbohydrates	8 g (6% of calories)
Cholesterol	124 mg
Sodium	130 mg
Fiber	1 g

Enchilada Casserole

Serves 8

Mexican food is a snap to prepare in the microwave. There is no need to "fry" tortillas in fat to soften as done in conventional preparation. Saves fat and calories, too.

1 pound extra lean ground beef
1/4 cup chopped onions
1 (16 oz.) can fat free refried beans
1/4 cup hot taco sauce
1/2 teaspoon salt
1/8 teaspoon garlic powder
8 (6-inch) corn tortillas
1 (10 oz.) can enchilada sauce
1/3 cup sliced pitted black olives
3/4 cup shredded lowfat cheddar cheese
3/4 cup shredded light Monterey Jack cheese

Place ground beef in microwave colander. Cook at 100% power for 3 minutes, covered. Stir to break apart. Mix in onion. Cook 2-3 minutes longer or until meat is no longer pink. Place hamburger in casserole or bowl and mix with refried beans, taco sauce, salt and garlic powder. Pour enchilada sauce in 8 x 12 inch casserole. Set aside. Place tortillas between dampened paper towels and microwave at 100% power for 30-45 seconds until pliable. Place 1/3 cup of meat/bean mixture down center of each tortilla and roll up. Roll filled tortillas in sauce to moisten. Place seam side down in casserole. Cover and microwave at 70% power for 10-15 minutes until very hot. Uncover and sprinkle with cheese and olives. Microwave uncovered an additional 1-3 minutes until cheese is melted.

Nutrition (per serving): 345 calories
Saturated fat	6 g
Total Fat	17 g (44% of calories)
Protein	24 g (27% of calories)
Carbohydrates	25 g (29% of calories)
Cholesterol	45 mg
Sodium	709 mg
Fiber	1 g

Fajitas

Serves 6

Chicken is a delicious substitute in this dish. Just remember, cook chicken 6 minutes per pound, covered, at 100% power. If you plan to store the guacamole for a while, cover tightly and place the seed into mixture until serving time. This helps prevent mixture from becoming dark. Top round or tip steaks may be substituted in this recipe.

1 1/2 pounds beef top loins
1 cup Picante sauce, mild to hot, divided
2 teaspoons lemon juice, divided
1 dash black pepper
1 dash garlic powder
1 large avocado
1/4 teaspoon salt
1 whole onion, thinly sliced
1 whole large green bell pepper, seeded and cut into rings
12 (10-inch) flour tortillas
1 large tomato, chopped
1/4 cup salsa, optional
1/4 cup nonfat sour cream, optional

Tenderize meat by pounding with mallet. Slice across grain into thin strips. Set aside. Mix 1/2 cup Picante sauce, 1 teaspoon lemon juice, pepper and garlic in refrigerator container. Place meat into mixture and refrigerate for 3-12 hours, turning occasionally. To make guacamole, peel, seed and mash avocado. Add remaining lemon juice, Picante sauce and salt. Stir well and refrigerate. Drain. Place onion and green pepper in microwave casserole. Microwave for 2-3 minutes, covered, at 100% power. Set aside. Place meat in colander or 2 quart casserole. Cover and microwave for 4 minutes at 100% power. Rearrange or stir meat. Cook an additional 3-5 minutes. Stir in onion and pepper and set aside to allow heat to distribute evenly. Place tortillas between two sheets of damp paper towels and microwave for 40 seconds to 1 minute at 100% power until hot and pliable. For each fajita, place some meat, onion and pepper down center of tortilla. Roll and serve with tomato, salsa and sour cream.

Lazy Day Stew

Serves 10

This is a recipe that takes about 8 hours in the conventional oven. It shows how to utilize slow cooking in your microwave and save many hours of cooking time. Try a few fresh mushrooms in this sometimes for a bit of a change. Also, do not drain vegetables if potatoes are used.

1 (28 oz.) can tomatoes
1 (8 oz.) can tomato sauce
6 ounces beef consomme
1/2 cup red wine
4 tablespoons tapioca
1 tablespoon brown sugar, optional
1 bay leaf
1/2 teaspoon seasoned salt
1/2 teaspoon beau monde seasoning
1/2 teaspoon pepper
1/4 teaspoon garlic powder
1/4 teaspoon basil
1/4 teaspoon marjoram
1/4 teaspoon dried thyme
1/4 teaspoon paprika
1/8 teaspoon allspice
1/8 teaspoon ground cloves
1/8 teaspoon cumin
3 potatoes, peeled and quartered, optional
1/2 cup dry bread crumbs
1 (16 oz.) can green beans drained
1 (16 oz.) can petite peas drained
1 (16 oz.) can small onions, drained

3 large carrots, cut into small chunks
3 pounds beef stew

Mix tomatoes, tomato sauce, consomme, wine, tapioca, sugar, spices, bread crumbs and potatoes together in large 5 quart casserole. Layer remaining vegetables and meat in order given. Cover and heat for 15-20 minutes until mixture is very hot. Lower power to 50%, cover and cook 45 minutes. Stir gently, cover and cook at 50% power for an additional 45 minutes to 1 hour or until vegetables and meat are tender. Stir and let stand a few minutes so heat will distribute.

```
Nutrition (per serving): 330 calories
    Saturated fat ......................................................... .2 g
    Total Fat ................................................................. .6 g (15% of calories)
    Protein ................................................................... 38 g (46% of calories)
    Carbohydrates ....................................................... 30 g (37% of calories)
    Cholesterol ............................................................ 78 mg
    Sodium .................................................................. 901 mg
    Fiber ...................................................................... 3 g
```

Liver Superb

Serves 4

Beef liver does not have to be cooked well done. It may be left "pink". If this is overcooked for your taste, lessen time. If it is undercooked, add time. Pork and poultry liver, however, needs to be fully cooked.

1 pound beef liver, sliced 3/4" thick
4 slices bacon
3/4 cup finely crushed wheat crackers
1 tablespoon minced fresh parsley
1 teaspoon paprika
1/2 teaspoon salt
1/8 teaspoon black pepper
1/3 cup thousand island dressing

Place bacon slices around edge of microwave casserole. Partially cover and cook at 100% power for 3 minutes, rearranging once if cooking is uneven. Remove bacon to paper towel. In a pie plate, mix cracker crumbs, parsley, paprika, salt and pepper. Spread liver slices on both sides with dressing. Thoroughly coat in seasoned crumbs. Place liver slices circle fashion in bacon drippings, thickest portions to outside of casserole. Cook for 4 minutes at 70% power. Turn liver slices over, sprinkle with more crumbs if desired and top with crumbled bacon. Rotate dish. Cook for 1-3 minutes or until liver is cooked as desired.

Meat Loaf

Serves 8

This mixture makes one very large meatloaf, two medium size meatloaves or 8 small individual meatloaves. This also makes wonderful stuffed peppers. Small loaves should be placed in circle fashion to cook. Remember they will take less time than a large loaf to cook.

2 pounds lean ground beef

11/2 cups herbed bread stuffing crumbs

2 eggs, slightly beaten

3/4 cup catsup

1/3 cup warm water

1 (3 oz.) package dehydrated onion soup mix

1 teaspoon creamed horseradish

1 teaspoon Worcestershire sauce

1/2 teaspoon seasoned pepper

4 ounces tomato sauce

1/4 cup brown sugar

Mix beef and stuffing mix. Stir in eggs, tomato sauce, water, soup mix, horseradish, Worcestershire sauce and pepper. Mix well and form into a ring or narrow loaf. Place on rack or in microwave colander or casserole. Cook for 8-24 minutes at 70% power. Drain off fat and top meatloaf with catsup/brown sugar mixture. Microwave another 3-5 minutes, or until meat is no longer pink. Let stand a few minutes before serving.

Party Meat Loaf

Serves 6

A "ring" is the perfect shape for cooking meatloaf , in the micro-wave. It has "4 way" even cooking (See Cooking Patterns). Placing meatloaf on a roasting rack in a ring shape or in a colander will drain off fat. An inverted glass (one that will take high heat such as a jelly glass, bar glass, etc.), if placed top down in the middle of a casse-role, will not only make a ring shaped casserole, but will also suction off grease during standing time. Of course you cannot remove the glass to serve the meatloaf as that would break the "suction" or seal and the grease will drain out. Simply serve family style from the pan leaving the glass in place.

2 cups fine dry bread crumbs
2/3 cup Picante sauce, mild to hot
1/3 cup chopped onions
1/3 cup chopped green bell peppers
1/4 cup chopped ripe olives
2 tablespoons pimiento-stuffed green olives
1 egg
1/2 teaspoon chili powder
1 teaspoon creamed horseradish
1 (4 oz.) can mushroom stems and pieces, drained
1 1/2 pounds extra lean ground beef
1 teaspoon salt
3 slices (1 oz. each) light Monterey Jack cheese

Mix breadcrumbs, Picante sauce, onion, green pepper, olives, egg, horseradish, chili powder, mushrooms and salt. Add beef and mix well. Place mixture in a ring casserole or in a ring shape in micro-wave casserole or colander. Cover with microwave wrap and cook at 70% power for 12-20 minutes, rotating once, if cooking is uneven. Drain off excess fat. Quarter cheese slices and form a pattern on top of meat loaf. Recover and let stand while cheese melts and meat has finished its "ongoing" cooking.

Nutrition (per serving): 436 calories
Saturated fat .... 9 g
Total Fat .... 23 g (48% of calories)
Protein .... 27 g (25% of calories)
Carbohydrates .... 29 g (26% of calories)
Cholesterol .... 116 mg
Sodium .... 1049 mg
Fiber .... 0 g

Pepper Steak

Serves 6

Vegetables may be cooked to "crisp tender" if desired. Recipes are a guide and should be adapted to your own taste. Beef round steak may be substituted in this recipe, but the longer it marinates the more tender it will become.

1 1/2 pounds beef sirloin steak
1/3 cup low sodium soy sauce
1 clove garlic, minced
1 teaspoon ground ginger
1/2 teaspoon salt, optional
1/4 teaspoon black pepper
2 large onions, thinly sliced
2 green bell peppers, seeded and sliced
1 cup diagonally sliced celery
1/2 teaspoon sugar
2/3 cup low sodium beef broth
2 tablespoons cornstarch
1 (8 oz.) can sliced water chestnuts, optional
1/4 cup water
1 1/2 tablespoons cornstarch
3 cups hot cooked rice
2 small tomato, peeled and cut into eighths

Freeze steak for at least one hour. Slice beef into strips 1/8" thick slices. Place in container with soy sauce, garlic, ginger, and pepper. Marinate for 30 minutes to 1 hour. When ready to cook, drain meat, reserving marinade, and place in 3 quart casserole. Cover and cook 4-7 minutes at 100% power, stirring once or twice until meat is partially cooked and begins to brown. Remove meat and set aside. Add green pepper, onions and celery. Microwave, covered, for 5-10 minutes until vegetables start to soften. Add meat and soy marinade, sugar, bouillon, water chestnuts and cornstarch dissolved in 1/4 cup of water. Cover and cook for 2-4 minutes at 100% power. Stir and lower power level to 70%. Cook 4-10 minutes until vegetables are crisp tender and sauce thickens. Add tomatoes and stir together. Microwave 1 additional minute and let stand a minute or two. Serve over rice.

Nutrition (per serving): 719 calories
```
Saturated fat ........................................................ 10 g
Total Fat .............................................................. 24 g (30% of calories)
Protein ................................................................ 30 g (17% of calories)
Carbohydrates ..................................................... 96 g (53% of calories)
Cholesterol .......................................................... 78 mg
Sodium ................................................................ 531 mg
Fiber ................................................................... 1 g
```

Pot Roast Supreme

Serves 8

Pick roasts of uniform shape for best results. The 6 minute per pound rule does not apply to muscular roasts (chuck, brisket, etc.) which need liquid to tenderize. The liquid "hides" the meat and changes cooking time. Once liquid around roast is hot, it takes approximately 55-60 minutes per pound at 30% power or 45-50 minutes at 50% power to tenderize roasts. Semi-muscular beef roasts (loin, eye or top round, rump, etc.), cook best on a rack both conventionally and microwave. They do not need liquid to tenderize, but cook best at 30% power, a slow heat. High power levels do not allow adequate time for development of tenderness and flavor. Cook at 100% power for a few minutes to seal in juices, then reduce power and cook 16-22 minutes per pound. This sauce thickened makes a wonderful gravy. The onion is delicious, but may be discarded if desired. Mashed potatoes instead of pieces of potato are great also!!

3 pound chuck roast
1 cup catsup
1 tablespoon freshly ground black pepper
1 1/2 teaspoons salt
1 tablespoon chili powder
1 tablespoon garlic powder
1 peeled onion
12 small red potatoes, peeled and halved
8 large carrots, scrubbed and halved
2 cups water

Mix catsup, pepper, salt, garlic powder. Pour over roast and add 1-2 cups of water to cover or nearly cover roast. Heat, covered at 100% power for 10-15 minutes until liquid is beginning to boil. Reduce power to 50% power. Cook, covered for 30 minutes. Turn meat over, add vegetables. Cook 50% power for additional 1-1 1/2 hours until meat and vegetables are tender.

Nutrition (per serving): 487 calories
```
Saturated fat ..................................................... 14 g
Total Fat .............................................................. 34 g (62% of calories)
Protein ................................................................ 25 g (20% of calories)
Carbohydrates .................................................... 26 g (18% of calories)
Cholesterol ......................................................... 19 mg
Sodium ............................................................... 744 mg
Fiber ................................................................... 1 g
```

Roast Beef

Serves 12

Microwave cooking extracts about 1/3 more fat from meats than conventional cooking does. It doesn't, however, extract the meat juices. There are very few drippings until you slice the meat, so be certain to save this juice for gravy. Although meat cooks satisfactorily by time, the most accurate way is by using a "probe" or thermometer made for the microwave. Elevate meat off the bottom of microwave so microwaves can get evenly under and around the meat. If you don't have a microwave rack, place on a casserole cover, etc. to lift meat out of its juices.

> 3 pounds sirloin beef tip roast
> 1/4 teaspoon garlic powder
> 1/2 teaspoon cracked black pepper
> 1/2 teaspoon browning powder, optional
> 3 slices bacon

Dampen roast slightly and rub with garlic powder. Press in pepper. If using browning powder, pierce with fork and sprinkle on powder. Wrap bacon slices around roast and place on meat rack, fat side down. Microwave at 100% power for 5 minutes. Reduce power to 30%, if time permits. Cook, partially covered, for 13-20 minutes per pound according to type of meat and desired doneness (See *Precepts of Meat)*. Turn the roast over halfway through the cooking time. When cooking time has finished or the internal temperature has been reached, remove from the microwave and "tent" with aluminum foil, shiny side to meat. Let stand 5 to 10 minutes before serving to allow "ongoing" cooking to finish.

Nutrition (per serving): 231 calories
```
Saturated Fat ..................................................... . 4 g
Total Fat, ............................................................ 11 g (43% of calories)
Protein ................................................................ 33 g (57% of calories)
Carbohydrates .................................................... ..0 g (0% of calories)
Cholesterol ......................................................... 93 mg
Sodium ............................................................... 116 mg
Fiber ................................................................... 0 g
```

Stuffed Hamburgers

Serves 4

Try variations other than listed. For example, other vegetables, sauces, etc. These are good as a main dish as well as a sandwich. Try Monterey Jack, cheddar or Roquefort cheese in these for a change.

1 onion, thinly sliced
1 pound lean ground beef
1/4 cup fine dried bread crumbs
1/4 cup barbecue sauce
1/2 cup shredded lowfat Swiss cheese
1 teaspoon browning powder, optional

Separate onion into rings. Place in small microwave casserole and cook, covered, for 2-3 minutes at 100% until tender. Set aside. Drain if onions contain excess moisture. Mix beef, crumbs and sauce. Form mixture into 8 flat patties. Divide onion among 4 patties. Sprinkle with cheese and top each filled patty with plain patty, crimping the edges together to seal. Dampen patties with water and sprinkle with browning powder. Place in circle fashion on microwave rack or in microwave casserole. Partially cover and microwave at 100% power for 6 minutes per pound, turning once during cooking.

Nutrition (per serving): 404 calories
Saturated fat .... 11 g
Total Fat .... 28 g (62% of calories)
Protein .... 27 g (26% of calories)
Carbohydrates .... 11 g (11% of calories)
Cholesterol .... 96 mg
Sodium .... 285 mg
Fiber .... 0 g

Tamale Casserole

Serves 6

1 (16 oz.) can tamales
1 onion, chopped
1 cup light Velveeta cheese, cubed
1/4 cup Picante sauce, mild to hot
1 (4 oz.) can chopped green chiles
1 1/2 cups tortilla chips

Drain tamales, unwrap. Cut tamales in half. Layer tamales, onion, cheese cubes, green chiles and Picante sauce in 2 quart casserole. Cook, covered, at 70% power for 18-22 minutes or until bubbly hot. Serve on top of tortilla chips.

Nutrition (per serving): 282 calories
Saturated fat .... .3 g
Total Fat .... 16 g (52% of calories)
Protein .... 10 g (14% of calories)
Carbohydrates .... 24 g (34% of calories)
Cholesterol .... 32 mg
Sodium .... 1397 mg
Fiber .... .1 g

Veal Marsala

Serves 4

Remember not to overcook meat as it will continue to cook about 20% more after the microwave shuts off. Veal and lamb need not be cooked well done like poultry. This dish is also very good made with beef, chicken or pork cutlets for a change.

> 4 4-ounce veal cutlets
> 1/2 cup seasoned bread crumbs
> 1/4 teaspoon dried parsley
> 2 cups sliced fresh mushrooms
> 1/2 cup chopped onions
> 1 clove garlic, minced
> 2 tablespoons melted lowfat margarine
> 2 tablespoons dry Marsala red wine
> 2 tablespoons sweet Marsala red wine
> 1/2 teaspoon salt
> 1/8 teaspoon black pepper
> 1/8 teaspoon paprika

Coat veal with crumbs and set aside. Place mushrooms, onion and garlic in 2 quart microwave casserole. Cover and microwave at 100% power for 2-4 minutes, stirring once, until vegetables start to soften. Stir in flour and margarine. add wine, salt, pepper and paprika. Place veal, circle fashion, on top of mushrooms and onions. Place in microwave partially covered and cook for 4 minutes at 100% power. Turn chops over and sprinkle with paprika. Rotate dish. Reduce power to 50%, cover and cook an additional 8-16 minutes or until meat is tender. Let stand a few minutes before serving. Stir mushroom mixture and spoon over cutlets.

Nutrition (per serving): 223 calories
```
Saturated fat ........................................................ ..2 g
Total Fat ............................................................... ..7 g (26% of calories)
Protein ................................................................. 26 g (46% of calories)
Carbohydrates ..................................................... 13 g (24% of calories)
Cholesterol .......................................................... 90 mg
Sodium ................................................................ 549 mg
Fiber .................................................................... .0 g
```

White Lasagne

Serves 12

If you wish to hurry this dish, noodles may be cooked convention-ally—or pour boiling water over pasta and let stand while combining other ingredients. Ground turkey may be substituted for beef.

8 ounces lasagne noodles, cooked
1 pound lean ground beef
2 cups finely chopped celery
2 cups finely chopped onions
1 clove garlic, minced
1 1/2 teaspoons dried basil
1 1/2 teaspoons dried oregano
1/2 teaspoon dried Italian seasoning
1 cup evaporated skim milk
1 (3 oz.) package softened light cream cheese
1/2 cup dry white wine
2 cups shredded lowfat cheddar cheese
1/2 cup shredded gouda cheese
12 ounces 1% lowfat creamed cottage cheese
2 ounces liquid egg substitute`
12 ounces lowfat mozzarella cheese
1/8 teaspoon paprika

Place noodles in 9 x 13 inch casserole and add 6 cups warm water and 1 tablespoon oil. Cook, covered, for 12-14 minutes at 100% power. Place ground beef in colander or 2 quart microwave casse-role. Cover and cook for 3 minutes at 100% power. Stir and add vegetables. Cover and cook additional 4-5 minutes at 100% power, stirring once. Drain. Add spices and set aside. Place cheese and milk in casserole and heat at 70% power for 3-5 minutes, stirring once or twice until cheese melts. Add wine and remaining cheese, except for mozzarella. Cook another few minutes until cheese melts.

Stir cottage cheese and egg into cheese mixture. Drain noodles. They will only be partially done. Wipe out casserole and layer 1/2 of noodles, 1/2 meat mixture, 1/2 cheese mixture and 1/2 mozzarella. Repeat. Sprinkle with paprika. Cook for 14-20 minutes at 70% power until mixture is bubbly hot. Let stand 10 minutes before cutting.

```
Nutrition (per serving): 408 calories
    Saturated fat ..................................................... 10 g
    Total Fat .............................................................. 21 g (46% of calories)
    Protein ................................................................ 31 g (31% of calories)
    Carbohydrates ................................................... 22 g (22% of calories)
    Cholesterol ......................................................... 86 mg
    Sodium ................................................................ 471 mg
    Fiber ..................................................................... 0 g
```

Egg/Cheese/Meatless

Be safe... Never Eat Nor Stir In Raw Eggs

Food safety experts say to remove all recipes calling for raw eggs from your files. Yolks may be contaminated with salmonella, a bacteria that can cause illness.

The risk is slight, but it is better not to take chances. The salmonella bacteria in eggs quickly multiplies at room temperature, but dies when cooked at 140 degrees for 3 1/2 minutes.

Here's the recipe from Harold McGee, a California-based author and food chemist, for safe egg yolks to use in uncooked foods.

Safe Egg Yolks

2 large raw egg yolks
2 1/2 tablespoons water
1 teaspoon lemon juice or vinegar

Mix yolks, water and lemon juice or vinegar in a small glass bowl. Cover with plastic wrap. Microwave at 100% power until mixture bubbles, about 20 seconds, and let bubble for 5-10 seconds more. Beat with another clean fork. As mixture cools, it should have the consistency of a stirred custard.

Breakfast Crepes

Serves 1

Remember that electrical power can fluctuate within your home according to time of day (See Power Fluctuation). A tortilla may be substituted for crepe if desired.

1 egg
1/3 cup minced cooked ham
2 tablespoons nonfat sour cream
1 tablespoon minced green onions
1 dash dry mustard
1 dash Greek seasoning, or your favorite spice
3 tablespoons shredded lowfat cheddar cheese

Microwave "hard boil" egg (See *Brunch/Eggs/Cheese*). Chop egg and combine with next five ingredients. Place mixture with cheese on a crepe. Roll and place seam side down on microwave rack or casserole. Microwave at 70% power for 30 seconds to 1 minute until hot and bubbly.

```
Nutrition (per serving): 237 calories
    Saturated fat ........................................................ ..4 g
    Total Fat ................................................................ 12 g (45% of calories)
    Protein ................................................................. 27 g (45% of calories)
    Carbohydrates .................................................. ..6 g (10% of calories)
    Cholesterol ........................................................ 248 mg
    Sodium ............................................................... 1587 mg
    Fiber ................................................................... ..0 g
```

Brunch Egg Casserole

Serves 8

Don't forget for low fat version of this dish or other egg dishes, use egg whites or egg substitute.

4 slices bacon, fried crisp
2 cups plain croutons
1 cup shredded lowfat cheddar cheese
4 eggs, slightly beaten
1 3/4 cups skim milk
1/2 teaspoon prepared mustard
1/2 teaspoon salt
1/8 teaspoon onion powder
1/8 teaspoon black pepper

Mix croutons and cheese and put into 8 x 12 inch casserole. Mix eggs, milk, mustard and spices until blended. Pour over crouton mixture. Crumble bacon and sprinkle over egg mixture. Microwave, uncovered, at 70% power for 14-18 minutes or until knife comes out clean when inserted near center. Let stand a few minutes before serving.

Nutrition (per serving): 225 calories

Saturated fat	..5 g
Total Fat	15 g (59% of calories)
Protein	13 g (23% of calories)
Carbohydrates	11 g (19% of calories)
Cholesterol	123 mg
Sodium	495 mg
Fiber	0 g

Casserole Relleno

Serves 12

When cooking eggs and cheese in the microwave, lower "heat" or power level as if cooking conventionally. Cheese will string and get tough if cooked at extremely high heat.

4 (8 oz.) cans whole mild green chiles
1 pound light Monterey Jack cheese
5 eggs
1 cup skim milk
1/4 cup flour
1/2 teaspoon salt
1/8 teaspoon black pepper
4 cups grated mild lowfat cheddar cheese

Slit chiles lengthwise on one side. Remove seeds and drain. Slice Jack cheese into 1/4 inch thick slices and place inside chiles. Place chiles in 3 quart casserole. Mix eggs, milk, flour, salt and pepper. Pour over chiles. Sprinkle with grated cheddar cheese and microwave, uncovered, at 70% for 12-20 minutes. Let stand a few minutes before serving.

Nutrition (per serving): 328 calories

Saturated fat	11 g
Total Fat	21 g (58% of calories)
Protein	27 g (33% of calories)
Carbohydrates	..8 g (10% of calories)
Cholesterol	143 mg
Sodium	685 mg
Fiber	1 g

Cheese and Mushroom Rarebit

Serves 4

Remember that cheese or egg type sauces may be started on "high" heat or 100% power, but for best results should finish on a medium or low heat. If cooked to boiling, sauces could curdle and string.

2 tablespoons minced onions
1 (8 oz.) can mushrooms, drained
1 (10 3/4 oz.) can cond. cheese soup
1/2 cup skim milk
1 teaspoon prepared mustard
1/3 teaspoon garlic powder
1/8 teaspoon ground nutmeg
1/8 teaspoon crushed red pepper
1/8 teaspoon paprika
4 slices toasted bread

Place onion in 2 quart casserole. Cover and cook 30 seconds at 100% power. Add mushrooms, soup, milk, mustard and spices. Stir until smooth. Cook at 100% power for 3 minutes. Stir and reduce power to 70%. Cook an additional 4-8, stirring once or twice, until mixture is very hot. Serve over toast. Sprinkle with paprika.

Nutrition (per serving): 249 calories
Saturated fat ....0 g
Total Fat .... 17 g (62% of calories)
Protein ....5 g (8% of calories)
Carbohydrates .... 19 g (30% of calories)
Cholesterol .... 44 mg
Sodium .... 1203 mg
Fiber ....1 g

Cheese Enchiladas

Serves 8

1 cup grated lowfat cheddar cheese
1 cup grated light jalapeño pepper cheese
1 cup grated light Monterey Jack cheese
1 (4 oz.) can chopped mild green chiles
1 (10 3/4 oz.) can enchilada sauce
3 chopped green onions including tops
8 (10-inch) flour tortillas

Mix all cheeses except for 1/4 cup cheddar cheese with green chiles and onions. Set aside. Soften tortillas (See Microwave Hints.) Fill tortillas equally with cheese mixture. Roll, envelope style. Place seam side down in 8 x 12 inch casserole. Top with enchilada sauce. Sprinkle with remaining cheddar cheese and microwave, covered, at 70% power for 10-15 minutes or until very hot.

```
Nutrition (per serving): 398 calories
    Saturated fat ........................................................ ..6 g
    Total Fat ............................................................. 15 g (33% of calories)
    Protein ............................................................... 24 g (24% of calories)
    Carbohydrates ..................................................... 43 g (43% of calories)
    Cholesterol ......................................................... 8 mg
    Sodium ............................................................... 608 mg
    Fiber .................................................................. ..0 g
```

Easy Souffle

Serves 6

If soup mixture is hot, pour a small amount of hot soup mixture into yolk mixture. Pour egg yolk mixture into remaining sauce, stirring to prevent lumpiness.

1 (10 3/4 oz.) can cond. cheese soup
1 dash cayenne pepper
1/4 teaspoon dried marjoram
6 eggs, separated

In 1 quart container blend soup and spices. Heat at 100% power for 2-4 minutes until hot, stirring occasionally. Beat egg whites until stiff peaks form. Set aside. Beat egg yolks in small bowl until yolks are thick and yellow colored. Gradually stir in soup mixture and fold in egg whites. Pour into ungreased 2 quart casserole or souffle dish. Microwave at 30% power for 20-35 minutes, rotating occasionally. Let stand a few minutes before serving.

```
Nutrition (per serving): 136 calories
    Saturated fat ....................................................... 4 g
    Total Fat ............................................................. 9 g (61% of calories)
    Protein ............................................................... 8 g (25% of calories)
    Carbohydrates ..................................................... 5 g (14% of calories)
    Cholesterol ......................................................... 224 mg
    Sodium ............................................................... 442 mg
    Fiber .................................................................. 0 g
```

Egg And Potato Casserole

Serves 8

Elevating delicate foods such as egg dishes and cakes help them to cook more evenly. Also, try using Swiss cheese in this recipe for a change.

6 ounces frozen hash brown potatoes
5 eggs, well beaten
1/2 cup 1% lowfat creamed cottage cheese
1 cup shredded light Monterey Jack cheese
4 drops Tabasco sauce
1 dash salt
1 dash black pepper
3/4 cup grated lowfat cheddar cheese
1 whole minced green onion
6 slices bacon, crisply fried
1/8 teaspoon paprika

Place potatoes in large mixing bowl. Add beaten eggs, cottage cheese, Jack cheese, Tabasco, salt and pepper. Put mixture into 10 inch quiche plate. Top with cheddar cheese, onion and bacon. Sprinkle with paprika. Place in microwave on inverted cover or casserole and microwave at 70% power 10-15 minutes or until knife inserted in center comes out clean. Let stand to become firm. Serve warm.

Nutrition (per serving): 287 calories
Saturated fat .... 10 g
Total Fat .... 22 g (70% of calories)
Protein .... 15 g (21% of calories)
Carbohydrates .... 6 g (9% of calories)
Cholesterol .... 167 mg
Sodium .... 480 mg
Fiber .... 0 g

Eggs Rockefeller

Serves 6

If desired, this casserole may be prepared except for the sauce and refrigerated overnight. When ready to cook, bring casserole to room temperature, heat sauce and proceed according to the recipe. Eggs may be "microwave hard boiled" if they are to be chopped and used in salads, etc. To hard boil eggs for deviled eggs or a dish such as this, use stove top method. Cooking time of this casserole will be shortened by heating sauce before covering eggs, as it is the liquid that will take so long to heat.

1 (10 oz.) package frozen chopped spinach
6 hard boiled eggs
1/2 cup nonfat mayonnaise
2 teaspoons tarragon vinegar
2 teaspoons prepared mustard
1/8 teaspoon black pepper
1 (10 3/4 oz.) can cond. cheese soup
3/4 cup skim milk
1/8 teaspoon paprika
1/2 teaspoon finely chopped parsley

Place spinach box on microwave-safe plate. Pierce several times and microwave at 100% power for about 3 minutes until defrosted and cooked. Gently squeeze box to drain. Peel eggs and cut in half lengthwise. Remove yolks and mash or puree. Mix yolks with mayonnaise, vinegar, mustard, salt, pepper and half of the spinach. Place the other half of spinach in a 8 x 8 inch square casserole or 2 quart casserole. Fill eggs and place in rows in casserole. Mix soup and milk and place in microwave container. Heat for 3-4 minutes at 100% power until hot. Pour over egg-spinach casserole and heat at 70% power partially covered for 5-10 minutes until bubbly hot. Sprinkle with paprika and parsley before serving.

Nutrition (per serving): 211 calories
Saturated fat ....2 g
Total Fat .... 16 g (68% of calories)
Protein ....9 g (17% of calories)
Carbohydrates ....8 g (15% of calories)
Cholesterol .... 242 mg
Sodium .... 1053 mg
Fiber .... 0 g

Eggs Sunny Side Up

Serves 2

By piercing egg yolks, the gas pressure is released somewhat and there is less chance of their exploding if overcooked.

1 tablespoon lowfat margarine
2 eggs
1 dash salt
1 dash black pepper

Preheat browning dish for 3-5 minutes, depending on size of dish (see manufacturers instructions). Add margarine. As margarine melts, tilt dish to coat. Break eggs into dish and gently pierce yolks. Cover or leave uncovered for more crisp egg. Cook for 30-60 seconds at 100% power until yolk is desired firmness. Egg may also be turned over for a second or two if "over easy" result is desired. Season to taste.

Nutrition (per serving): 100 calorie
Saturated fat .... 2 g
Total Fat .... 8 g (71% of calories)
Protein .... 6 g (25% of calories)
Carbohydrates .... 1 g (4% of calories)
Cholesterol .... 213 mg
Sodium .... 327 mg
Fiber .... 0 g

Fettuccine Sour Cream

Serves 4

This dish may be made ahead. Place food in casserole, reheat, covered, at 50% power and toss before serving. Fresh vegetables, meats, poultry and seafood may be used in this dish also.

8 ounces fettuccine noodles
1/4 cup melted lowfat margarine
1/2 cup nonfat sour cream
3/4 cup grated parmesan cheese
1/8 teaspoon freshly ground black pepper

Cook noodles in the microwave or conventionally, according to directions being careful, however, not to overcook. Drain noodles. Toss noodles with margarine and remaining ingredients. Serve immediately or place in chafing dish to keep warm.

Frittata

Serves 6

This freezes well. Also, you may add other vegetables or meat in place of artichoke hearts if you desire. An aluminum foil ring may be used for shielding (a circle with no center), if edges start to overcook (See Shielding).

> 4 whole eggs
> 2 (6 oz.) jars marinated hearts of artichokes
> 1 cup shredded lowfat Swiss cheese
> 2 teaspoons dried Italian herbs
> 1 teaspoon onion salt
> 1 teaspoon chopped chives
> 1 teaspoon chopped fresh parsley

Place eggs in mixing bowl. In a food processor, finely chop artichoke hearts. Mix chopped artichoke hearts and remaining ingredients into well beaten eggs. Pour mixture into 9 inch pie plate. Place on inverted microwave dish to elevate and microwave at 70% power for 12-14 minutes or until metal knife inserted in center comes out clean. Allow frittata to stand and cool before cutting. Reheat at 50% power for several minutes if desired and serve.

Happy Day Potatoes

Serves 6

This recipe will show the diversity of the microwave. We can bake our potatoes, make our white (cheese) sauce, "microwave hard boil" our eggs as well as finish the dish in our "friend", the microwave.

4 potatoes, baked, cooled and sliced
2 hard boiled eggs, peeled and sliced
1 small onion, thinly sliced
4 tablespoons lowfat margarine, divided use
2 tablespoons flour
1 cup skim milk
1/2 cup light Velveeta cheese, cubed
3/4 teaspoon salt, divided
1/4 teaspoon black pepper, divided
1/4 teaspoon dry mustard
1/2 cup shredded lowfat cheddar cheese

Spread 2 teaspoons of margarine in 2 quart casserole. Layer 1/2 potatoes, chopped eggs, onion, 1/2 teaspoon salt and 1/8 teaspoon pepper. Top with remaining potatoes and set aside. In 2 cup measure, melt margarine for 30 seconds at 100% power. Whip in flour and mustard. Gradually add milk, mixing thoroughly. Heat for 3-4 minutes at 100% power, stirring once. Add cheese and remaining salt. Stir until cheese is melted. Pour cheese sauce over potatoes. Cover and cook for 5-10 minutes at 100% power or until bubbly hot. Sprinkle with cheese and heat for 1 minute, uncovered, at 100% power.

Nutrition (per serving): 305 calories	
Saturated fat	..4 g
Total Fat	10 g (30% of calories)
Protein	14 g (18% of calories)
Carbohydrates	39 g (51% of calories)
Cholesterol	87 mg
Sodium	781 mg
Fiber	..1 g

Hard Boiled Eggs

Serves 1

This is an excellent way to prepare eggs for salads, etc. You won't have to peel them either. Several eggs may be done at once, circle fashion, but need to be rotated to cook evenly. Eggs take 1-1 1/2 minutes per egg. A shorter time is required for several eggs (See Dealing With Multiples).

1 egg
nonstick cooking spray

Lightly spray custard cup. Crack egg and place liquid eggs into proper container. Pierce egg yolk gently. Cover and cook at 50% power for 1-1 1/2 minutes. Let stand and cool before slicing or chopping.

```
Nutrition (per serving): 82 calories
     Saturated fat ....................................................... 2 g
     Total Fat .............................................................. 6 g (66% of calories)
     Protein ................................................................ 6 g (31% of calories)
     Carbohydrates ................................................... 1 g (3% of calories)
     Cholesterol ......................................................... 213 mg
     Sodium ................................................................ 63 mg
     Fiber .................................................................... 0 g
```

Lone Star Eggs

Serves 10

Food from the refrigerator may be brought to room temperature by heating at 20-30% power for a few minutes before cooking.

12 whole eggs
1/4 cup skim milk
1/4 teaspoon salt
1/8 teaspoon black pepper
1 (10 3/4 oz.) can lowfat cond. cream of mushroom soup
1 (4 oz.) can sliced mushrooms, drained
1 cup grated lowfat cheddar cheese
1/8 teaspoon paprika

Mix eggs and milk. Place in round casserole and microwave at 100% power, approximately 8-10 minutes, stirring occasionally until eggs are moist and partially set, but not overdone. Mix all remaining ingredients except cheese and paprika in mixing bowl. In 2 quart casserole layer eggs, soup and cheese. Sprinkle with paprika. Let stand overnight. Warm to room temperature and then microwave, partially covered, for 10-15 minutes at 50% power or until very hot throughout. Let stand a few minutes for heat to distribute evenly.

```
Nutrition (per serving): 138 calories
     Saturated fat ....................................................... 3 g
     Total Fat .............................................................. 8 g (56% of calories)
     Protein ................................................................ 12 g (35% of calories)
     Carbohydrates ................................................... 3 g (9% of calories)
     Cholesterol ......................................................... 262 mg
     Sodium ................................................................ 304 mg
     Fiber .................................................................... 0 g
```

Mexican Scrambled Eggs

Serves 6

You may scramble eggs at 100% power as the high fat of the yolks and the low fat egg whites are blended. For uniform cooking, however, it is necessary to stir eggs occasionally as they cook more around the outside of the dish than in the middle (See Cooking Patterns). Heating the cheese at 100% power until it melts is like placing cheese under the broiler when cooking conventionally. Cook only until it melts. Prolonged cooking at high heat level would cause the cheese to string.

2 small tomatoes, chopped and drained
1 (4 oz.) can diced mild green chiles
2 tablespoons finely minced onions
6 eggs
1/8 teaspoon garlic powder
1/8 teaspoon salt
1 dash black pepper
1 cup grated lowfat sharp cheddar cheese
1/2 teaspoon minced fresh parsley

Place vegetables in round 2 quart casserole dish. Cover and cook for 1-2 minutes at 100% power until vegetables soften. Beat eggs and milk with garlic powder, salt and pepper. Microwave, uncovered, at 100% power for 4-6 minutes, stirring several times until eggs are set, but still moist. Sprinkle cheese over top and cook for 1-2 minutes at 100% power until cheese is melted. Sprinkle with parsley and serve.

Nutrition (per serving): 148 calories
Saturated fat ....3 g
Total Fat ....9 g (54% of calories)
Protein .... 13 g (36% of calories)
Carbohydrates ....4 g (10% of calories)
Cholesterol .... 223 mg
Sodium .... 243 mg
Fiber ....0 g

Pasta With Green Sauce

Serves 4

This is a delicious pasta, but a step from the ordinary spaghetti with red sauce. Remember, spaghetti may also be cooked in your microwave (See Side Dish-Pasta).

2 tablespoons lowfat margarine
2 tablespoons chopped fresh basil
2 tablespoons chopped fresh parsley
1 clove garlic, minced
1/2 teaspoon ground black pepper
1/3 cup grated parmesan cheese
1 (8 oz.) package softened light cream cheese
2/3 cup boiling water
8 ounces cooked spaghetti

Melt margarine in 4 cup measure for 1 minute at 100% power or until melted. Add herbs to margarine. Blend in garlic, pepper and cheeses. Stir in boiling water and heat at 50% power until hot and cheese is melted. Place hot spaghetti on plate and top with sauce.

```
Nutrition (per serving): 416 calories
    Saturated fat ....................................................... 10 g
    Total Fat ............................................................. 19 g (41% of calories)
    Protein ................................................................ 16 g (15% of calories)
    Carbohydrates ................................................... 45 g (43% of calories)
    Cholesterol ......................................................... 48 mg
    Sodium ................................................................ 427 mg
    Fiber ................................................................... 0 g
```

Penne With Spicy Sauce

Serves 4

Pasta may be cooked in the microwave (See Side Dish-Pasta). Also, slow cooking in the microwave only takes 1/4-1/3 of the time of slow cooking conventionally.

1/4 cup finely chopped onions
2 tablespoons olive oil
6 cloves garlic, slightly crushed
1/4 cup finely chopped celery
1/4 cup finely chopped green bell peppers
1 (16 oz.) can undrained tomatoes
1 cup chopped fresh parsley
1/4 teaspoon dried red pepper
1/4 teaspoon salt
1/3 teaspoon freshly ground black pepper
1/2 teaspoon dried basil
2 jalapeño peppers, seeded and minced, optional
1/2 pound cooked Penne tube pasta
Grated parmesan cheese

Place olive oil, celery, green pepper, onion and garlic in 2 quart microwave casserole. Cover and cook for 4-6 minutes at 100% power. Stir in tomatoes with liquid, 3/4 cup parsley and red pepper. Break up tomatoes with a spoon. Season with salt and pepper. Heat for 5 minutes at 100% power. Reduce power to 30% and simmer for 12-20 minutes until tomatoes are thick and pulpy, stirring occasionally. Discard garlic and mix in remaining parsley. Pour sauce over pasta and toss well. Sprinkle with parmesan cheese and serve.

```
Nutrition (per serving): 282 calories
    Saturated fat ........................................................ 1 g
    Total Fat ............................................................. 9 g (28% of calories)
    Protein ............................................................... 9 g (13% of calories)
    Carbohydrates ..................................................... 42 g (59% of calories)
    Cholesterol ......................................................... 42 mg
    Sodium ............................................................... 381 mg
    Fiber .................................................................. 1 g
```

Puffy Cheese Omelet

Serves 2

If eggs do not want to cook in the center, gently lift edges and allow uncooked eggs to flow underneath. You may also add cooked vegetables or meats instead of cheese or at the same time as cheese is added. Cook an additional 30 seconds—1 minute to thoroughly heat through. Margarine may be omitted if you are watching fat intake. Just spray dish lightly with no-fat cooking spray.

3 eggs, separated
1/3 cup nonfat mayonnaise
2 tablespoons water
1 tablespoons margarine, optional
3/4 cup grated lowfat cheddar cheese
1 dash salt
1/8 teaspoon black pepper
1/4 teaspoon chopped fresh parsley

Beat egg whites in large bowl until soft peaks form. In separate bowl beat yolks, mayonnaise and water. Gently fold yolks into whites, blending well. Place margarine in 9 inch pie plate and microwave for about 45 seconds at 100% power. (This step may be omitted if you are watching your fats by simply greasing dish lightly.) Tilt dish to coat completely. Pour egg mixture into dish and cook at 50% power, partially covered, for 7-8 minutes, rotating dish if eggs appear to be cooking unevenly. When eggs are set but still a bit moist on top, sprinkle with cheese. Cook 1 minute at 50% power until cheese is melted. Gently fold omelet in half and slide onto serving plate. Sprinkle with parsley and serve immediately.

```
Nutrition (per serving): 279 calories
     Saturated fat ...................................................... ..6 g
     Total Fat .......................................................... 16 g (51% of calories)
     Protein .............................................................. 24 g (35% of calories)
     Carbohydrates ................................................... 10 g (14% of calories)
     Cholesterol ....................................................... 342 mg
     Sodium .............................................................. 947 mg
     Fiber .................................................................. ..0 g
```

Shirred Eggs

Serves 2

Wattage of microwave and power fluctuation within homes can make times vary quite a bit. (See Power Fluctuation)

2 lowfat margarine
2 eggs
1 dash salt
1 dash black pepper

Place 1 teaspoon margarine in each of 2 custard cups. Set cups on microwave-safe dinner plate. Heat at 100% power for about 30 seconds. Break 1 egg into each cup. Pierce yolk gently. Cover and cook at 50% power for 1 1/2-2 minutes, rotating plate if eggs appear to be cooking unevenly. Allow eggs to stand, covered, for a moment or two. Serve in cups or invert into bowl.

```
Nutrition (per serving): 91 calories
     Saturated fat ...................................................... 2 g
     Total Fat .......................................................... 7 g (68% of calories)
     Protein .............................................................. 6 g (28% of calories)
     Carbohydrates ................................................... 1 g (4% of calories)
     Cholesterol ....................................................... 213 mg
     Sodium .............................................................. 303 mg
     Fiber .................................................................. 0 g
```

Sour Cream Enchilada

Serves 12

Prepare white sauce earlier in day if desired. Assemble casserole all but sour cream and heat before serving. More time may be required to heat casserole if white sauce is room temperature rather than hot. Heat gently—as cheese/dairy products can "curdle" if cooked at high temperatures.

6 tablespoons melted lowfat margarine
6 tablespoons flour

3 cups evaporated skim milk
1/2 teaspoon black pepper
1 (8 oz.) can chopped mild green chiles
12 (6-inch) corn tortillas
4 cups grated Longhorn lowfat cheddar cheese
4 cups grated light Monterey Jack cheese
1/2 cup minced onions
1 3/4 cups lowfat sour cream

Mix margarine, flour, milk, and pepper. Blend well and cook at 70% power for 9-15 minutes, stirring occasionally until mixture thickens. Stir in green chiles. Set aside. Place tortillas between 2 sheets of dampened paper towel and microwave for 30 seconds to 1 minute at 100% power until tortillas are pliable and soft. Divide mixture of cheese and onion equally between tortillas. Roll and place seam side down in 9 x 13 inch microwave casserole. Pour white sauce mixture over top. Heat at 50% power for 10 minutes or until very hot. Serve with sour cream.

```
Nutrition (per serving): 457 calories
    Saturated fat ....................................................... 11 g
    Total Fat ............................................................. 23 g (45% of calories)
    Protein ................................................................ 33 g (29% of calories)
    Carbohydrates ................................................... 30 g (26% of calories)
    Cholesterol ......................................................... 56 mg
    Sodium ............................................................... 636 mg
    Fiber .................................................................... 1 g
```

Southwestern Eggs

Serves 6

This dish may be brought to "room" temperature by microwaving at 20-30% power for several minutes. Egg dishes should be cooked at lower power levels or "heat" for best quality. Remember to cook for the least time at lower power when time permits. Time may always be added, but if overcooked, food is ruined.

6 eggs
1 (16 oz.) can canned cream-style corn
2 cups grated lowfat cheddar cheese
1 (4 oz.) can chopped mild green chiles
2 teaspoons Worcestershire sauce
1/4 teaspoon salt
1/2 teaspoon black pepper

Mix all ingredients, beating well. Pour into a 3 quart casserole. Cover and refrigerate for 24 hours, if possible—otherwise, overnight. Bring to room temperature and microwave for 10-15 minutes at 50-70% power, uncovered. Let stand a minute or two and then serve.

```
Nutrition (per serving): 265 calories
    Saturated fat ..................................................... 5 g
    Total Fat .............................................................. 13 g (43% of calories)
    Protein .................................................................. 21 g (32% of calories)
    Carbohydrates ................................................... 17 g (25% of calories)
    Cholesterol .......................................................... 233 mg
    Sodium ................................................................. 589 mg
    Fiber ..................................................................... 1 g
```

Zucchini Lasagne

Serves 8

If you wish a "crisper" top on the casserole, wait and sprinkle with toasted crumbs after cooking.

4 large zucchini
1 (16 oz.) can tomatoes
1 (6 oz.) can tomato paste
1/2 cup apple cider
2 cloves garlic, minced
1/2 cup chopped onions
1 1/2 teaspoons dried oregano
1/2 teaspoon dried thyme
1/2 teaspoon dried basil
1 dash salt
1 dash black pepper
1 (8 oz.) package sliced lowfat mozzarella cheese
8 ounces lowfat creamed cottage cheese
1/2 cup grated parmesan cheese
1/4 cup toasted bread crumbs

Combine tomatoes, tomato paste, cider, garlic, onion and spices in medium size bowl. Peel and cut zucchini into long 1/4" thick strips. Place 1/2 zucchini in 8 x 12 inch casserole. Top with 1/2 mozzarella and cottage cheese. Spoon 1/2 of sauce over this and repeat layers. Sprinkle with parmesan cheese and crumbs. Cover and cook for 30 minutes at 50% power. Let stand a few minutes before serving.

```
Nutrition (per serving): 194 calories
    Saturated fat ..................................................... 4 g
    Total Fat .............................................................. 7 g (34% of calories)
    Protein .................................................................. 15 g (33% of calories)
    Carbohydrates ................................................... 16 g (34% of calories)
    Cholesterol .......................................................... 23 mg
    Sodium ................................................................. 522 mg
    Fiber ..................................................................... 1 g
```

Cajun Baked Fish

Serves 4

Be careful not to overcook fish as it will become very tough. Meat, vegetables and fruit cook in approximately 6 minutes per pound, but fish and seafood take approximately 3 minutes per pound. Orange roughy may also be substituted for catfish if desired.

> 1 pound catfish
> 1 1/4 cups nonfat mayonnaise dressing
> 1/4 teaspoon crushed red pepper
> 1/2 teaspoon ground cumin
> 1/4 teaspoon onion powder
> 1/4 teaspoon garlic powder
> 1/2 cup crushed crackers

Mix mayonnaise and spices. Coat fish with spice/mayonnaise mixture and coat with cracker crumbs. Arrange fish on microwave rack with thickest portions to outside. Cover with microwave wrap. Microwave at 100% power for 3-4 minutes. Let stand a few seconds and check for doneness. Fish will flake easily when done.

Nutrition (per serving): 185 calories
Saturated fat	1 g
Total Fat	6 g (30% of calories)
Protein	22 g (47% of calories)
Carbohydrates	11 g (23% of calories)
Cholesterol	66 mg
Sodium	366 mg
Fiber	0 g

Florentine Flounder

Serves 8

As fish cooks so much more quickly than meats, partially cook spinach so fish will not overcook. Fish will flake when properly cooked. Arranging the fish in a circle allows it to cook more evenly, as microwaves can enter the food from the center as well as the sides and bottoms (See Cooking Patterns).

> 1 (10 oz.) package frozen spinach, defrosted
> 1/2 cup sliced fresh mushrooms

1/2 cup shredded mozzarella cheese
1/4 teaspoon ground nutmeg
1/4 teaspoon salt
1 dash black pepper
8 firm white fish fillets, approximately 1 1/2 pounds
1/4 cup white wine
1 pinch paprika

Place frozen spinach in microwave-safe casserole. Microwave for 5-6 minutes at 50% power until spinach is defrosted and hot, stirring once to break apart. Drain thoroughly. Mix spinach, mushrooms, cheese, nutmeg, salt and pepper. Stir until cheese is melted. On a flat surface lay fillets side by side. Place 2 tablespoons of spinach mixture on each fillet. Beginning at the small end, roll fillet. Place in casserole circle fashion with seam side down. Pour wine over fillets and cook, covered at 100% power for 6-8 minutes. Sprinkle with paprika and let stand a minute or two before serving.

```
Nutrition (per serving): 217 calories
    Saturated fat ...................................................... 1 g
    Total Fat ............................................................. 3 g (14% of calories)
    Protein ............................................................... 44 g (80% of calories)
    Carbohydrates .................................................... 2 g (4% of calories)
    Cholesterol ......................................................... 105 mg
    Sodium ............................................................... 251 mg
    Fiber .................................................................. 0 g
```

Golden Fish Fillets

Serves 6

Fish is done if it appears translucent and flakes easily with a fork. Do not overcook as fish will become tough. This recipe sounds very hot and spicy, but after cooking, the flavor is wonderful rather than hot. Orange roughy or catfish fillets are delicious in this dish.

1/3 cup prepared mustard
1 tablespoon hot pepper sauce
1/4 cup yellow corn meal
3/4 cup dry bread crumbs
1/4 teaspoon salt
1/4 teaspoon black pepper
1/4 teaspoon paprika
1 1/2 pounds firm white fish fillets

Blend mustard and pepper sauce. Set aside. Mix cornmeal, breadcrumbs and seasonings. Wash fillets and cut into uniform pieces if necessary. Pat dry. Coat all sides with mustard mixture. Roll in dry mixture. Compute time at 3 minutes per pound. Arrange in circle fashion on microwave rack, thickest portions to the outside. Cook at 100% power for computed time. Cover with paper towel and let stand a minute or two. Check for doneness. If necessary, add more cooking time.

Nutrition (per serving): 168 calories
Saturated fat ....0 g
Total Fat .... .2 g (11% of calories)
Protein .... 23 g (54% of calories)
Carbohydrates .... 15 g (35% of calories)
Cholesterol .... 49 mg
Sodium .... 420 mg
Fiber ....0 g

Non-fishlovers Bake

Serves 4

Fish only takes a few minutes (3 minutes per pound) to cook. Sauce is then added and protects the fish from overcooking. With a sour cream sauce it is important to heat gently so that sour cream will not curdle.

1/2 cup skim milk
2 tablespoons lemon juice
4 firm white fish fillets
1/4 teaspoon black pepper
1/4 cup chopped onions
3/4 cup lowfat sour cream
2 tablespoons chopped fresh parsley
2 tablespoons chopped pimientos
1 teaspoon Worcestershire sauce
2 dashes Tabasco sauce
1/4 cup grated parmesan cheese
1 pinch paprika

Soak fish in milk/lemon juice for at least 30 minutes. Place fish fillets in microwave casserole, thickest portions to the outside. Cover and microwave 3 minutes per pound at 100% power or until fish flakes. Drain any liquid that remains. In 2 cup microwave measure, cook onion covered for 1 minute at 100% power. Stir in sour cream, parsley, pimiento, Worcestershire sauce and Tabasco sauce. Top fish with sour cream sauce. Heat at 50% power for 10-15 minutes until all is hot, but not boiling. Sprinkle with parmesan and paprika.

Scallops Exceptional

Serves 4

Scallops will be translucent when done... do not overcook or scallops will be tough. If fresh scallops are not available, frozen defrosted ones will do.

8 ounces large fresh scallops
1 cup florets broccoli
1/2 red bell pepper, cut into strips
1 clove garlic, minced
1 teaspoon crushed fresh basil
1/4 pound light Velveeta cheese, cubed
1 tablespoon dry sherry
2 cups cooked rice

Drain scallops and set aside. Place broccoli, pepper strips, garlic clove and basil in 2 quart microwave casserole. Cook for 1-1 1/2 minutes, covered at 100% power until vegetables begin to soften. Add scallops and cook 2-3 minutes or until tender. Stir in cheese and sherry. Heat 30 seconds- 1 minute until hot. Serve over rice.

Seafood Au Gratin

Serves 8

This recipe has several steps, but is an elegant dish for company or that special family dinner. If you wish, assemble casserole early in the day, refrigerate and heat until hot before serving. Remember, however, refrigerated food takes longer to heat than food at room temperature.

2 cups hot cooked rice
1/2 cup cooked peas
1/2 cup grated Romano cheese
1 (4 oz.) can sliced mushrooms, drained
1/2 teaspoon white pepper
1/4 cup lowfat margarine
1/4 cup flour
1 3/4 cups evaporated skim milk
1 /4 teaspoon salt
1 dash white pepper
2 cups shredded lowfat sharp cheddar cheese
1 cup shredded American cheese
1/3 cup dry sherry
2 ounces fresh scallops
1/3 cup small fresh mushrooms, sliced
3 ounces cooked lump crabmeat
2 tablespoons lemon juice
4 whole green onions including tops, chopped
2 tablespoons white wine

Mix rice, peas, Romano cheese, drained mushrooms and 1/2 teaspoon white pepper and set aside. Place margarine in 4 cup measure, heat at 100% power for 30 seconds or until melted. Stir in flour. Add milk, salt and dash of white pepper. Cook at 70% power, uncovered, for 5-7 minutes, stirring once, until mixture thickens. Add cheddar, American cheese and sherry. Stir until cheese melts. If necessary, heat another few seconds. Set aside. Place scallops and fresh mushrooms in small microwave casserole. Microwave for 1 minute, covered at 100% power. Mix and add other seafood, lemon juice, onion and white wine. Set aside. In large microwave casserole place rice mixture. Top with seafood mixture and cheese sauce. Sprinkle with paprika. Heat at 50% power for 12-18 minutes or until mixture is very hot.

```
Nutrition (per serving): 629 calories
    Saturated fat ........................................................ ..9 g
    Total Fat ............................................................. 20 g (29% of calories)
    Protein ............................................................... 35 g (23% of calories)
    Carbohydrates ..................................................... 72 g (46% of calories)
    Cholesterol ......................................................... 67 mg
    Sodium ............................................................... 1090 mg
    Fiber .................................................................. ..0 g
```

Seafood Gumbo

Serves 10

When possible, hold gumbo until the next day and reheat. Flavor will be much better. Add filé just before serving. Serve over hot rice.

4 tablespoons light salad oil
4 tablespoons flour
1/2 pound pork or Italian sausages
1 green bell pepper, chopped
1 onion, chopped
4 stalks celery, chopped
8 ounces chicken broth
1 (6 oz.) can tomato paste
1 (16 oz.) can chopped Italian tomatoes
1 (10 oz.) package cut frozen okra
1 1/2 cups cooked peeled shrimp
1 pound cooked lump crabmeat
1 tablespoon lemon juice
1 tablespoon Worcestershire sauce
1/4 cup chopped fresh parsley
1/2 teaspoon dried thyme
2 bay leaves
3 tablespoons gumbo filé

Place oil and flour in 2 cup microwave container. Microwave at 100% power for 2-4 minutes until dark brown stirring once. In 2 quart casserole crumble sausage and add celery, onion and green pepper. Cook, covered, at 100% power for 6-8 minutes, stirring once or twice until sausage is done and vegetables tender. Add broth, tomatoes, tomato paste, okra, seafood and spices other than filé. Microwave at 100% power for 4-5 minutes. Reduce power to 30% and simmer for 30-45 minutes, stirring occasionally. If serving right away, stir in filé. Serve over rice if desired.

Nutrition (per serving): 357 calories
Saturated fat ....6 g
Total Fat .... 18 g (46% of calories)
Protein .... 19 g (22% of calories)
Carbohydrates .... 29 g (32% of calories)
Cholesterol .... 119 mg
Sodium .... 1069 mg
Fiber ....4 g

Seafood Imperial

Serves 8

Again, notice all of the ingredients in this recipe which can be cooked, melted or toasted in the microwave. Try various types of seafood in this dish... shrimp, lobster, crab or assorted white fish. For a complete change, use pieces of hard boiled egg. Also, for variation, try substituting curry for dry mustard and nutmeg.

4 tablespoons flour
3 tablespoons melted lowfat margarine
2 cups skim milk
1/2 pound cooked shrimp
1/2 pound lump crabmeat, cooked
1/2 pound white fish, cut into chunks
1/2 pound sliced fresh mushrooms
1/2 pound grated lowfat cheddar cheese
2 ounces chopped pimientos
1/4 cup white wine
1 teaspoon dry mustard
1/8 teaspoon cayenne pepper
1/8 teaspoon garlic powder
1/8 teaspoon ground nutmeg
1/8 teaspoon salt
1/8 teaspoon black pepper
1 tablespoon lemon juice
1 teaspoon Worcestershire sauce
1/4 cup green onions including tops, chopped
1/4 cup toasted slivered almonds
1 pinch paprika

Place flour margarine and milk in 2 quart Casserole. Microwave for 5-7 minutes at 100% power, stirring occasionally until mixture thickens. Add seafood, mushrooms, cheese, pimientos, wine, spices, lemon juice and Worcestershire sauce to white sauce. Sprinkle with green onion. Microwave covered, at 50% power for 12-20 minutes until bubbly hot. Sprinkle with almonds before serving.

Nutrition (per serving): 279 calories	
Saturated fat	..4 g
Total Fat	13 g (41% of calories)
Protein	29 g (41% of calories)
Carbohydrates	11 g (16% of calories)
Cholesterol	126 mg
Sodium	527 mg
Fiber	..1 g

Shrimp Chafing Dish

Serves 16

This dish allows many uses of your microwave. Not only is white sauce made easily, without lumping, but the shrimp may be cooked, covered, in circle fashion for 3 minutes per pound. You may also microwave hard boil eggs (See Eggs) as well as toast the almonds (See Microwave Hints). The conventional cook will also find the microwave to be a great friend in the kitchen. Use this as a great brunch dish, too.

1/4 pound lowfat margarine
2 tablespoons flour
2 cups skim milk
1/4 teaspoon dry mustard
1 (8 oz.) can sliced mushrooms, drained
2 (10 3/4 oz.) can cond. cheese soup
1/4 pound light Velveeta cheese, cubed
4 hard cooked eggs
1 pound peeled cooked shrimp
1 cup toasted sliced almonds
8 cups Rice Chex cereal

Melt margarine in 1 quart container for 45 seconds to 1 minute at 100% power. Stir with flour, mustard and add milk, blending thoroughly. Heat at 100% power for 5-7 minutes, stirring once until mixture thickens. Stir in soup and cheese. Heat, approximately 10 minutes at 70% power until hot, stirring occasionally. Add shrimp, eggs and 3/4 cup almonds, reserving 1/4 cup. Continue to heat another 10 minutes or so until mixture is very hot. Place in serving dish or chafing dish and sprinkle with remaining almonds. Serve over rice chex.

```
Nutrition (per serving): 300 calories
    Saturated fat ................................................. ..2 g
    Total Fat .............................................. 18 g (54% of calories)
    Protein ................................................ 13 g (17% of calories)
    Carbohydrates ................................... 21 g (28% of calories)
    Cholesterol ........................................... 134 mg
    Sodium .................................................. 1002 mg
    Fiber ..................................................... . 0 g
```

Shrimp Curry Au Gratin

Serves 8

To cook shrimp, place in circle fashion, cover and microwave at 100% power for 3 minutes per pound or until shrimps turn pink. Do not overcook or they will be tough.

- 1 cup minced onions
- 1 cup chopped celery
- 1 tablespoon melted lowfat margarine
- 6 tablespoons flour
- 1/4 teaspoon ground ginger
- 1 teaspoon seasoned salt
- 1 teaspoon curry powder
- 1 teaspoon sugar
- 2 1/2 cups evaporated skim milk
- 1 1/2 pounds cooked shelled shrimp
- 3 tablespoons lemon juice
- 1 cup grated lowfat sharp cheddar cheese

Place onion and celery with melted margarine in 2 quart casserole. Cook for 3-5 minutes at 100% power until vegetables soften. Stir in flour, spices and sugar. Gradually add milk, mixing well. Cook at 70% power for 8-10 minutes, stirring occasionally until mixture thickens. Stir in shrimp, lemon juice and cheese. Stir and continue to heat another few minutes until cheese is melted and shrimp is hot. Serve over rice.

```
Nutrition (per serving): 233 calories
    Saturated fat ......................................................... 2 g
    Total Fat ............................................................... 5 g (18% of calories)
    Protein ................................................................. 30 g (51% of calories)
    Carbohydrates ..................................................... 18 g (31% of calories)
    Cholesterol .......................................................... 176 mg
    Sodium ................................................................ 903 mg
    Fiber .................................................................... 0 g
```

Spanish Shrimp

Serves 12

If using shrimp in shells, cook shrimp before starting recipe, 3-4 minutes per pound, covered. It will take more than 3 pounds of shrimp in shells to make 3 pounds of cooked, peeled shrimp. Bacon may also be cooked ahead, 1-2 minutes per slice on microwave rack. This dish is delicious with rice.

3 pounds cooked shelled shrimp
1/4 pound cooked crumbled bacon
1 onion, diced
1 green bell pepper, seeded and chopped
1/2 cup chopped celery
2 cloves garlic, minced
1 pound fresh mushrooms, sliced
1 cup dry white wine
3/4 cup chicken broth
2 cups cooked plum tomatoes
1 bay leaf
1 teaspoon dried basil
1/4 teaspoon salt
1 teaspoon black pepper

When ready to prepare recipe, place onion, green pepper, celery and garlic in 5 quart casserole. Cover and cook for 2-3 minutes at 100% power until vegetables soften. Add mushrooms. Cook an additional 1-2 minutes, covered, to soften mushrooms. Add wine, broth, tomatoes and spices. Heat for 8-10 minutes at 100% power until mixture is very hot. Add shrimp, reduce power to 50% power and continue to cook covered for 5-10 minutes until very hot. Sprinkle with crumbled bacon to serve.

Nutrition (per serving): 204 calories
Saturated fat .... .2 g
Total Fat .... .7 g (31% of calories)
Protein .... 26 g (51% of calories)
Carbohydrates .... .6 g (11% of calories)
Cholesterol .... 227 mg
Sodium .... 474 mg
Fiber .... .1 g

Bacon Bits

Serves 8

Bacon does exceptionally well in the microwave. The microwave also rids bacon of the cancer-causing agents that are produced when cooking conventionally. Cooking times, however, vary tremendously with bacon. Bacon is thick and thin, lean and fat. Neither the 6 minutes per pound rule nor the 1 minute per slice rule is successful. Therefore, cook 3/4 to 1 minute per slice and add more time if necessary.

1 pound thick sliced bacon
3/4 cup packed brown sugar
3/4 teaspoon dry mustard

Place bacon slices in single layer on roasting rack. Cover with a paper towel. Microwave for approximately 1 minute per slice at 100% power until bacon is partially cooked. Mix sugar and mustard. Place bacon in microwave casserole and sprinkle with sugar mixture. Microwave at 100% power for 45 seconds to 1 minute per slice until bacon is thoroughly cooked and crisp to your likeness. Break into bite size pieces to serve if desired.

Nutrition (per serving): 357 calories
Saturated fat .... 12 g
Total Fat .... 33 g (82% of calories)
Protein .... .5 g (6% of calories)
Carbohydrates .... 11 g (12% of calories)
Cholesterol .... 38 mg
Sodium .... 423 mg
Fiber .... .0 g

Barbecued Pork Chops

Serves 6

Remember to check pork for doneness. It must reach 160 degrees throughout to be done. It may still have a light pink interior, but overcooking pork will make it tough.

1 (16 oz.) can stewed tomatoes
1/2 cup packed brown sugar
1/4 cup vinegar
1/2 teaspoon ground nutmeg

1/4 teaspoon ground cloves
1 tablespoon cornstarch
2/3 cup dried bread crumbs
1/4 teaspoon dried parsley flakes
1/4 teaspoon paprika
6 boneless pork chops, 1" thick

Place tomatoes, brown sugar, vinegar, spices and cornstarch in microwave casserole. Mix well. Microwave at 100% power for 6-10 minutes, stirring once. Mix parsley, crumbs and paprika. Moisten pork chops and coat with crumb mixture. Place pork chops in casserole on top of sauce, meatiest portions to outside. Cover and microwave at 70% power for 15-18 minutes. Let stand a few minutes. Spoon sauce over chops to serve.

```
Nutrition (per serving): 448 calories
    Saturated fat ....................................................... 10 g
    Total Fat ................................................................ 28 g (56% of calories)
    Protein .................................................................. 25 g (22% of calories)
    Carbohydrates ..................................................... 25 g (22% of calories)
    Cholesterol .......................................................... 87 mg
    Sodium ................................................................. 347 mg
    Fiber ..................................................................... .0 g
```

Barbecued Ribs

Serves 8

After basting "uncooked" meats and poultry, the marinade should not be served. Juices may have contaminated it. Always reserve fresh marinades and glazes that you plan to serve.

4 pounds pork ribs, cut into 3" pieces
1 whole onion, sliced
1 3/4 cups low sodium chicken stock
1 cup low sodium soy sauce
3/4 cup catsup
1/2 cup pineapple juice
1 1/4 cups honey, divided
1/2 cup dry sherry
2 tablespoons sugar
2 tablespoons ginger, divided
1/2 teaspoon black pepper, divided
1/4 teaspoon garlic powder

Arrange ribs around side of baking dish, meatiest portions to outside. Top with onion rings. Cover with microwave wrap and cook for 5 minutes at 100% power. Reduce heat to 50% power and continue to cook for 15 minutes, rearranging half way through cooking time. Drain ribs. Mix chicken stock, soy sauce, catsup, pineapple juice, 1/2 cup honey, sherry, sugar, 1/4 teaspoon ginger and 1/4 teaspoon black pepper. Reserve 1/4 cup and pour remaining marinade into shallow pan. If possible, add ribs and marinate in refrigerator for 24 hours, turning occasionally. When ready to cook, remove ribs from marinade, place in baking dish, meatiest portions to outside. Micro-wave for 5 minutes at 100% power. For glaze, mix 1/4 cup reserved marinade with remaining honey, ginger and black pepper. Reserve part of glaze mixture to serve with ribs if desired. Baste ribs with remaining mixture. Cook, covered with microwave wrap for 20-25 minutes at 50% power, basting once. Rearrange ribs and baste again. Cook, uncovered, for 10 minutes at 50% power. Serve with remaining glaze if you wish.

```
Nutrition (per serving): 835 calories
    Saturated fat .......................................................... 19 g
    Total Fat ................................................................ 54 g (58% of calories)
    Protein ................................................................... 45 g (21% of calories)
    Carbohydrates ...................................................... 40 g (19% of calories)
    Cholesterol ........................................................... 145 mg
    Sodium .................................................................. 1362 mg
    Fiber ...................................................................... 1 g
```

Cajun Pork Roast

Serves 8

The National Pork Producers Council say that pork cooked to an internal temperature of 160 degrees or medium is now considered "done" and safe to eat as trichinosis is no longer a threat in today's fresh pork supply. Even with the rare chance that consumers buy food tainted by trichanea, it is destroyed at 137 degrees F.

3 tablespoons paprika
1 tablespoon garlic powder
2 teaspoons dried thyme
2 teaspoons dried oregano
1/2 teaspoon cayenne pepper
1/2 teaspoon ground cumin
1/2 teaspoon white pepper
1/2 teaspoon salt
1/4 teaspoon ground nutmeg
2 pounds pork tenderloin, 3" diameter

Mix all spices in small container. Rub spices generously into pork loin. Curve roast in "circle fashion" around the edge of a microwave casserole. If necessary for fit, cut roast in half so that two uniform pieces face one another around the edge of the casserole. Cover and cook for 11 minutes per pound at 50% power. Let stand several minutes and check for doneness in several spots.

```
Nutrition (per serving): 195 calories
     Saturated fat ...................................................... ..3 g
     Total Fat ............................................................ ..9 g (42% of calories)
     Protein ............................................................... 25 g (52% of calories)
     Carbohydrates ................................................... ..3 g (6% of calories)
     Cholesterol ........................................................ 62 mg
     Sodium .............................................................. 200 mg
     Fiber .................................................................. ..1 g
```

Cheese And Sausage Grits

Serves 4

This recipe may be doubled, but cooking time will need to be doubled also.

8 ounces ground pork sausages

1/2 cup quick cooking grits

1 cup hot water

2 tablespoons lowfat margarine

1/4 teaspoon garlic powder

1 dash salt

1/2 cup grated sharp lowfat cheddar cheese

1 egg, well beaten

1 (4 oz.) can chopped mild green chiles

1/4 teaspoon dried parsley flakes

Place sausage in microwave colander and cook for 3 minutes at 100% power, stirring once to crumble. Set aside. In 2 quart casserole microwave water, covered, approximately 2-3 minutes at 100% power until boiling. Add grits, stir and partially cover. Microwave for 2-3 minutes at 100% power. Stir. Add margarine and spices. Blend in cheese, sausage, egg and chiles. Sprinkle with parsley. Microwave, uncovered, at 50% power for 10-15 minutes or until firm. Cover with paper towel and allow mixture to stand for 3-4 minutes before serving.

```
Nutrition (per serving): 361 calories
     Saturated fat ...................................................... ..9 g
     Total Fat ............................................................ 25 g (62% of calories)
     Protein ............................................................... 17 g (19% of calories)
     Carbohydrates ................................................... 17 g (19% of calories)
     Cholesterol ........................................................ 96 mg
     Sodium .............................................................. 856 mg
     Fiber .................................................................. ..0 g
```

Cranberry Ham

Serves 6

When cooking a whole 3-4 pound ham, baste all sides before placing it in the microwave. Cover with vented casserole cover or microwave wrap and heat for 6 minutes per pound at 50% power. Half way through the cooking period, turn ham over, rotisserie style. Ham is precooked and only needs to be reheated... not actually cooked. If desired, this recipe may be basted and cooked with thickened sauce poured over ham right before serving.

1 cup fresh cranberries
1/2 cup sugar
1/4 cup red wine
1 teaspoon grated orange rind
2 teaspoons cornstarch
2 tablespoons water
1 1/2 pounds cured ham, cut into 2-3" slice

Place berries, sugar, wine, and orange peel in 4 cup measure. Mix cornstarch and water. Stir into berry mixture. Microwave for 2-3 minutes at 100% power, stirring once, until sugar dissolves. Place ham in microwave casserole and top with berry mixture. Microwave for 12-15 minutes until ham is hot throughout and sauce has thickened.

Nutrition (per serving): 288 calories
Saturated fat	..4 g
Total Fat	12 g (38% of calories)
Protein	20 g (28% of calories)
Carbohydrates	23 g (32% of calories)
Cholesterol	65 mg
Sodium	1494 mg
Fiber	..0 g

Ham Loaf

Serves 10

1 1/2 pounds smoked ham
1 pound lean ground pork
2 eggs
1/2 cup skim milk
1/3 cup tomato juice
2 tablespoons creamed horseradish
1 tablespoon prepared mustard, divided

1/2 teaspoon black pepper
1 cup crushed crackers
3/4 cup brown sugar
1/4 cup vinegar
1/2 cup water

Mix ham, pork, eggs, milk, tomato juice, horseradish, 1 teaspoon mustard, pepper and crackers. Shape meat loaf into a ring. Place on microwave rack. Mix brown sugar, vinegar, water and remaining mustard in 2 cup measure. Microwave at 100% power for 1-3 minutes until boiling. Boil 1 minute, stir and set aside. Place ham loaf in microwave and cook for 12-15 minutes at 70% power. Top with glaze 10 minutes before loaf is done. Let stand to finish cooking.

```
Nutrition (per serving): 260 calories
    Saturated fat ........................................................ ..3 g
    Total Fat ............................................................. ..9 g (32% of calories)
    Protein ............................................................... 28 g (43% of calories)
    Carbohydrates ................................................... 16 g (25% of calories)
    Cholesterol ........................................................ 107 mg
    Sodium ............................................................... 1224 mg
    Fiber ................................................................... ..0 g
```

Maple Pork Chops

Serves 4

Remember, it is important to cook pork slowly in a covered container to insure even and thorough cooking.

4 (4 ounce) boneless pork chops, 1" thick
1/2 cup chopped onions
1/3 cup maple syrup
1/4 cup water
1 1/2 tablespoons vinegar
1 1/2 tablespoons Worcestershire sauce
2 teaspoons chili powder
1/4 teaspoon salt
1/8 teaspoon black pepper
1/8 teaspoon garlic powder

Arrange chops in microwave casserole, circle fashion, with thickest portions to the outside of dish. Cover with vented microwave casserole cover or microwave wrap. Microwave at 30% power for 7-8 minutes. Mix syrup, water, vinegar, Worcestershire sauce, chili powder, salt, pepper and garlic. Turn pork chops over and pour sauce over chops. Sprinkle with onion. Cover and microwave an additional 7-8 minutes at 30% power until meat is done.

```
Nutrition (per serving): 388 calories
    Saturated fat ..................................................... ..9 g
    Total Fat ........................................................... 25 g (58% of calories)
    Protein ............................................................. 21 g (22% of calories)
    Carbohydrates ................................................. 20 g (20% of calories)
    Cholesterol ...................................................... 79 mg
    Sodium ............................................................ 224 mg
    Fiber ................................................................ ..0 g
```

Pineapple Lamb Chops

Serves 4

Lamb may be cooked rare to well done according to taste. Check for desired doneness, being careful not to overcook. Remember, 20-25% of the cooking takes place during standing time.

> 4 lamb chops, 3/4 " thick
> 1/4 cup pineapple juice
> 1 tablespoon soy sauce
> 2 teaspoons cornstarch
> 1/2 cup chopped green onions including tops

Place lamb chops, circle fashion, in microwave casserole, meatiest pieces to outside of pan. Make a paste of pineapple juice, soy sauce and cornstarch. Heat in small microwave dish for 30 seconds at 100% power until thickened. Spread each chop with sauce and sprinkle with green onion. Partially cover and cook at 70% power for 6-9 minutes. Let stand a minute or two before serving so heat will distribute evenly.

```
Nutrition (per serving): 208 calories
    Saturated fat ..................................................... ..3 g
    Total Fat ........................................................... 10 g (42% of calories)
    Protein ............................................................. 25 g (49% of calories)
    Carbohydrates ................................................. ..5 g (9% of calories)
    Cholesterol ...................................................... 86 mg
    Sodium ............................................................ 349 mg
    Fiber ................................................................ ..0 g
```

Plan Over Casserole

Serves 6

Pasta may be cooked conventionally or microwaved. Also, this is a great casserole for all kinds of leftovers such as pasta, rice, vegetables, poultry, seafood and meats. Simply substitute the proper amounts needed of the desired ingredients for those listed in recipe.

1/2 cup finely diced celery

1/2 cup chopped onions

2 cups cooked drained pasta

2 cups cooked diced pork

1 cup drained peas

1 (10 3/4 oz.) can lowfat cond. cream of chicken soup

1/3 cup skim milk

2 tablespoons water

2 tablespoons chicken bouillon granules

2 tablespoons dried seasoned bread crumbs

1/4 cup grated lowfat cheddar cheese

Place onion and celery in 3 quart microwave casserole. Cover and cook for 2-3 minutes until vegetables begin to soften. Stir in meat, pasta and peas. Mix bouillon which has been dissolved in water with soup and milk. Mix with meat/pasta mixture. Partially cover with microwave wrap or vented casserole cover. Cook at 70% power for 15-20 minutes. Uncover and sprinkle with crackers/chips and cheese. Cook an additional 1-2 minutes uncovered until cheese is melted.

```
Nutrition (per serving): 196 calories
    Saturated fat .......................................................2 g
    Total Fat ...........................................................5 g (24% of calories)
    Protein ............................................................. 16 g (33% of calories)
    Carbohydrates .................................................... 21 g (43% of calories)
    Cholesterol ........................................................ 50 mg
    Sodium ............................................................. 248 mg
    Fiber .................................................................1 g
```

Pork With Mustard Sauce

Serves 12

This roast takes several steps... but it is delicious!!!

3 pounds tied boneless pork tenderloin

3/4 cup dry white wine

1/4 cup Dijon mustard

1 tablespoon mustard seed

2 cloves garlic, pressed

Freshly ground black pepper

1/4 cup mashed soft tofu

1/4 teaspoon dried rosemary

1/4 teaspoon cornstarch

1 tablespoon water

6 whole green onions including tops, chopped

Place pork in microwave casserole. Pour wine over pork. Microwave, uncovered, at 100% power for 5 minutes to "sear" in juices. Mix mustard, mustard seeds and garlic in small bowl. Season with pepper. Rub all but 1 tablespoon of mustard mixture over pork. Cover with vented casserole cover or microwave wrap and cook for 11 minutes per pound at 50% power until meat is done. Transfer pork to platter. Cover loosely with foil for on going cooking. Mix tofu and remaining mustard mixture in 2 cup measure. Using electric mixer, gradually add pan juices and beat until sauce is smooth. Add rosemary and cornstarch/water mixture. Microwave for 1-3 minutes at 100% power until mixture thickens. In small microwave dish place onions and microwave, covered, for 2-3 minutes. Cut strings on pork. Slice pork and arrange. Spoon sauce over and sprinkle with onions.

Nutrition (per serving): 199 calories

Saturated fat	..3 g
Total Fat	..9 g (41% of calories)
Protein	26 g (52% of calories)
Carbohydrates	..1 g (2% of calories)
Cholesterol	71 mg
Sodium	202 mg
Fiber	..0 g

Sportsman's Sausage

Serves 6

This recipe can easily be doubled. Cooking time will double, too. This is a great brunch dish. Also, the skins may be left on apples if you prefer.

1 pound link sausages

6 apples, pared and sliced

1/4 teaspoon salt

1/4 teaspoon black pepper

1 tablespoon lemon juice

3 tablespoons brown sugar

1 teaspoon browning powder, optional

Place sausage on microwave rack and sprinkle with browning powder. Cook 3 - 4 minutes or until meat starts to brown. Cut each link in half, lengthwise. Combine apples and sausage links in 2 quart casserole. Sprinkle with salt, pepper, lemon and sugar. Cover and cook at 70% power for 8-12 minutes.

Stuffed Pork Cutlets

Serves 4

It is important to cook muscular pork slowly to get a moist and evenly cooked product. It is recommended that pork be cooked in closed container to keep the heat uniform. Fresh pork should be cooked to an internal temperature of 160-170 degrees. As standing time will allow meat to cook about 20%, undercook slightly. Cover and let stand a few minutes to complete cooking.

> 4 (4 oz.) boneless lean pork cutlet, 1/2 inch thick
> 2 slices lowfat mozzarella cheese, 4" x 8"
> 1 beaten egg
> 2 tablespoons water
> 1/3 cup flour
> 3/4 cup crushed cracker crumbs
> 1/4 cup grated parmesan cheese
> 1/2 teaspoon dried Italian seasoning
> 1 (10 3/4 oz.) can lowfat cond. cream of mushroom soup
> 1/4 cup skim milk

Place pork cutlets on waxed paper. Place 1/2 slice of cheese on each cutlet. Fold steaks over and seal by pressing together. Mix egg and water in small bowl. In a pie plate mix crumbs, parmesan cheese and Italian seasoning. Dip each cutlet in flour, then egg mixture and coat with crumb mixture. Place in microwave baking dish. Microwave, covered, for 15-20 minutes at 30% power. Turn meat over and cook an additional 12-18 minutes until meat is no longer pink. Mix soup and milk in microwave casserole and cook, covered, for 3 minutes at 100% power. Pour over cutlets to serve.

Poultry/Game

Apricot Chicken

Serves 8

Precook chicken about 3 minutes per pound before adding the remaining ingredients. This is similar to browning on top of the stove when cooking conventionally. Juice of the chicken will run clear when the dish is done. By arranging chicken with meatiest pieces to outside of the pan, chicken will not need rearranging during the cooking as pieces are placed according to cooking pattern of the microwave (See Cooking Pattern). Also, skin chicken for a lower fat dish.

3 pound whole chicken, cut up
1/3 cup Russian salad dressing
1/3 cup apricot preserves
1 (3 oz.) package dehydrated onion soup mix

Wash chicken and pat dry. Arrange chicken in 2 quart casserole, meatiest pieces to outside of dish, boney pieces to the middle. Cook, uncovered, at 100% power for 8-9 minutes. Combine Russian dressing, preserves and soup mix. Spread evenly over chicken. Reduce power to 70% and continue to cook for 15-18 minutes. Check chicken for doneness after it stands a minute or two.

Nutrition (per serving): 486 calories
Saturated fat ....9 g
Total Fat .... 33 g (61% of calories)
Protein .... 32 g (27% of calories)
Carbohydrates .... 15 g (12% of calories)
Cholesterol .... 154 mg
Sodium .... 1139 mg
Fiber ....0 g

Chestnut Chicken

Serves 8

Divide this recipe into two casseroles. Freeze one for later. Remember small casseroles take less cooking time than larger ones. Defrost frozen foods before cooking for best results. Keep microwave techniques similar to conventional cooking techniques. Example: If certain foods are cooked at medium heat conventionally, they should also be cooked at medium heat or power in the microwave.

4 cups cooked chicken, diced
2 cups uncooked noodles
1 (4 oz.) can chopped pimientos
1 (6 oz.) can water chestnuts, drained and chopped
3/4 cup chopped celery
2/3 cup chopped onions
1 (10 3/4 oz.) can lowfat cond. cream of mushroom soup
1 cup chicken broth
1/2 teaspoon salt
1/2 teaspoon black pepper
1/3 cup sliced almonds

Mix all ingredients and place in 8 x 12 inch microwave casserole. Cover tightly and cook at 70% power for 20-30 minutes or until mixture is hot, bubbly and noodles tender. Sprinkle with almonds and paprika. Recover and allow casserole to stand a few minutes before serving.

```
Nutrition (per serving): 258 calories
    Saturated fat ....................................................... ..3 g
    Total Fat ............................................................. 13 g (46% of calories)
    Protein ................................................................ 20 g (31% of calories)
    Carbohydrates ................................................... 15 g (23% of calories)
    Cholesterol ......................................................... 76 mg
    Sodium ............................................................... 476 mg
    Fiber ................................................................... ..1 g
```

Chicken Alfredo

Serves 4

Following conventional techniques, saute vegetables and brown or partially cook chicken before assembling casserole. By heating liquid before adding it to the casserole, microwave cooking time will be greatly shortened.

1 whole onion, chopped
1 whole green bell pepper, chopped
2 cloves garlic, minced
4 skinless boneless chicken breast halves
1/2 cup dry white wine
1 (16 oz.) can tomato sauce
1 1/2 teaspoons dried basil
1/2 teaspoon dried oregano
1/8 teaspoon dried thyme
1 tablespoon Worcestershire sauce

1 cup sliced fresh mushrooms
2 tablespoons low sodium soy sauce
6 ounces lowfat mozzarella cheese, cut into strips

Place onion, green pepper and garlic in 4 cup measure. Cover and cook for 2-5 minutes at 100% power, stirring once until vegetables soften. Place chicken breasts in microwave casserole. Arrange with thickest portions to outside of casserole. Cover and cook 5-6 minutes per pound at 100% power until chicken is nearly done. Drain excess liquid if needed and top with vegetable mixture. In 4 cup measure place wine, tomato sauce, spices and Worcestershire sauce . Mix well. Heat for 6-7 minutes at 100% power until boiling. Pour sauce over chicken/vegetables and cook at 50% power for 10-15 minutes until vegetables and chicken are tender and done. Mix mushrooms and soy sauce. Top with mushroom mixture and cheese. Cook, uncovered, for 1-2 minutes at 100% power until cheese is melted and mushrooms tender.

Nutrition (per serving): 332 calories
Saturated fat .... .5 g
Total Fat ....9 g (24% of calories)
Protein .... 41 g (50% of calories)
Carbohydrates .... 17 g (21% of calories)
Cholesterol .... 93 mg
Sodium .... 1215 mg
Fiber ....1 g

Chicken Asparagus

Serves 8

Sauce may be heated a bit to shorten cooking time if desired. This is a good " fix ahead" casserole. Make two and freeze one. Remember, however, to shorten cooking time for smaller amounts when cooking. Add bread crumbs after casserole is defrosted and ready to cook. If desired, two boxes of frozen defrosted asparagus may be substituted for canned asparagus in this casserole.

6 skinless boneless chicken breast halves
1 1/2 cups instant rice
1 (10 3/4 oz.) can lowfat cond. cream of mushroom soup
1 (10 3/4 oz.) can lowfat cond. cream of chicken soup
1/3 cup nonfat mayonnaise
1/3 cup skim milk
2 (16 oz.) cans asparagus, drained
1 (8 oz.) can water chestnuts, drained and sliced

4 ounces fresh mushrooms, sliced
1/4 cup dried bread crumbs

Wash chicken and pat dry. Place breasts, circle fashion, in micro-wave-safe casserole. Cover and cook 6 minutes per pound. Set aside and cool. Slice chicken after cool. Cover the bottom of 8 x 12 inch casserole with rice. Set aside. Blend soups, mayonnaise and milk. Stir about 1/3-1/2 of mixture through rice. Spread evenly in pan. Layer chicken, mushrooms, chestnuts and asparagus. Pour remaining soup over top. Sprinkle with crumbs. Cook, uncovered, at 70% power for 15-25 minutes. Cover with paper towel for standing time if removed from oven. Casserole should be bubbly hot when served. Cooking times may vary slightly according to starting temperature of ingredients.

```
Nutrition (per serving): 317 calories
    Saturated fat .......................................................... ..0 g
    Total Fat ................................................................. ..2 g (7% of calories)
    Protein .................................................................... 28 g (36% of calories)
    Carbohydrates ........................................................ 46 g (57% of calories)
    Cholesterol ............................................................. 53 mg
    Sodium ................................................................... 378 mg
    Fiber ....................................................................... ..1 g
```

Chicken Divan

Serves 8

This is not expensive or hard to make, but makes great company fare.

2 (10 oz.) packages frozen broccoli spears
2 cups cooked, sliced chicken breast
2 (10 3/4 oz.) cans lowfat cond. cream of chicken soup
3/4 cup nonfat mayonnaise
1 teaspoon lemon juice
1/2 teaspoon ground curry powder
2 (4 oz.) cans mushroom stems and pieces, drained
1/2 cup shredded lowfat sharp cheddar cheese
1/2 cup dried bread crumbs

Arrange broccoli in 8 x 12 inch casserole dish, alternating directions of spears for even cooking. Place cooked chicken on top of broccoli. Mix soup, mayonnaise, lemon juice and spice. Pour over chicken and broccoli. Sprinkle with mushrooms. Cover partially and cook for 15-25 minutes at 70% power until mixture is bubbly hot. Sprinkle with cheese and top with crumbs. Microwave, uncovered, for an additional 2-3 minutes until cheese is melted. Cover loosely and allow food to stand a few minutes before serving.

Chicken Risotto

Serves 4

This dish may be made ahead and reheated, covered, at 50% power until hot. Food reheated in the microwave tastes fresh cooked and should not be considered leftovers. Chicken breasts may be substituted for thighs if lower fat content is desired.

1/2 cup chopped onions

1 clove garlic, minced

2 tablespoons lowfat margarine

3/4 cup converted white rice

1 (14 oz.) can chicken broth

1 cup water

1/2 teaspoon salt

1 pound skinless chicken thighs, cooked and cut into 1" cubes

1 cup julienned carrots

1/2 cup sliced celery

1/4 cup minced fresh parsley

2 tablespoons parmesan cheese

Place onion, garlic and margarine in 3 quart microwave casserole. Cover and cook for 2 minutes at 100% power. Stir in rice, broth, water and salt. Microwave at 100% power for 10-12 minutes until boiling. Add remaining ingredients, except for parsley and cheese. Lower power to 70% power and cook for additional 12-18 minutes until vegetables are "crisp" tender and rice is done. Stir in parsley and sprinkle with parmesan cheese.

Chicken Tetrazzini

Serves 10

Excellent for freezing. Make an extra or save half for use later. Defrost before cooking. Remember smaller quantities take less time than the full casserole. Cooking times can vary slightly due to the temperature of the food when starting cooking.

3 cups cooked chicken, skinned and chopped
1/4 cup chopped green bell peppers
1/8 cup chopped onions
2 cloves garlic, minced
3/4 pound thinly sliced fresh mushrooms
1 pound spaghetti, cooked and drained
1 (10 3/4 oz.) can lowfat cond. cream of chicken soup
1 (10 3/4 oz.) can lowfat cond. cream of mushroom soup
2 cups chicken broth
1/2 cup dry white wine
1 teaspoon dried parsley flakes
1/2 teaspoon paprika
1/8 teaspoon black pepper
1 dash ground nutmeg
1 dash salt
1 1/2 cups shredded lowfat cheddar cheese
1/2 cup grated parmesan cheese

Prepare chicken and set aside. Place green pepper, onion, garlic and mushrooms in a 2 quart microwave container. Cover and cook for 1 - 3 minutes at 100% power, stirring once or twice. Set aside. Mix soups, broth, wine and spices. Place 1/2 of spaghetti in bottom of 8 x 12 inch casserole. Add 1/3 of sauce, stirring gently. Sprinkle with 1/2 of parmesan, layer with mushroom mixture, then chicken. Sprinkle with remaining parmesan and top with 1/3 more sauce. Add remaining spaghetti and sauce. Sprinkle with cheddar cheese. Partially cover with microwave wrap and cook at 70% power for 15-30 minutes until bubbly hot.

Nutrition (per serving): 371 calories
Saturated fat ....4 g
Total Fat ....12 g (28% of calories)
Protein ....25 g (27% of calories)
Carbohydrates ....40 g (43% of calories)
Cholesterol ....53 mg
Sodium ....645 mg
Fiber ....0 g

Chicken Tostadas

Serves 8

Cook chicken breasts and sauce, prepare lettuce, tomato, cheese, etc. ahead of time. Refrigerate and later quickly assemble, heat and serve as an easy supper. Remember, however, if ingredients are cold, it may take a few seconds extra to heat to serving temperature. A prepared canned bean dip may also be substituted for refried beans if desired.

4 skinless boneless chicken breast halves
1 (8 oz.) can tomato sauce
1 1/4 ounces taco seasoning mix
1 (4 oz.) can chopped green chiles
1/4 cup water
9 ounces fat free refried beans
8 tostada shells
2 cups shredded lettuce
1 cup chopped tomatoes
1/2 cup shredded lowfat cheddar cheese
1/2 cup nonfat sour cream
1/2 cup taco sauce

Place chicken breasts in microwave casserole, thickest portions to the outside. Cover and cook 6 minutes per pound until chicken is no longer pink. Set aside. Mix tomato sauce, seasoning mix, chiles and water in 2 quart casserole. Cool at 100% power for 3-4 minutes. Shred or finely chop chicken. Add to tomato mixture and cook 3-4 minutes at 100% power until mixture is very hot. Spread 1-2 tablespoon refried beans over each tostada shell. Top with chicken mixture. Heat each 20-30 seconds at 100% power and top with lettuce, tomatoes, cheese, sour cream and taco sauce as desired.

Nutrition (per serving): 169 calories	
Saturated fat	..1 g
Total Fat	..3 g (16% of calories)
Protein	20 g (48% of calories)
Carbohydrates	15 g (36% of calories)
Cholesterol	38 mg
Sodium	971 mg
Fiber	..1 g

Chicken With Lobster

Serves 6

This is a very elegant dish. If lobster is too expensive, crab meat or a seafood mixture may be substituted. Serve with wild rice or wild rice mixture.

1/3 cup dried bread crumbs
1 tablespoon paprika
6 skinless boneless chicken breast halves
1/3 pound chunked lobster meat
1 cup finely chopped onions
1 (10 3/4 oz.) can lowfat cond. cream of chicken soup
1/4 cup skim milk
1 cup lowfat sour cream

Mix breadcrumbs and paprika. Coat chicken breasts with crumb mixture and place on microwave rack, thickest portions to the outside. Cook 5-6 minutes per pound until chicken is nearly done. Place chicken in 8 x 12 inch microwave casserole. Place lobster chunks over chicken breasts, sprinkle with green onions. Mix soup and milk in 4 cup measure. Heat for 3-4 minutes at 100% power, stirring once until mixture is hot. Pour over chicken, reduce power to 50%. Partially cover and heat for 5-8 minutes until contents are very hot. Gently blend sour cream into sauce mixture. Heat another 2-3 minutes until sour cream is hot. Be careful, however, not to boil as cream can curdle.

```
Nutrition (per serving): 253 calories
    Saturated fat ........................................................ 2 g
    Total Fat ............................................................. 5 g (19% of calories)
    Protein .............................................................. 36 g (58% of calories)
    Carbohydrates .................................................... 15 g (24% of calories)
    Cholesterol ........................................................ 101 mg
    Sodium .............................................................. 353 mg
    Fiber ................................................................ 0 g
```

Dirigibles

Serves 4

These potatoes will store in the refrigerator for 2-3 days. By eliminating the meat in these potatoes and preparing a half potato shell this is a wonderful side dish.

4 large Idaho potatoes
1/4 cup melted lowfat margarine

1/4 pound cooked cubed turkey
1/4 pound cooked cubed ham
1/4 pound grated lowfat sharp cheddar cheese
1 small green bell pepper, seeded and chopped
3/4 cup lowfat sour cream
1/4 teaspoon minced chives
4 slices bacon, cooked and crumbled, optional

Place potatoes in circle fashion or preferably standing in circle fashion. Cook 6 minutes per pound or until potatoes are firm but softening when squeezed. Wrap potatoes in foil and let stand until very soft. While potatoes are standing, mix meats and vegetables. Cut potatoes lengthwise but not quite in half. Loosen pulp and remove 1/4 of potato. Divide margarine evenly and mash into potatoes. Mix reserved potato with remaining ingredients and mound onto potatoes. Wrap tightly in foil or plastic wrap and store in refrigerator. When ready to serve, unwrap and place potatoes, circle fashion, in microwave dish. Heat at 70% power for approximately 9 minutes per pound or until heated through. Top with sour cream and chives and generously sprinkle with bacon.

Nutrition (per serving): 600 calories

Saturated fat	..5 g
Total Fat	15 g (22% of calories)
Protein	32 g (22% of calories)
Carbohydrates	84 g (56% of calories)
Cholesterol	48 mg
Sodium	760 mg
Fiber	..3 g

Duck a' La Orange

Serves 6

More fat cooks out of microwaved meats and poultry than any other cooking method. Heart Healthy! Ducklings are very fat so skin browns naturally. Fat should be drained several times during cooking as it attracts microwave energy and will also make the dish difficult to handle.

3 pound whole duck,
1 small onion, quartered
2 stalks celery, cut into thirds
1 orange
1 cup orange juice
2 tablespoons cornstarch
2 tablespoons low sodium soy sauce

1/4 cup dry sherry
3 tablespoons honey

After duckling is defrosted, remove giblets and wash. Place breast side down on microwave rack in microwave roaster. Make orange sauce by placing orange juice, cornstarch and soy sauce in 2 cup measure. Mix well and microwave for 2-3 minutes at 100% power. Peel orange thinly, being careful not to take white membrane. Quarter orange and reserve for stuffing duckling. Julienne peel. Stir sauce. Mix in orange peel, sherry and honey. Microwave 2 minutes at 100% power or until sauce is thick and glossy. Estimate cooking time for duck at 8-9 minutes per pound. Divide time in half. Microwave first 10 minutes at 100% power. Let stand for 5 minutes to allow fat to drain. Drain fat from casserole. Secure neck skin in back with wooden picks. Fill cavity with orange, onion and celery. Return duckling to rack, breast side down and reduce power to 50%. Microwave the remaining first 1/2 of the time. Drain fat. Turn duckling breast side up. Spoon on 1/3 of glaze. Microwave remaining time. Drain. Spoon on another 1/3 of glaze. Let stand, tented with foil, shiny side in for 5 minutes. Serve duck with remaining glaze.

Nutrition (per serving): 976 calories
Saturated fat .... .28 g
Total Fat .... 84 g (77% of calories)
Protein .... .27 g (11% of calories)
Carbohydrates .... 26 g (10% of calories)
Cholesterol .... 161 mg
Sodium .... 563 mg
Fiber ....3 g

Fiery Chicken

Serves 8

If a spicier dish is desired, add 1/4 teaspoon cayenne pepper. Also, 8 skinless boneless chicken breast halves may be used instead of chicken pieces.

3 pounds skinned meaty chicken pieces
1 onion, peeled and chopped
1 teaspoon browning powder
1/2 teaspoon paprika
1 tablespoon flour
1 cup nonfat sour cream
1 (4 oz.) can chopped green chiles
1/8 teaspoon ground cayenne pepper
3/4 teaspoon salt

Rinse chicken and pat dry. Place chicken, meatiest pieces to the outside of a microwave casserole. Sprinkle with browning spice if desired. Cover loosely. Cook 10-15 minutes at 100% power, until chicken is nearly done, rearranging if necessary. Add onion and cook a few more minutes until onion begins to soften. Sprinkle with paprika and flour. Stir together. Cover and cook at 70% power for about 10-12 more minutes, until juices of chicken run clear. Mix sour cream, chiles, salt and cayenne pepper. Pour over chicken and gently stir through. Heat at 50% power for 5-10 minutes until very hot, but not boiling. Serve with rice or noodles.

```
Nutrition (per serving): 393 calories
    Saturated fat ........................................................ ..7 g
    Total Fat ............................................................. 25 g (58% of calories)
    Protein ................................................................ 34 g (35% of calories)
    Carbohydrates ..................................................... ..7 g (7% of calories)
    Cholesterol .......................................................... 153 mg
    Sodium ................................................................ 570 mg
    Fiber ................................................................... ..1 g
```

Garden Turkey Breast

Serves 6

Use this same method when cooking a whole breast or turkey. Simply cook for the first 1/3 of the time at 100% power. Remember to check in meatiest or thickest parts with meat thermometer to insure that it is well done. If boney area begins to overcook, you may shield or protect with a small amount of aluminum foil (See Shielding).

2 large carrots, julienne sliced
2 stalks celery, julienne sliced
2 small onions, julienne sliced
2 small whole potatoes, julienne sliced
2 tablespoons minced fresh parsley
4 tablespoons melted lowfat margarine
1/4 teaspoon salt
1/4 teaspoon black pepper
3 pounds skinless turkey breast
1 pinch paprika

Place first five ingredients close together in small microwave dish. Top with 1 tablespoon margarine. Season with salt and pepper if desired. Microwave at 100% power for 7 minutes, stirring once. Place turkey breast top down on vegetables. Melt remaining margarine. Brush with margarine/paprika mixture. Cover with microwave wrap or casserole cover. Calculate cooking time at 11 minutes per pound at 50% power. Cook for 5 minutes at 100% power. Turn breast over, baste and cook remaining time at 50% power. Let stand a few minutes, covered, so that turkey will finish cooking. Check in several areas to make certain that internal temperature has reached 170 degrees.

```
Nutrition (per serving): 374 calories
    Saturated fat .......................................................... ..2 g
    Total Fat .................................................................. .8 g (19% of calories)
    Protein .................................................................... 57 g (61% of calories)
    Carbohydrates ........................................................ 19 g (20% of calories)
    Cholesterol ............................................................. 136 mg
    Sodium .................................................................... 611 mg
    Fiber ........................................................................ ..3 g
```

Mexican Casserole

Serves 8

Remember to lower the microwave temperature or power level when cooking a cheese type sauce, just as you would in conventional cooking. Also, cream of mushroom soup is good in this and the nonfat version will cut the fat content quite a bit.

9 (6-inch) corn tortillas
3 skinless boneless chicken breast halves
1 (4 oz.) can chopped green chiles
3 cups grated sharp lowfat cheddar cheese
2 (6 oz.) cans sliced mushrooms, drained
1/3 cup dry white wine
1 dash dry sherry
1 (10 3/4 oz.) can lowfat cond. cream of chicken soup
1/4 teaspoon dry mustard

Tear tortillas in quarters and set aside. Place chicken breasts, circle fashion, meatiest portions to outside of casserole. Cook covered for 6 minutes per pound. Cool and shred breasts. In 2 quart casserole layer tortillas, chicken, chiles, cheese and mushrooms. Mix soup, wine and mustard. Pour soup mixture over casserole and cook for 15-20 minutes at 70% power or until mixture is very hot and bubbly.

```
Nutrition (per serving): 298 calories
    Saturated fat .......................................................... ..4 g
    Total Fat .................................................................. 11 g (32% of calories)
    Protein .................................................................... 29 g (39% of calories)
    Carbohydrates ........................................................ 20 g (27% of calories)
    Cholesterol ............................................................. 50 mg
    Sodium .................................................................... 759 mg
    Fiber ........................................................................ ..1 g
```

Pheasant With Sauerkraut

Serves 6

When cooking game in the microwave, use conventional techniques. For example, if meat is browned conventionally, cook at 100% power in the microwave for a few minutes. After browning, heat may be lowered to finish. The same would be true for microwave cooking (See Converting Recipes).

2 whole pheasants, halved
1 large onion, sliced
2 stalks celery, thinly sliced
1/4 teaspoon salt
1/8 teaspoon black pepper
1/4 cup melted lowfat margarine
1/4 teaspoon paprika
3 cups drained sauerkraut
1 teaspoon caraway seeds

Rinse pheasants and pat dry. Rub cavities of birds with salt and pepper. Layer onions and celery in bottom of 9 x 13 inch microwave casserole. Place birds in casserole, thickest portions to the edge. Mix melted margarine and paprika and baste birds. Microwave at 100% power for 4 minutes per pound. Mix sauerkraut and caraway. Cover birds with sauerkraut. Cover with plastic wrap or casserole cover. Cook for 20-30 minutes at 50% power or until juice of pheasants run clear when pierced. Let stand a few minutes.

Nutrition (per serving): 477 calories	
Saturated fat	.4 g
Total Fat	13 g (25% of calories)
Protein	69 g (58% of calories)
Carbohydrates	21 g (17% of calories)
Cholesterol	155 mg
Sodium	1324 mg
Fiber	.4 g

Picante Chicken

Serves 6

Foods that are cooked in the microwave need standing time to finish cooking properly. They have on going cooking after the microwave shuts off. Skinless chicken pieces will also reduce fat content of this recipe.

3 pound broiler-fryer chicken, rinsed and cut up
1 thinly sliced lemon
1 onion, thinly sliced
1/3 cup Picante sauce
1/2 cup catsup
1 tablespoon soy sauce
1 tablespoon brown sugar

Place chicken in shallow microwave baking dish, meatiest pieces to outside so they will receive more concentrated microwaves and cook more easily. Top with lemon and onion slices. Cook at 100% power for 12 minutes. Drain liquid. Mix Picante, catsup, soy sauce and brown sugar while chicken is cooking. Blend well. Spoon sauce over chicken. Microwave, partially covered, for additional 10-15 minutes or until chicken is no longer pink. Let stand for 5 minutes to finish cooking before serving.

```
Nutrition (per serving): 524 calories
    Saturated fat ....................................... .10 g
    Total Fat ............................................. 34 g (58% of calories)
    Protein ............................................... .43 g (33% of calories)
    Carbohydrates .................................... 12 g  (9% of calories)
    Cholesterol ........................................ 204 mg
    Sodium .............................................. 666 mg
    Fiber .................................................. 0 g
```

Raspberry Praline Hens

Serves 6

If you wish to use only 1 or 2 hens instead of 3, compute time (See 6 Minute Per Pound Rule and Lowering Power Levels). Proceed with recipe as written. When hens are done, juices will run clear when pierced.

2 teaspoons lowfat margarine
1/3 cup black raspberry preserves
1 1/2 tablespoons dry sherry
2 ounces frozen concentrate orange juice
3 tablespoons brown sugar
1 1/2 teaspoons tarragon vinegar
1 1/2 teaspoons prepared mustard
3 whole Rock Cornish game hens
1 teaspoon dried parsley flakes
1/ 3 cup chopped pecans

Mix margarine, preserves, sherry, orange juice, brown sugar, vinegar and mustard in 1 cup measure. Heat for 1-2 minutes at 100% power until boiling. Set aside. Split cornish hens and remove backbones. Wash and pat dry. Arrange cut side down in large rectangular microwave casserole. Place legs to outside of dish. Brush generously with sauce. Sprinkle with parsley flakes. Cover partially with microwave wrap or casserole cover. Cook 30-35 minutes at 70% power. Let stand several minutes before serving and check for doneness. Spoon sauce over cornish hens and sprinkle with pecans to serve.

```
Nutrition (per serving): 481 calories
    Saturated fat ............................................... ...8 g
    Total Fat ................................................... .35 g (66% of calories)
    Protein .................................................... 23 g (19% of calories)
    Carbohydrates ............................................. 18 g (15% of calories)
    Cholesterol ............................................... 215 mg
    Sodium .................................................... ..95 mg
    Fiber ..................................................... ..0 g
```

Roquefort Chicken

Serves 6

This chicken is delicious served with a wild rice mixture.

    6 skinless boneless chicken breast halves
    1/4 teaspoon white pepper
    4 ounces Roquefort cheese
    1 clove garlic
    1 cup nonfat sour cream

Season chicken with pepper and place in circle fashion in microwave casserole. Cover and cook 6 minutes per pound until chicken is no longer pink. In 2 cup measure, mix cheese, garlic and sour cream. Heat mixture for 2-3 minutes at 50% power until mixture is warm. Pour over chicken breasts, cover and cook at 50% power for another 8-12 minutes until mixture is very hot, but not boiling.

```
Nutrition (per serving): 223 calories
    Saturated fat ............................................. ..4 g
    Total Fat ................................................. .. 7 g (29% of calories)
    Protein .................................................. 34 g (62% of calories)
    Carbohydrates ............................................ ..5 g (9% of calories)
    Cholesterol .............................................. ...85 mg
    Sodium ................................................... 448 mg
    Fiber .................................................... .. 0 g
```

Sherried Chicken

Serves 8

This casserole may be divided into two smaller casseroles and frozen for use later if desired. Remember to defrost and cook smaller casseroles for about half the time of the larger one, however.

8 skinless boneless chicken breast halves
1/2 cup sliced fresh mushrooms
1 (3 oz.) package brown gravy mix
1 cup chicken broth
2 tablespoons tomato paste
1 tablespoon dry sherry
1 teaspoon Dijon mustard
1/3 cup evaporated skim milk
1/4 cup dried bread crumbs

Wash chicken and pat dry. Place in circle fashion in large microwave casserole. Cook chicken covered for 4 minutes per pound. Drain excess liquid. Sprinkle mushrooms over chicken. Stir mix, broth, sherry, mustard, tomato paste and milk in 2 cup measure. Heat mixture for 2 1/2-3 minutes at 100% power until mixture is hot. Pour over chicken and mushrooms. Partially cover with vented casserole cover or microwave wrap. Cook at 70% power for 10-20 minutes or until chicken is no longer pink. Allow food to stand a few minutes to finish cooking. Sprinkle with crumbs before serving.

```
Nutrition (per serving): 189 calories
    Saturated fat .......................................................... ..1 g
    Total Fat ................................................................ ..3 g (12% of calories)
    Protein .................................................................. 29 g (61% of calories)
    Carbohydrates ..................................................... 12 g (25% of calories)
    Cholesterol ........................................................... .69 mg
    Sodium .................................................................. 748 mg
    Fiber ..................................................................... ..0 g
```

Tarragon Cream Chicken

Serves 4

This is very good served with rice.

4 skinless boneless chicken breast halves
2 tablespoons olive oil
1 teaspoon freshly ground black pepper
1/3 cup honey
1/4 cup Dijon mustard

2 tablespoons prepared mustard
1 clove garlic, minced
2 teaspoons lemon juice
1/4 teaspoon salt
1 teaspoon dried tarragon
1/2 cup Creme Fraiche or whipping cream
1/4 cup chopped fresh chives

Gently pound chicken breasts to flatten. Place chicken in refrigerator container. Coat with olive oil, sprinkle with pepper and press into chicken. Refrigerate until ready to use. Mix honey, mustards, garlic, lemon juice, salt, tarragon and cream. Whisk thoroughly. Place chicken in microwave casserole, circle fashion. Microwave for 6-8 minutes at 100% power, turning once. Drain juices. Whisk sauce and pour over chicken. Sprinkle with chives. Microwave 5-8 minutes, partially covered, at 70% power until chicken is thoroughly done and juices run clear.

```
Nutrition (per serving): 363 calories
    Saturated fat ..................................................8 g
    Total Fat ............................................. 21 g (51% of calories)
    Protein ...............................................29 g (32% of calories)
    Carbohydrates ....................................15 g (17% of calories)
    Cholesterol ....................................... 109 mg
    Sodium .............................................. 708 mg
    Fiber ................................................ 0 g
```

Turkey a La Orange

Serves 8

Many times we forget how delicious the thigh meat is, and less expensive too. If you wish to use turkey breast, however, you may do so as it contains less fat than the thigh meat.

4 cups frozen chopped broccoli
1 teaspoon instant granules chicken bouillon
1 teaspoon ginger, divided
1/2 cup frozen concentrate orange juice
3/4 cup water
1 1/2 tablespoons soy sauce
1 1/2 tablespoons chopped pimientos
3 1 pound skinned turkey thighs, boned
1/2 teaspoon paprika
1 large onion, sliced
2 tablespoons brown sugar
2 tablespoons chopped fresh parsley

Mix broccoli, chicken granules, 1/3 teaspoon ginger, 2 tablespoon orange juice concentrate, 1/2 cup water, soy sauce and pimientos. Spread mixture into large 9 x 13 inch casserole. Rinse turkey thighs and pat dry. Place thighs, circle fashion, on top of broccoli mixture with meatiest portions to the outside of the casserole. Top with onion rings. Mix remaining orange juice concentrate, water, remaining ginger, brown sugar and parsley. Mix thoroughly and pour over thighs and onions. Cover and cook at 70% power for 28-35 minutes or until juices run clear when thigh is pierced.

Nutrition (per serving): 254 calories
Saturated fat ....3 g
Total Fat .... .8 g (28% of calories)
Protein .... .36 g (57% of calories)
Carbohydrates .... 10 g (15% of calories)
Cholesterol .... 117 mg
Sodium .... 370 mg
Fiber ....1 g.

notes:

_____
_____
_____
_____
_____
_____
_____
_____
_____
_____
_____
_____
_____
_____
_____
_____
_____
_____
_____
_____

Sweets and Baking

DID YOU KNOW?

♥ Do not frost cakes until cool.

♥ Baking powder biscuits will have better texture if you knead the dough for half a minute after mixing.

♥ A dash of Worcestershire sauce adds zip to hot mulled cider, pumpkin pie, spiced cookies and cakes.

♥ Measure liquid shortening into measuring cup first before sticky substance such as honey is added, and X will pour out easily.

♥ Crumbled cookies, graham crackers and sugar-type cereal that remain in the bottom of their containers may be placed in a food processor and reduced to crumbs. Save in either an airtight container or freeze for use later as "great" pie crusts or to extend chopped nuts on desserts for topping.

♥ Crackers, bread, chips and regular cereals may also be reduced to crumbs in the food processor and kept for casserole toppings and crumb coatings.

♥ Coat berries, raisins or nuts with flour before adding to batter to prevent them from sinking to the bottom.

♥ A cake that is lightly buttered on top while cooling will not get crumbly when you frost the completely cooled cake.

♥ Use powdered gelatin mix for colored sugar when decorating baked goods.

♥ Cookie dough stored in cans in the refrigerator can be pushed out for easy slicing after removing second end from can.

♥ Dip cheese slicer in flour to cut uniform cookies from a roll of dough.

♥ A cake rack covered with a paper towel lets the cake "breathe" as it cools. The cake won't stick to the paper towel, either.

♥ Sift dry cake mix before you add other ingredients so it won't be lumpy.

♥ So they will be easy to remove from the pan, place a pie or cake on a wet hot towel for a few minutes.

Candy and Frosting Charts	
Temperature of Syrup	
Thread	230-234 degrees
Soft ball	234-240 degrees
Firm ball	244-248 degrees
Hard ball	250-266 degrees

Sweets and Baking

Bars, Cookies and Candy

Chocolate Chip Fudge
Chocolate Drops
Chocolate Pizza
Date Cookies
Divinity
Fudge Nougats
Lemon Squares
Pecan Cheesecake Squares
Poppy Cock
Sauce Pan Brownie
Truffles

Breads/Rolls/Etc.

Beer Bread
Chilli Corn Bread
Pumpkin Bread
Rolled Tortillas
Steamed Breads
Strawberry Bread
Swiss Bread Loaf
What's In A Muffin
Yeast Breads

Cakes

Angel Cloud Cake
Angel Food Cake
Blueberry Cake
Bundt Cake Variations
Bundt Coffee Cake
Cheesecake
Chocolate Cream Cupcakes
Cream Cheese Frosting
Earthquake Cake
Fabulous Cake
Hot Fudge Pudding Cake
Pumpkin Cake
Raspberry Cheese Cake
Sour Cream Cocoa Cake

Desserts & Miscellaneous

Berry Cobbler
Chocolate Crinkle Cups
Cran-Apple Sauce
Delightful Dessert
Dessert Cheese Ball
Fudge Pudding
Vanilla Pudding
Williamsburg Trifle

Pies and Pie Doughs

Banana Split Pie
Canned Berry Pie
Chocolate Mousse Pie
Custard Pie
Favorite Liqueur Pie
French Apple Pie
Fresh Berry Pie
Peach Pie
Pecan Pie
Shake A Pie Crust
Sonja's Pie Crust
Strawberry Pie

Chocolate Chip Fudge

Serves 36

Use any flavor or blend flavors of chips, such as 12 ounces peanut butter chips and 6 ounces semi-sweet chocolate chips. Also, add other ingredients, such as raisins or marshmallows if desired. Freezes well.

18 ounces semi-sweet chocolate chips
1 (12 oz.) can sweetened condensed milk
1/2 cup chopped nuts

Place chips in large microwave measure. Microwave 4-6 minutes at 50% power, stirring once or twice. If chocolate is not melted, microwave a few more minutes until soft. Add milk, stirring well. Add nuts. Pour into 8 x 12 inch buttered casserole. Refrigerate until firm.

Nutrition (per serving): 123 calories
Saturated fat ....3 g
Total Fat ....7 g (50% of calories)
Protein ....2 g (5% of calories)
Carbohydrates .... 14 g (44% of calories)
Cholesterol .... 3 mg
Sodium .... 13 mg
Fiber ....0 g

Chocolate Drops

Serves 48

Melt chocolate chips at 50% power, uncovered, for 3-5 minutes until chips liquefy when touched. Chips will hold their shape and won't melt down as when melting conventionally. Be certain not to overcook.

2 cups peanut butter
3 cups Rice Krispies cereal
1 (16 oz.) package powdered sugar
1/4 cup softened butter or margarine
1 (12 oz.) package chocolate chips, melted

Mix peanut butter, cereal, powdered sugar and butter. Form into small balls. Dip peanut butter balls in melted chocolate and let harden on wax paper.

Chocolate Pizza

Serves 20

Notice the large amount of chocolate/bark is started at 100% power and then turned down. Reduce power level when melting chocolate so that it won't burn. It takes a few minutes more, but has less chance of burning. Remember, when melting chocolate conventionally, a double boiler which gives an indirect heat is used. Similar techniques when microwaving applies, but it need not be placed over boiling water, simply lower heat. Remember, smaller circles may be formed on cookie sheet for small pizzas if desired.

1 (12 oz.) package semisweet chocolate chips
1 pound almond bark white chocolate
2 cups miniature marshmallows
1 cup Rice Krispies cereal
1 cup peanuts
1 (6 oz.) jar red maraschino cherry
3 tablespoons green maraschino cherry
1/3 cup flaked coconuts
1 teaspoon vegetable oil

Place chips and 14 oz. of almond bark in 2 quart microwave measure or casserole. Microwave for 2 minutes at 100% power. Stir. Microwave at 50% power for 5-8 minutes, stirring every 2 minutes until mixture is smooth. Stir in marshmallows, cereal and peanuts. Pour into an oiled 12 inch pizza pan. Drain cherries. Halve red cherries and quarter green cherries. Top mixture with cherries and sprinkle with coconut. Place remaining 2 ounces of almond bark and oil in 1 cup measure. Microwave 1-3 minutes at 50% power, stirring until smooth. Drizzle over coconut and refrigerate till firm. Store at room temperature.

Cinnamon Crisps

Serves 8

Foods have a hard time becoming "crisp" when cooked in the microwave. For better results, place them on paper towels, leave product uncovered while cooking and covered with paper towels to absorb extra moisture during the standing time. Remember, we are again using a technique similar to the conventional technique of not covering cakes, cookies, etc. we wish "brown" or "crisp".

1 ready-to-bake pie crust
1 tablespoon butter or margarine
2 tablespoons sugar
1/4 teaspoon cinnamon

Place pie crust on a microwave rack or in a large microwave pan which has been covered with several pieces of paper towels. Prick crust several times with a fork and set aside. Melt butter in small container for 30-45 seconds at 100% power. Brush pie crust with melted butter and sprinkle with cinnamon-sugar. Microwave at 100% for 5-6 minutes or until no longer doughy. Rotate once if crust seems to be cooking unevenly. Let cool slightly and cut into wedges. Serve warm as a snack, with brunch or entree.

```
Nutrition (per serving): 139 calories
    Saturated fat ........................................................ ..3 g
    Total Fat ............................................................. ..9 g (58% of calories)
    Protein ............................................................... ..1 g (4% of calories)
    Carbohydrates ..................................................... 13 g (38% of calories)
    Cholesterol .......................................................... ....4 mg
    Sodium ................................................................ 152 mg
    Fiber ................................................................... ..0 g
```

Date Cookies

Serves 30

These will keep in the refrigerator for weeks. Both pecans and walnuts are good in these.

1/4 cup melted lowfat margarine
1 cup sugar
2 eggs, well beaten
1 (8 oz.) package chopped dates
1 1/2 cups Rice Krispies cereal
1 cup chopped nuts

1 teaspoon vanilla
1 cup flaked coconut

Mix margarine, sugar, eggs and dates. Place in 3 quart microwave casserole. Microwave at 100% power for 3-6 minutes until mixture boils. Stir and continue to boil for 1-2 minutes. Stir in cereal, nuts and vanilla. When cool enough to handle roll into small balls the size of walnuts and roll in coconut flakes. 5 dozen.

Nutrition (per serving): 107 calories
Saturated fat ....1 g
Total Fat ....4 g (37% of calories)
Protein ....2 g (6% of calories)
Carbohydrates .... 15 g (57% of calories)
Cholesterol .... 14 mg
Sodium .... 43 mg
Fiber ....0 g

Divinity

Serves 36

4 cups sugar
1 cup light corn syrup
3/4 cup cold water
1/4 teaspoon salt
3 egg whites
1 teaspoon vanilla
1/2 cup chopped nuts

Mix together first 4 ingredients in 1 1/2 quart microwave casserole. Microwave at 100% power for 22 minutes (hard ball stage), stirring once or twice while cooking. Beat egg whites stiff in a very large mixing bowl. Pour the hot mixture into egg whites and beat for 12 minutes. Fold in the nuts and vanilla. Continue beating until mixture commences to lose its shine and will just hold its shape. Put into a buttered pan. Cool and cut into squares.

Nutrition (per serving): 129 calories
Saturated fat ....0 g
Total Fat ....1 g (7% of calories)
Protein ....1 g (2% of calories)
Carbohydrates .... 29 g (91% of calories)
Cholesterol .... 0 mg
Sodium .... 28 mg
Fiber .... 0 g

Fudge Nougats

Serves 40

2 cups sugar
1/2 cup lowfat margarine
1 cup evaporated skim milk
1 (6 oz) package semisweet chocolate chips
3/4 cup flour
1 cup finely crushed graham crackers
3/4 cup chopped walnuts
1 teaspoon vanilla

Mix sugar, margarine and milk in large microwave measure. Microwave at 100% power for about 6 minutes or until mixture is boiling, stirring once. Boil for an additional 10 minutes, stirring occasionally. Stir in chocolate chips, cracker crumbs, walnuts and vanilla. Spread in well buttered 12x8 inch pan. Top with walnut halves, one for each piece, if desired. Cool and cut into 40 squares.

Nutrition (per serving): 112 calories
Saturated fat ....1 g
Total Fat ....4 g (34% of calories)
Protein ....1 g (5% of calories)
Carbohydrates .... 17 g (61% of calories)
Cholesterol ....0 mg
Sodium .... 50 mg
Fiber ....0 g

Lemon Squares

Serves 32

1 cup room temperature lowfat margarine
3/4 cup powdered sugar, divided
2 1/3 cups flour
4 eggs
1 3/4 cups sugar
1/3 cup lemon juice
1/2 teaspoon baking powder

In medium size mixing bowl, cream margarine and 1/2 cup of powdered sugar. Add 2 cups flour and stir until well combined. Pat evenly into 8 x 12 inch microwave dish. Microwave at 70% power for 5-10 minutes until firm. Blend eggs, granulated sugar, remaining 1/3 cup flour, lemon juice and baking powder in blender or food processor. Mix for 5 seconds. Scrape down sides and blend another 5 seconds. Pour over partially baked crust. Bake for 5-15 minutes at 70% power until done. Sprinkle with remaining powdered sugar.

```
Nutrition (per serving): 123 calories
    Saturated fat ........................................................ ..1 g
    Total Fat .............................................................. ..4 g (26% of calories)
    Protein ................................................................. ..2 g (6% of calories)
    Carbohydrates ................................................... 21 g (68% of calories)
    Cholesterol ........................................................ 27 mg
    Sodium ............................................................... 83 mg
    Fiber .................................................................. ..0 g
```

Pecan Cheesecake Squares

Serves 16

To toast crumb mixture, place in small microwave container. Microwave for 1 - 1 1/2 minutes at 100% power, stirring once or twice.

1/3 cup lowfat margarine

1/3 cup packed brown sugar

1 cup flour

1/2 cup chopped pecans

1 (8 oz.) package light cream cheese

1/2 cup sugar

1 egg

1 tablespoon skim milk

1 teaspoon lemon juice

1 teaspoon vanilla

Blend sugar, flour and pecans with melted margarine. Press mixture into 8 x 8 inch microwave dish, reserving 1/2 cup for later. Microwave for 2 minutes at 100% power. Blend softened cream cheese, sugar, egg, milk, lemon and vanilla. Spread over base. Sprinkle with toasted crumb mixture. Microwave for 5-6 minutes at 100% power.

```
Nutrition (per serving): 146 calories
    Saturated fat ........................................................ ..3 g
    Total Fat .............................................................. ..8 g (49% of calories)
    Protein ................................................................. ..3 g (8% of calories)
    Carbohydrates ................................................... 16 g (43% of calories)
    Cholesterol ........................................................ ..24 mg
    Sodium ............................................................... 108 mg
    Fiber .................................................................. 0 g
```

Picnic Bars

Serves 24

These will microwave more evenly if baked in 2 small pans (round or 8 x 8 inch) and cooked a shorter time. Some shielding may be needed if cooked in large pan as directed.

> 2 eggs
> 1/4 cup softened lowfat margarine
> 1/4 cup packed brown sugar
> 1 package (18.5 oz.) butter brickle or butter pecan chocolate cake mix
> 1 (6 oz.) package semisweet chocolate chips
> 3/4 cup chopped nuts

Beat eggs, water, margarine, sugar and half the cake. Mix thoroughly. Stir in remaining cake mix, chips and nuts. Spread into 8x12 inch microwave casserole. Microwave 70% power for 7-8 minutes, rotating once, until no longer doughy. Shield corners of cake if cake starts to overcook.

```
Nutrition (per serving): 87 calories
    Saturated fat ....................................................... 2 g
    Total Fat ............................................................. 6 g (63% of calories)
    Protein ............................................................... 2 g (7% of calories)
    Carbohydrates .................................................... 6 g (30% of calories)
    Cholesterol ........................................................ 18 mg
    Sodium ............................................................... 29 mg
    Fiber .................................................................. 0 g
```

Poppy Cock

Serves 24

> 2 quarts freshly popped popcorn
> 1 1/3 cups pecans
> 2/3 cup almonds
> 2/3 cup sugar
> 1 cup lowfat margarine
> 1/2 cup light corn syrup
> 1/2 teaspoon vanilla

Mix popcorn and nuts on cookie sheet. In large glass measure, combine sugar, margarine and syrup. Microwave at 100% power for 2-6 minutes until mixture boils. Continue to boil for 8-10 minutes, stirring once or twice until mixture turns light caramel in color. Remove from heat. Stir in vanilla. Pour over popcorn and nuts. Mix to coat and spread out on cookie sheet to dry. Break apart and store in air tight container.

```
Nutrition (per serving): 155 calories
    Saturated fat ......................................................... ..1 g
    Total Fat ................................................................ 10 g (60% of calories)
    Protein ................................................................... ..2 g (4% of calories)
    Carbohydrates ..................................................... 14 g (36% of calories)
    Cholesterol ........................................................... ..0 mg
    Sodium .................................................................. 98 mg
    Fiber ...................................................................... ..0 g
```

Sauce Pan Brownies

Serves 12

A round pan cooks more evenly in the microwave than a square one. If you wish to have square brownies, you may use the square pan and shield the corners if they start to overcook (See Shielding). If a round pan is used, cut as pie and serve with a bit of ice cream if desired.

2 (1 oz.) squares unsweetened chocolate

1/2 cup lowfat margarine

1 cup sugar

2 eggs

1 teaspoon vanilla

3/4 cup plus 2 Tbsp. flour

1/4 teaspoon baking powder

1/2 cup chocolate chips

1/2 cup chopped nuts

In large microwave measure, place chocolate and margarine. Microwave at 70% power, for 1-2 minutes until melted, stirring once. Add remaining ingredients except for chocolate chips and nuts. Pour into microwave round 9 inch cake pan or 8 x 8 inch microwave baking dish. Microwave 5-8 minutes at 70% power until brownies are done, but not overcooked. While hot, top with chocolate chips and nuts. Let stand a few moments, spread chips as icing if desired.

```
Nutrition (per serving): 247 calories
    Saturated fat ......................................................... ..4 g
    Total Fat ................................................................ 13 g (46% of calories)
    Protein ................................................................... ..4 g (6% of calories)
    Carbohydrates ..................................................... 30 g (48% of calories)
    Cholesterol ........................................................... 35 mg
    Sodium .................................................................. 112 mg
    Fiber ...................................................................... ..0 g
```

Truffles

Serves 36

Truffles are very expensive when purchased. They are easy to make and also freeze well if you need to keep them more than a month. For an elaborate truffle, add 1/4 cup Grand Marnier and 1 teaspoon grated orange rind before shaping chocolate mixture. If chocolate is thick, it will melt a bit when handled.

1 1/4 cups whipping cream
1 pound semisweet chocolate
1/2 cup unsalted butter
1/2 cup unsweetened cocoa
3/4 cup chopped nuts

In microwave measure, heat cream for 3-4 minutes at 100% power until it boils. Add chocolate in small bits. Microwave at 50% power for 1-2 minutes until all chocolate is melted. Add butter a little at a time. Stir until smooth. Heat another minute at 50% power if necessary to melt all ingredients. Cover and chill 8 hours or overnight. Sift cocoa onto plate. Place chopped nuts onto second plate. Scoop up chocolate mixture in teaspoonfuls. With hands shape into 3/4 inch balls. Roll in cocoa or nuts and set on another plate. Store, covered, in refrigerator until ready to serve. Truffles keep up to 1 month in the refrigerator. Makes about 3-4 dozen truffles.

```
Nutrition (per serving): 145 calories
    Saturated fat ......................................................... ..6 g
    Total Fat ................................................................. 12 g (73% of calories)
    Protein ................................................................... ..1 g (49% of calories)
    Carbohydrates ...................................................... ..9 g (24% of calories)
    Cholesterol ............................................................ 18 mg
    Sodium .................................................................. 35 mg
    Fiber ...................................................................... ..0 g
```

Breads/Rolls

Beer Bread

Serves 8

Let dough stand for a few minutes so leavening will start to react and you will get its full benefit. Also, bread may appear slightly damp on top when done, but should not be wet. Standing time will allow bread to finish "cooking". Remember that crushed cracker crumbs or dried breadcrumbs may be substituted for cereal.

3 cups self-rising flour
4 tablespoons sugar
1 (12 oz.) can beer
3 tablespoons crushed Wheaties cereal

Mix flour, sugar and beer in large container. Let stand for 3 or 4 minutes. Place in greased 10 inch pie plate. Sprinkle with crumbs and microwave at 70% power for 6-9 minutes or until bread is done, turning once. Let stand 10 minutes or so, covered with a paper towel. Serve in wedges.

```
Nutrition (per serving): 212 calories
    Saturated fat ............................................................... ..0 g
    Total Fat ...................................................................... ..0 g (2% of calories)
    Protein ......................................................................... ..5 g (10% of calories)
    Carbohydrates ............................................................. 44 g (83% of calories)
    Cholesterol .................................................................. ..0 mg
    Sodium ........................................................................ 10 mg
    Fiber ............................................................................ ..0 g
```

Chili Corn Bread

Serves 8

Harder to cook foods, such as cake or quick breads, cook more evenly if elevated off of the bottom of the microwave. By placing an "invisible" inverted microwave dish in the microwave with food on its top, the food "floats" in the center of the oven and microwaves can enter more uniformly from all directions. This compares to placing food in the center of conventional ovens for more uniform heat.

1 (8 oz.) package cornbread mix
2 tablespoons hot pepper sauce
1 tablespoon dried parsley flakes
1 (16 oz.) can chili without beans

Place all ingredients in a large mixing bowl and stir until fairly smooth. Pour into 9 inch round microwave dish and smooth the top of the batter. Microwave for 11-13 minutes at 70% power, rotating once, or until toothpick inserted in the center comes out clean.

```
Nutrition (per serving): 213 calories
    Saturated fat ............................................................... ....1 g
    Total Fat ...................................................................... ..10 g (44% of calories)
    Protein ......................................................................... ....6 g (12% of calories)
    Carbohydrates ............................................................. ..24 g (45% of calories)
    Cholesterol .................................................................. ..34 mg
    Sodium ........................................................................ 546 mg
    Fiber ............................................................................ ....0 g
```

Pumpkin Bread

Serves 12

Bread will pull away from sides of pan and look dry on the bottom when done. In the microwave, use a "heat" or power level similar to that used when cooking the same food conventionally. You get better results. For example, 70% power will give much the same heat as a 350% oven, which is the temperature used to cook the recipe conventionally.

1 cup canned pumpkin
1 1/2 cups sugar
1/2 cup vegetable oil
2 eggs
1 3/4 cups sifted flour
1/2 teaspoon ground cinnamon
1/2 teaspoon ground nutmeg
1 pinch ground ginger
1 pinch ground cloves
1 teaspoon baking soda
1/3 cup water
1/2 cup chopped pecans
1/2 cup powdered sugar
2 tablespoons undiluted orange juice concentrate
1 pinch ground allspice

Mix pumpkin and sugar in a medium size mixing bowl. Add oil and eggs and mix thoroughly. Sift flour, spices, other than allspice, baking soda and water. Add to the pumpkin mixture and mix well. Stir in the chopped nuts. Let batter stand a minute or two and then pour into a 9x5x3 inch microwave-safe loaf pan. Microwave at 70% power for 11-15 minutes. Let stand 5 minutes before turning out to cool. For glaze, mix powdered sugar, orange juice and allspice until smooth and drizzle over cooled bread.

```
Nutrition (per serving): 328 calories
    Saturated fat ....................................................... ..2 g
    Total Fat ............................................................. 14 g (37% of calories)
    Protein ............................................................... ..4 g (4% of calories)
    Carbohydrates .................................................... 48 g (58% of calories)
    Cholesterol ......................................................... 35 mg
    Sodium ............................................................... 82 mg
    Fiber .................................................................. ..1 g
```

Rolled Tortillas

Serves 8

The hot water will warm the tortillas. The foil protects them from getting over-cooked and tough. The foil does not "arc" or spark because there is enough water to attract the microwaves. Remember when "protecting" foods by shielding with aluminum foil, use a large proportion of water or food content to small amounts of foil, 80% food weight and no more than 20% foil weight.

8 flour tortillas
2 tablespoons lowfat margarine
2 tablespoons grated lowfat cheddar cheese
1 1/2 cups water

Mix margarine and cheese. Spread tortillas with mixture. Roll and place on a piece of foil. Smoothly wrap tortillas in foil and place in microwave colander. Put water in 3 quart casserole and place colander on top and cover. Microwave for 10 minutes at 100% power. Serve warm.

```
Nutrition (per serving): 251 calories
    Saturated fat ........................................................ ....2 g
    Total Fat ............................................................. ....6 g (22% of calories)
    Protein ............................................................... ....9 g (15% of calories)
    Carbohydrates ..................................................... ..40 g (64% of calories)
    Cholesterol ......................................................... ....1 mg
    Sodium ............................................................... 316 mg
    Fiber .................................................................. ....0 g
```

Steamed Breads

Serves 4

When warming foods in foil, it is important that there is enough water to attract the microwaves so that foil will not "spark". Use at least 80% food or water weight and no more than 20% foil. Also, you can apply this method for warming buns or bread slices.

4 whole French rolls
2 pieces aluminum foil
1 1/2 cups water

Place sheet of aluminium foil in microwave colander or 2 quart casserole. Place bread products on foil, cover with another sheet of foil and securely wrap, sealing all seams smoothly so that bread is totally enclosed. Place water in 3 quart casserole. Set colander on top of 3 quart casserole. Cover with casserole cover if available.

Place in microwave oven and cook at 100% power for 5-10 minutes until bread is warm.

```
Nutrition (per serving): 81 calories
    Saturated fat ........................................................ ....0 g
    Total Fat .............................................................. ....0 g (3% of calories)
    Protein ................................................................. ...3 g (14% of calories)
    Carbohydrates ..................................................... ..17 g (84% of calories)
    Cholesterol .......................................................... ....0 mg
    Sodium ................................................................ 176 mg
    Fiber ................................................................... ....0 g
```

Strawberry Bread

Serves 10

Bread will pull away from sides of pan and look dry on the bottom when done. When microwaving products containing leavening such as baking powder or baking soda, let mixture stand a few minutes before baking. As leavening causes a chemical reaction taking a certain length of time and microwave ovens cook so quickly, letting batter stand a few minutes will give leavening a head start on its reaction time.

3/4 cup vegetable oil
1 cup sugar
2 eggs
1 (10 oz.) package frozen strawberries, defrosted
1 1/2 cups flour
1/2 teaspoon baking soda
1 teaspoon ground cinnamon
1 dash salt
1/2 cup chopped pecans

Mix oil, sugar and eggs in medium mixing bowl. Gently stir in strawberries and dry ingredients. Place mixture into a lightly greased 9x5x3 inch microwave-safe loaf pan. Before baking, let batter stand for a few minutes. Microwave at 70% for 10-14 minutes or until done. Let stand for 5 minutes and turn out to cool.

```
Nutrition (per serving): 301 calories
    Saturated fat ........................................................ ..2 g
    Total Fat .............................................................. 18 g (54% of calories)
    Protein ................................................................. ..3 g (4% of calories)
    Carbohydrates ..................................................... 32 g (42% of calories)
    Cholesterol .......................................................... 35 mg
    Sodium ................................................................ 78 mg
    Fiber ................................................................... ..0 g
```

Swiss Bread Loaf

Serves 12

It is very easy to overcook breads when warming them in the microwave. As there is not much liquid content in bread, the microwaves do not find the liquid content easily. Therefore, the tendency is to cook the bread until it feels warm. If this is done, the bread will be hard and tough after standing time. Undercook breads when warming. They become warm during standing time.

1 loaf French bread
1/2 cup lowfat margarine
1/3 cup finely chopped onions
3 tablespoons prepared mustard
3/4 tablespoon poppy seeds
2 teaspoons celery seed
1/2 teaspoon beau monde seasoning
2 teaspoons lemon juice
4 drops tabasco sauce
1/2 cup shredded Swiss cheese
1/4 cup cooked crumbled bacon
1/2 teaspoon paprika

Slice bread into 3/4 inch slices and set aside. Mix softened margarine with all remaining ingredients except for paprika. Spread 3/4 of mixture on bread slices. Places slices together to form a loaf. Spread top with remaining mixture. Line a microwave-safe wicker basket or other utensil with paper towels. Place bread in container and sprinkle with paprika. Cover with another paper towel and microwave at 100% power for 45 seconds to 1 minute. Serve immediately.

```
Nutrition (per serving): 85 calories
   Saturated fat ........................................... 2 g
   Total Fat ................................................. 7 g (78% of calories)
   Protein ................................................... 2 g (11% of calories)
   Carbohydrates ........................................ 2 g (12% of calories)
   Cholesterol ............................................ 6 mg
   Sodium .................................................. 362 mg
   Fiber ..................................................... 0 g
```

What's In A Muffin

Serves 8

Muffins may appear slightly damp on top when done, but let stand to finish cooking. Also, when baking cupcakes and muffins, place them in a circle so they will cook evenly. For a change try cheddar or other types of cheese in these muffins.

1 cup flour
1 tablespoon sugar
1 1/2 teaspoons baking powder
1/2 teaspoon paprika
1/4 teaspoon salt
1/2 cup shredded lowfat Swiss cheese
2 slices bacon, cooked and crumbled
2 tablespoons chopped onions
2 tablespoons chopped green bell peppers
1/2 cup skim milk
1/4 cup vegetable oil
1 egg, slightly beaten

Mix all ingredients until lightly blended. Let batter stand. Place two muffin papers for each muffin in microwave muffin pan or other microwave utensil. Fill each paper half full. Microwave at 100% power as follows: 1 muffin: 20- 40 seconds; 2 muffins: 40 - 90 seconds; 4 muffins: 1 - 2 1/2 minutes; 6 muffins: 2 1/2 - 4 1/2 minutes.

Nutrition (per serving): 200 calories
Saturated fat ....3 g
Total Fat .... 13 g (58% of calories)
Protein ....6 g (12% of calories)
Carbohydrates .... 15 g (30% of calories)
Cholesterol .... 36 mg
Sodium .... 213 mg
Fiber ....0 g

Yeast Breads

Serves 8

Yeast breads in the microwave are possible but not satisfactory. I suggest they be cooked the conventional way. The microwave is, however, an excellent way to "proof" the dough as it provides an even heat environment with no drafts and the warmth will hasten the rising of the dough. The method below can be used with a mix, frozen dough or your favorite yeast dough recipe.

1 package yeast dough mix

Prepare dough according to directions. Place the dough in a large glass container, cover with plastic wrap and place in microwave for 10 minutes. Microwave for 1 minute at 100% power. With door closed allow dough to remain in oven, without power, for 10 minutes. Repeat the process if needed to increase the volume of the dough. Dough should be doubled in size. It is ready when an indention of your finger remains. Bake conventionally.

Nutrition (per serving): 10 calories
Saturated fat	..0 g
Total Fat	..0 g (13% of calories)
Protein	..0 g (13% of calories)
Carbohydrates	..2 g (74% of calories)
Cholesterol	..0 mg
Sodium	.. 18 mg
Fiber	..0 g

Cakes

Angel Cloud Cake

Serves 12

Store in refrigerator or freezer until time to serve. This cake will freeze for several weeks. Remember that you can bake you own angel food cake in the microwave if desired (See Bread/Cake/ Dessert/Pie). To frost cake, you may use nondairy whipped topping instead of whipped cream if desired.

1 whole (9 inch) angel food cake
1 pint whipping cream, divided
1 (14 oz.) can sweetened condensed milk
1/3 cup lemon juice
1 teaspoon almond extract
3 drops red food color, optional
3 tablespoons sugar
1 teaspoon vanilla
12 whole strawberries

Slice top off of angel food cake about 2-3 inches down. Hollow a "tunnel" in bottom section of cake, being certain to leave inside and outside walls intact. Whip 1/2 cup cream and blend in condensed milk, lemon juice and almond extract. If desired, add a few drops of red food coloring for a pink color. Fill "tunnel" in bottom layer of cake with milk/cream mixture. Whip remaining cream to stiff peaks. Stir in sugar and vanilla. Put top of cake on bottom layer. Frost with whipped cream. Garnish with fresh strawberries before serving.

Nutrition (per serving): 270 calories
    Saturated fat .... 11 g
    Total Fat .... 18 g (59% of calories)
    Protein .... 4 g (5% of calories)
    Carbohydrates .... 24 g (36% of calories)
    Cholesterol .... 66 mg
    Sodium .... 57 mg
    Fiber .... 0 g

Angel Food Cake

Serves 12

This cake has too much volume to bake the entire cake mix at one time in the microwave. You may wish to make half of the cake mix at a time. This is excellent to use in desserts calling for angel cake and is done in a jiffy.

1 (16 oz.) package one step angel food cake mix

Mix cake with electric mixer according to directions on box. Place 1/2 of batter in microwave tube pan or 3 quart casserole with cone. Tap several times on counter to remove air bubbles. Microwave, covered, for 2 minutes at 100% power. Reduce power to 70% power and cook another 3 minutes. Let stand on rack. Cool and remove. Cook other half.

Nutrition (per serving): 102 calories
    Saturated fat .... 0 g
    Total Fat .... 0 g (1% of calories)
    Protein .... 3 g (10% of calories)
    Carbohydrates .... 23 g (89% of calories)
    Cholesterol .... 0 m
    Sodium .... 107 mg
    Fiber .... 0 g

Blueberry Cake

Serves 8

Cake may appear slightly damp on top, but will finish cooking during standing time. This is an excellent breakfast cake.

1/4 cup softened lowfat margarine
1/2 cup sugar
2 eggs
1 cup sifted flour
1/2 teaspoon baking powder
1/4 teaspoon salt
1/2 cup lowfat sour cream
1/2 teaspoon vanilla
1/2 teaspoon ground cardamom, optional

1 cup unsweetened blueberries, divided
1/4 cup packed brown sugar

Cream margarine and sugar. Add eggs one at a time, beating well after each addition. Sift dry ingredients together. Add gradually to egg mixture, alternating with sour cream and ending with flour. Stir in vanilla and cardamom. Fold in 1/2 cup blueberries. Pour half of batter into 9 inch round cake pan. Top with remaining blueberries and sprinkle with brown sugar. Top with remaining batter. Bake for 5-10 minutes at 70% power or until cake tests done.

```
Nutrition (per serving): 186 calories
    Saturated fat ............................................................ ...1 g
    Total Fat ................................................................ ...4 g (21% of calories)
    Protein .................................................................. ...4 g (9% of calories)
    Carbohydrates ........................................................ ..32 g (70% of calories)
    Cholesterol ............................................................ ..53 mg
    Sodium ................................................................. 193 mg
    Fiber ................................................................... ...0 g
```

Bundt Cake Variations

Serves 14

This recipe gives you many dessert variations by using any flavor cake mix, pudding and liquid.

1 package (18.5 oz.) chocolate cake mix
1 (3 oz.) package instant pudding mix
1/2 cup vegetable oil
3/4 cup liquid (milk, coffee or juice)
4 eggs

Mix ingredients together in order given. Pour into bundt pan and bake at 70% power for 12-18 minutes or until done. Cool 10 minutes and remove from pan. VARIATIONS: Use same amount of oil and eggs but substitute the following: DARK CHOCOLATE PECAN: Devils food cake mix, chocolate pudding mix, 1 cup double strength coffee, 1/2 cup chopped pecans; COCONUT PECAN: Yellow cake mix, vanilla pudding mix, orange, apple or pineapple juice, 1/2 cup chopped pecans; POPPY SEED: Yellow cake mix, vanilla pudding, 1 cup sour cream, 1 tsp. vanilla, 1/4 cup poppy seeds.

```
Nutrition (per serving): 115 calories
    Saturated fat ..................................................... 2 g
    Total Fat ......................................................... 9 g (73% of calories)
    Protein ........................................................... 2 g (7% of calories)
    Carbohydrates .................................................... 6 g (20% of calories)
    Cholesterol ...................................................... 61 mg
    Sodium ........................................................... 43 mg
    Fiber ............................................................ 0 g
```

Bundt Coffee Cake

Serves 14

When cooking cakes in the microwave, the bottoms occasionally do not get done. If you elevate the cake on an inverted microwave casserole or cover to form an "invisible" shelf on which to place the cake, microwaves can "bounce" or flow more uniformly instead of getting trapped underneath. The cake will cook more evenly. This is similar to placing cakes in the center of the conventional oven where they will get even heat. When done, cake may appear slightly moist on top, but sides will pull away and bottom will be done. Top will finish cooking during standing time.

1 (18 oz.) yellow cake mix
1 (3 oz.) package instant lemon pudding mix
3/4 cup vegetable oil
2/3 cup water
4 eggs
1 teaspoon vanilla extract
1 teaspoon butter flavored extract
2/3 cup chopped pecans
2/3 teaspoon cinnamon
1/3 cup softened lowfat margarine
1/4 cup sugar
1 cup powdered sugar
3 tablespoons milk
1/2 teaspoon vanilla extract
1/2 teaspoon almond extract

Combine cake mix, pudding, oil and water in large mixing bowl. Add eggs one at a time and beat 4 or 5 minutes until very well blended. Add extracts. Set aside. Grease a microwave-safe bundt pan with some of the softened margarine. In small bowl mix sugar, 1/2 of nuts and remaining margarine. Sprinkle remaining nuts into pan and shake so that nuts will stick to margarine and coat the pan. Pour half of batter into the pan and cover with cinnamon mixture. Add remaining batter. Place cake in microwave and cook at 70% power for 15-18 minutes or until done. While cake is baking prepare glaze by mixing powdered sugar, milk, vanilla and almond extract. Let cake stand for 5-10 minutes before turning out. Pour glaze over top of cake and let it drizzle down the sides.

```
Nutrition (per serving): 402 calories
    Saturated fat ........................................................ ....3 g
    Total Fat ............................................................. ..23 g (50% of calories)
    Protein .............................................................. ....4 g (4% of calories)
    Carbohydrates ...................................................... ..46 g (45% of calories)
    Cholesterol ......................................................... ..61 mg
    Sodium .............................................................. 371 mg
    Fiber ................................................................ ....0 g
```

Cheesecake

Serves 12

1 cup of miniature chocolate chips may be added to batter for a change.

3 (8 oz.) packages light cream cheese, softened

1 cup sugar

4 eggs

1 teaspoon vanilla

1 tablespoon lemon juice

1 dash salt

2 cups cinnamon graham cracker crumbs

2 tablespoons melted lowfat margarine

2 tablespoons cream

2 cups non-fat sour cream

1 tablespoon sugar

1/2 teaspoon vanilla

Thoroughly mix cream cheese, sugar, eggs, vanilla, salt and lemon juice. Set aside. Mix cracker crumbs, margarine and cream. Press into bottom and up the sides of microwave spring form pan or casserole. Pour cheese mixture into crust and bake at 70% power for 10-20 minutes until nearly firm. Mix sour cream, sugar and vanilla. Top cooled cake and microwave for 1-3 minutes at 100% power. Cool thoroughly before serving.

```
Nutrition (per serving): 217 calories
    Saturated fat ........................................................ ....7 g
    Total Fat ............................................................. .12 g (51% of calories)
    Protein .............................................................. ....8 g (15% of calories)
    Carbohydrates ...................................................... ..18 g (34% of calories)
    Cholesterol ......................................................... ....0 mg
    Sodium .............................................................. 250 mg
    Fiber ................................................................ ....0 g
```

Chocolate Cream Cupcakes

Serves 16

Cupcakes will not be tough unless overcooked. Remember, they may appear slightly damp looking on top when done, but will finish cooking while standing.

1 (8 oz.) package light cream cheese, softened
1 egg
1 1/3 cups sugar, divided
1/8 teaspoon salt
1 cup mini chocolate chips
1 1/2 cups flour
1/4 cup cocoa
1/2 teaspoon salt
1/3 cup vegetable oil
1 tablespoon vinegar
1 teaspoon baking soda
1 cup water
1 teaspoon vanilla

Mix cream cheese, egg, 1/3 cup sugar and salt. Mix well. Blend in chips and set aside. Sift together flour, remaining sugar, cocoa, baking soda and salt. Stir in water, oil, vanilla and vinegar. Fill double cupcake papers 1/3 full of batter. Top with 1 1/2 tsp. cheese mixture. Microwave six at a time, circle fashion, at 70% power for 2-5 minutes until no longer doughy, but a bit shiny on top. Let stand to finish cooking. Repeat.

```
Nutrition (per serving): 257 calories
    Saturated fat ........................................................ ....5 g
    Total Fat ............................................................... ..12 g (43% of calories)
    Protein ................................................................. ....4 g (6% of calories)
    Carbohydrates ..................................................... ..33 g (51% of calories)
    Cholesterol .......................................................... ..24 mg
    Sodium ................................................................. 214 mg
    Fiber .................................................................... ....0 g
```

Cakes Cream Cheese Frosting

Serves 8

1 (3 oz.) package light cream cheese, softened
3 tablespoons skim milk
1 teaspoon vanilla
2 cups powdered sugar

Cream cheese and milk. Add remaining ingredients. Beat well. Let stand 3 minutes. Beat until creamy.

```
Nutrition (per serving): 150 calories
    Saturated fat ........................................................ ..2 g
    Total Fat ............................................................ ..3 g (15% of calories)
    Protein .............................................................. ...1 g (3% of calories)
    Carbohydrates ....................................................... .31 g (82% of calories)
    Cholesterol ......................................................... ..8 mg
    Sodium .............................................................. 46 mg
    Fiber ............................................................... ..0 g
```

Earthquake Cake

Serves 8

This is a sinfully rich cake. I have used low fat/calorie ingredients when possible. You may use egg substitute also, if desired. Better yet ... just enjoy it occasionally in small amounts. Also, this will cook well in a large bundt type cake pan.

1/2 cup chopped pecans
1/2 cup shredded coconut
9 ounces German chocolate cake mix
1/3 cup water
1/4 cup vegetable oil
3 eggs
1 (8 oz.) package light cream cheese
1/2 teaspoon vanilla
1/4 cup lowfat margarine
8 ounces powdered sugar

Mix pecans and coconut and spread in bottom of 9 inch round microwave pan. Mix cake mix, water, oil and eggs. Pour cake mix over coconut and pecans. Soften cream cheese and margarine. Mix with vanilla and sugar and spoon over cake batter. Microwave at 70% power for 10-15 minutes. Cake will erupt and have craters. Serve topped with ice cream if desired.

```
Nutrition (per serving): 382 calories
    Saturated fat ........................................................ ....8 g
    Total Fat ............................................................ ..25 g (59% of calories)
    Protein .............................................................. ....6 g (6% of calories)
    Carbohydrates ....................................................... ..33 g (35% of calories)
    Cholesterol ......................................................... 101 mg
    Sodium .............................................................. 228 mg
    Fiber ............................................................... ....0 g
```

Fabulous Cake

Serves 12

This is a fabulous but simple cake that will bring people back for seconds. Try using other flavors of cake mixes and frostings for change.

1 (18.5 oz.) package chocolate cake mix
3/4 -1 cup water
1/3 cup vegetable oil
3 eggs
1 (8 oz.) can pecan coconut frosting

Mix cake according to directions on box, but notice the water has been cut back 25% (See Converting Recipes). Place frosting mix in bottom in bundt cake pan or 3 quart casserole with cone. Place cake mix on top of frosting. Let stand a minute or two before baking. Microwave at 100% power for 15 minutes. Cool a few minutes and invert on serving dish.

```
Nutrition (per serving): 73 calories
    Saturated fat ........................................................ ..1 g
    Total Fat .............................................................. ..7 g (91% of calories)
    Protein ................................................................ ..2 g (9% of calories)
    Carbohydrates .................................................... ..0 g (1% of calories)
    Cholesterol .......................................................... 53 mg
    Sodium ................................................................ 16 mg
    Fiber ................................................................... ..0 g
```

Hot Fudge Pudding Cake

Serves 8

Frozen dessert topping, frozen yogurt or ice cream may be served with this if desired.

3/4 cup flour
1 1/4 cups sugar, divided
6 tablespoons cocoa, divided
1 1/2 teaspoons baking powder
1/3 cup skim milk
3 tablespoons melted lowfat margarine
1 1/2 teaspoons vanilla
1/4 cup chopped pecans
1 cup hot water

In mixing bowl stir together 1/2 cup sugar, flour, 2 tablespoons cocoa and baking powder. Stir in milk, margarine and vanilla. Blend in nuts and pour batter into 3 quart casserole. In a small mixing bowl, mix 3/4 cup sugar and 1/4 cup cocoa. Stir in hot water and pour evenly over batter. Do Not Stir!! Cook, uncovered, at 100% power for 5-8 minutes or until cake springs back when lightly touched. Let stand 15-20 minutes before serving.

```
Nutrition (per serving): 231 calories
    Saturated fat ........................................................1 g
    Total Fat ..............................................................5 g (20% of calories)
    Protein ..................................................................3 g (4% of calories)
    Carbohydrates .....................................................44 g (75% of calories)
    Cholesterol ...........................................................0 mg
    Sodium ............................................................. 153 mg
    Fiber .....................................................................0 g
```

Pumpkin Cake

Serves 16

This is a very moist cake. Cake may appear damp on top when done, but should be done on bottom. Check with long pick for bottom doneness. Cool for 10-12 minutes before turning out. This is good with a cream cheese/powdered sugar glaze.

2 cups sugar
1 1/4 cups vegetable oil
4 eggs
2 cups canned pumpkin
3 cups flour
2 teaspoons baking soda
2 teaspoons baking powder
1/2 teaspoon salt
1 teaspoon ground cinnamon
1/2 teaspoon ground nutmeg
1/2 teaspoon ground allspice
1/8 teaspoon ground cloves
1/8 teaspoon ground ginger
3/4 cup chopped pecans

Cream sugar and oil, add eggs, stirring well. Mix in pumpkin and dry mixture alternately. Stir in pecans. Place cake in large 10 inch microwave bundt pan and microwave at 70% power for 12-15 minutes or until cake is done.

Raspberry Cheese Cake

Serves 12

This is a most elegant dessert and worth the effort. Save your fat grams for this one!! Splurge occasionally!!

3/4 cup crushed cookie crumbs

1 1/4 cups lightly toasted pecans

1/4 cup packed brown sugar

1/4 teaspoon ground cinnamon

1/8 teaspoon ground cloves

3 tablespoons unsalted butter or margarine

2 (8 oz.) packages light cream cheese, softened

1/2 cup whipping cream

1 cup sugar, divided

1 teaspoon vanilla

1 tablespoon cornstarch

6 tablespoons water

4 cups fresh raspberries

CRUST: Blend cookie crumbs, pecans, brown sugar, cinnamon and cloves to coarse crumbs in food processor. Transfer to medium size mixing bowl and mix in melted butter. Mound crumbs in bottom of 9 inch microwave springform pan or 9 inch cake pan. Cover crumbs with plastic wrap and press firmly into bottom and up sides of pan. Chill 30 minutes. Microwave for 3-5 minutes at 100% power and set aside to cool completely. FILLING: Using electric mixer, beat cream cheese, cream, 1/2 cup sugar and vanilla. Pour into crust. Cover and refrigerate for at least 4 hours. TOPPING: In small cup, mix 2 teaspoons water with cornstarch in small cup. In large microwave measure, stir 2 1/2 cups berries with 1/2 cup sugar and remaining 1/4 cup water. Stir together and heat at 100% power for 1-2 minutes, stirring once, until sugar is dissolved. Continue to cook, stirring frequently, for about 4-5 minutes until berries are thoroughly crushed and have extruded their juices. Add cornstarch mixture and boil for another minute or two until slightly thickened. Strain through sieve set over large bowl, pressing on berries with back of spoon. Discard berry skins. Cool sauce. Cover and refrigerate until chilled. Mix remaining 1 1/2 cups whole berries into sauce right before serving. Cut pie into wedges. Spoon berry sauce over all and serve.

```
Nutrition (per serving): 375 calories
    Saturated fat ..................................................... ..11 g
    Total Fat ........................................................... ..25 g (60% of calories)
    Protein ............................................................. ....6 g (6% of calories)
    Carbohydrates ................................................... ..32 g (35% of calories)
    Cholesterol ....................................................... ..53 m
    Sodium .............................................................. 201 mg
    Fiber ................................................................. ...1 g
```

Sour Cream Cocoa Cake

Serves 9

This cake will cook more evenly in a round pan rather than an 8 x 8 inch square pan (See Cooking Patterns). This cake may be frosted.

1 cup sugar
1/2 cup lowfat margarine
1 egg
1 1/2 cups flour
3 tablespoons cocoa
3 tablespoons water
8 ounces lowfat sour cream
1/4 cup nuts
2 tablespoons powdered sugar

In medium size mixing bowl, cream sugar and margarine. Beat in egg. Blend flour alternately with cocoa that has been dissolved in water. Blend in sour cream and nuts. Place in 1 quart microwave casserole or cake pan. Microwave at 70% power for 8-12 minutes until cake is done. Frost or sprinkle with powdered sugar and nuts.

```
Nutrition (per serving): 288 calories
    Saturated fat ..................................................... ....2 g
    Total Fat ........................................................... ..10 g (30% of calories)
    Protein ............................................................. ....6 g (8% of calories)
    Carbohydrates ................................................... ..45 g (62% of calories)
    Cholesterol ....................................................... ..28 mg
    Sodium .............................................................. 173 mg
    Fiber ................................................................. ....0 g
```

Berry Cobbler

Serves 8

Drained canned berries may be substituted for fresh. They will not have to be cooked to form juice. While baking, the fruit mixture goes to bottom of dish and a cake-like layer forms on the top.

1/4 cup softened lowfat margarine
1/2 cup sugar
1 cup flour
2 teaspoons baking powder
1 dash salt
1/3 cup skim milk
1 1/2 cups fresh berries
1/2 cup sugar
1/2 teaspoon ground cinnamon
1/2 cup berry juice

Cream together margarine and sugar. Mix in flour, baking powder and salt alternately with milk. Pour into 2 quart oblong or round microwave casserole. Put berries and 1/2 cup sugar in microwave measure. Heat for 2-3 minutes at 100% power so that berries will start to make juice. Mix juice into berry mixture and spoon over dough. Microwave at 70% power for 12-15 minutes. Serve with cream, whipped cream or ice cream.

Nutrition (per serving): 195 calories
Saturated fat ...... 1 g
Total Fat ...... 3 g (14% of calories)
Protein ...... 2 g (4% of calories)
Carbohydrates ...... 40 g (81% of calories)
Cholesterol ...... 0 mg
Sodium ...... 212 mg
Fiber ...... 0 g

Chocolate Crinkle Cups

Serves 10

These shells may be filled with any filling desired. Makes a special dessert. Freeze if desired.

6 ounces semisweet chocolate

2 tablespoons lowfat margarine

1 quart vanilla lowfat ice cream

1/2 cup toasted shredded coconut

Place chocolate and margarine in 2 cup measure. Microwave at 50% power for 3-6 minutes until chocolate is melted. Blend together. Place 10 aluminum foil baking cups in muffin tins. Using a teaspoon, spread chocolate mixture over inside of cups to thoroughly cover. Chill until firm. Peel off foil. Roll ice cream in coconut and place in cups to serve.

```
Nutrition (per serving): 180 calories
    Saturated fat ....................................................... ..6 g
    Total Fat ............................................................... 10 g (52% of calories)
    Protein ................................................................. ..2 g (5% of calories)
    Carbohydrates .................................................... 20 g (43% of calories)
    Cholesterol. ........................................................ ..2 mg
    Sodium ................................................................ 68 mg
    Fiber ................................................................... ..0 g
```

Cran-Apple Sauce

Serves 10

Any type flavoring may be used if orange liqueur is not available.

4 cups sliced cooking apples

1 cup fresh cranberries

1/4 cup raisins

1/2 cup sugar

1/2 tablespoon cornstarch

2 tablespoons orange flavored liqueur

2 cups frozen dessert topping

1/2 teaspoon ground cinnamon

Mix apples, cranberries, raisins, sugar and cornstarch in 1 1/2 quart casserole. Cover and cook at 100% power, stirring once, for 7-8 minutes or until apples are tender. Stir in liqueur. Cool. Serve warm or chilled in dessert dishes topped with spoonfuls of whipped topping and dash of cinnamon.

```
Nutrition (per serving): 146 calories
    Saturated fat ....................................................... ..3 g
    Total Fat ............................................................... ..4 g (25% of calories)
    Protein ................................................................. ..0 g (1% of calories)
    Carbohydrates .................................................... .26 g (71% of calories)
    Cholesterol ......................................................... ..0 mg
    Sodium ................................................................ ..5 mg
    Fiber ................................................................... ..1 g
```

Delightful Dessert

Serves 16

This is a very rich dessert but a show stopper!

   2 cups flour
   1 1/2 cups pecans, chopped, divided
   1 cup melted lowfat margarine
   2 1/2 cups whipping cream, divided
   4 ounces light cream cheese, softened
   1/2 cup sifted powdered sugar
   2 (3 oz.) packages vanilla instant pudding mix
   2 1/2 cups skim milk
   1 whole banana, thinly sliced
   1/2 cup flaked coconut

Mix flour, 1 cup nuts and margarine. Place in 9 x 13 inch micro-wave casserole and bake for 5-6 minutes at 70% power. Beat 1 1/2 cups whipping cream with cream cheese and sugar until thoroughly blended. Spread over crust. Cover and chill. Whisk together pudding mix and milk until thickened. Spread over cheese layer and chill. Arrange thinly sliced banana in single layer over pudding. Whip 1 cup whipping cream and fold in remaining pecans. Spread over banana and sprinkle with coconut. Chill well before serving.

Nutrition (per serving): 418 calories	
Saturated fat	..12 g
Total Fat	..30 g (64% of calories)
Protein	....6 g (5% of calories)
Carbohydrates	..32 g (31% of calories)
Cholesterol	..57 mg
Sodium	245 mg
Fiber	....0 g

Dessert Cheese Ball

Serves 16

   1 (9 oz.) package crumbled mincemeat
   1/2 cup orange juice
   1 (8 oz.) package light cream cheese, softened
   1/2 cup chopped nuts

In microwave measure, combine mincemeat and juice. Microwave at 50% power for 6-8 minutes, stirring once. Chill. In medium bowl, beat cheese until fluffy. Stir in mincemeat. Chill and shape into a ball. Coat with nuts. Chill. Serve with cookies, crackers or chilled apples, pears or grapes. Makes 5 inch ball.

Fudge Pudding

Serves 4

1 1/4 cups skim milk, divided

1 tablespoon vegetable oil

2/3 cup sugar

1 egg, well beaten

2 ounces unsweetened chocolate

1 cup flour

1 teaspoon baking powder

Mix 2/3 cup milk, oil, sugar and egg. Heat remaining 1/2 cup milk and chocolate at 70% power for 2-4 minutes until chocolate melts. Mix with flour and baking powder and remaining ingredients. Bake at 70% power for 7-10 minutes until hot and bubbly.

Vanilla Pudding

Serves 4

This is a basic recipe for vanilla pudding. Chocolate or other flavors may be added. This also makes a good base for a pie. Egg substitute or 4 egg whites and skim milk may be substituted in this recipe if you are watching fats in your diet.

1/2 cup sugar

2 tablespoons cornstarch

1 tablespoon flour

1 dash salt

2 cups milk

2 whole eggs, slightly beaten

1 teaspoon vanilla

In 2 quart casserole or large microwave measure, mix sugar, cornstarch and flour. Stir in milk. Cook at 100% power for 7-10 minutes until thickened, stirring once or twice.

```
Nutrition (per serving): 234 calories
        Saturated fat ......................................................... ....3 g
        Total Fat ................................................................ ....7 g (25% of calories)
        Protein ................................................................... ....7 g (13% of calories)
        Carbohydrates ...................................................... ..36 g (62% of calories)
        Cholesterol ........................................................... 123 mg
        Sodium ................................................................. 189 mg
        Fiber ..................................................................... ....0 g
```

Williamsburg Trifle

Serves 20

This is a spectacular dessert I used in my catering business. The recipe may be halved, doubled or even tripled according to the size of your group and your container. Dessert keeps for 10 days. Try variations of white or yellow cake, miscellaneous pudding flavors, coconut, almonds or fruit.

1 (18.2 oz.) package chocolate cake mix
3 (3 oz.) packages instant chocolate cake mix
1/4 cup rum
1 pint whipping cream
1 cup chopped pecans
1 (8 oz.) can instant whipped cream
1 (6 oz.) jar maraschino cherries with stems

Prepare cake mix and bake at 70% power in microwave bundt casserole for 10-15 minutes or until cake is done. Prepare instant pudding as directed for pies. Stir in rum flavoring. Whip cream. In large glass serving bowl or brandy snifter, put thin layer of crumbled cake pieces. Spread this with a thin layer of pudding followed by a thin layer of whipped cream. Sprinkle with nuts and repeat several times ending with whipped cream and nuts. Refrigerate for at least 4 days before serving. Garnish with dollops of whipped cream topping and red cherries with stems.

```
Nutrition (per serving): 217 calories
        Saturated fat ......................................................... ..8 g
        Total Fat ................................................................ 16 g (64% of calories)
        Protein ................................................................... ..2 g (3% of calories)
        Carbohydrates ...................................................... 16 g (29% of calories)
        Cholesterol ........................................................... 41 mg
        Sodium ................................................................. 76 mg
        Fiber ..................................................................... ..0 g
```

Pies

Facts About Microwaving Pie Crust

1. Pie crust should always be pre-cooked in the microwave. Crusts will be very flaky although they do not brown. Spices or some of the sauces in Potpourri (Definitive Microwave Cookery) may be added for coloring.
3. Give savory pastry color by using a glaze made of egg and Worcestershire sauce or soy sauce and water or gravy browning brushed over the shell before baking.
4. Give sweet pastry color by sprinkling a mixture of cinnamon and sugar or brown sugar dissolved in water brushed over the shell before baking.
5. Use whole wheat flour to improve color.
6. For two crust pies, microwave crust separately; then assemble and microwave again.
7. Frozen pie shells may be removed from container and placed upside down over the bottom of pie dish and microwaved. This will prevent poorly shaped or warped bottoms. They may also be placed loosely in the plate and pricked on bottom and sides. Cook, rotating when necessary. After cooking, a mixture of egg and water may be brushed on and cooked another minute to seal the holes.

TIPS

♥ If bottom of pastry is not cooking dry, elevate pie plate on overturned saucer or casserole cover.

♥ A pie crust is easier to make if all the ingredients are cool.

♥ Substitute crusted cornflakes in a pecan pie if you don't have any nuts. They will rise to the top like nuts and give a great crunch and flavor.

♥ When making a cream pie, sprinkle with powdered sugar to prevent crust from becoming soggy.

♥ Put a layer of marshmallows in the bottom of a pumpkin pie before you add the filling. While cooking, the marshmallows will become the topping as they rise to the top.

♥ A teaspoon of vinegar added to pecan pie syrup will cut the sugary sweetness and bring out the flavor.

♥ When fresh fruit is plentiful, try this: Mix the fruit as you would for your favorite pie. Put the filling in several pie plates lined with plastic wrap, waxed paper or foil. Cover and freeze. Remove and keep frozen until you have time to prepare your crusts. Just pop your pie-shaped fillings into the crust and bake.

♥ Add a spoonful of tapioca to pie fillings that contain especially juicy fruits. Tapioca absorbs the excess juice and keeps the filling in the crust.

Shake A Pie Crust

Serves 16

Try some variations of this pie crust.

    2 cups flour
    1/2 teaspoon salt
    3/4 cup solid shortening
    1/4 cup ice water

Place flour and salt in medium mixing bowl. Seal and shake to mix. Add shortening and shake until mixture is uniform size, about the size of peas. Sprinkle with water, tablespoon at a time. Seal and shake. Repeat until dough forms a ball. A thudding sound will be heard. Divide into two equal parts. Flatten, cover and refrigerate for 30 minutes. Place on lightly floured surface. Roll to 1/8" thickness. Fold into fourths, being careful not to stretch dough. Let rest on baking dish for 5 minutes before baking or adding mixture to allow for shrinkage. Prick pastry and microwave at 100% power for 5-7 minutes, rotating dish 1/2 turn after 3 minutes. Pastry is done when it looks dry and blistered and is not doughy. VARIATIONS: To enhance pie crust color, flavor and texture, add the following to flour and salt mixture; COCONUT CRUST—1/2 cup flaked coconut (cherry, rhubarb, cream pies); SPICE CRUST—1 T. sugar, 1 t. cinnamon, 1/4 t. nutmeg (cream, custard, pumpkin, mincemeat, apple pies); CHEESE CRUST—omit shortening and add 1/2 cup shredded cheddar cheese (apple, pear, main dish pies); COFFEE CRUST—Add 1-2 t. instant coffee to water and 2 Tbsp. finely chopped pecans or walnuts to flour (cream, chiffon pies); NUT CRUST—Add 1/4 cup finely chopped nuts and 1/4 t. nutmeg (cream, chiffon, mince pies); CHOCOLATE CRUST—Add 1 T. sugar and 2 T. cocoa (chocolate chiffon, cream pies); WHOLE WHEAT CRUST— Substitute whole wheat flour for all purpose flour (cream, chiffon, mincemeat, apple, fruit pie).

```
Nutrition (per serving): 151 calories
    Saturated fat ..................................................... 2 g
    Total Fat .......................................................... 11 g (64% of calories)
    Protein ............................................................ 2 g (4% of calories)
    Carbohydrates ................................................. 12 g (32% of calories)
    Cholesterol ...................................................... 0 mg
    Sodium ............................................................ 74 mg
    Fiber ............................................................... 0 g
```

Sonja's Pie Crust

Serves 16

Do not be afraid to pat crust into pan if it begins to "slip" or "bubble" while cooking. Simply stop microwave, shape crust correctly and start microwave again. This could not be done when cooking conventionally.

> 2/3 cup vegetable oil
> 1/2 cup water
> 2 1/2 cups flour
> 1 teaspoon baking powder
> 1/4 teaspoon salt

Mix with fork. Divide dough into two parts. Flatten into thick circle, wrap and place in refrigerator for 30 minutes. Put one part between wax paper. Roll out. Fit into dish. Microwave 4-7 minutes at 100% power.

```
Nutrition (per serving): 152 calories
    Saturated fat ............................................... ..1 g
    Total Fat .................................................... ..9 g (55% of calories)
    Protein ...................................................... ..2 g (5% of calories)
    Carbohydrates ............................................ 15 g (39% of calories)
    Cholesterol ................................................ ..0 mg
    Sodium ...................................................... 59 mg
    Fiber ........................................................ ..0 g
```

Banana Split Pie

Serves 8

Remember you may soften ice cream in the microwave for 30 seconds to 1 minute at 100% power (See Microwave Tips). Pie shell may be baked in the microwave (See Bread/Cake/Dessert/Pie).

> 3 whole bananas, peeled and sliced
> 1 tablespoon lemon juice
> 1 pint strawberry lowfat ice cream
> 1 1/2 cups frozen dessert topping
> 1 cup chocolate sauce
> 1 baked pie shell
> 1/4 cup finely chopped nuts
> 2 tablespoons grated chocolate candies
> 1 red maraschino cherry

Sprinkle bananas with lemon juice, turning to coat. Arrange on bottom of pie shell. Spread ice cream over bananas. Spread with whipped topping. Decorate with nuts or chocolate sprinkles and maraschino cherry. Freeze. Remove from freezer 20 minutes before serving. Cut and serve with chocolate sauce.

```
Nutrition (per serving): 370 calories
        Saturated fat .......................................................... ....7 g
        Total Fat ............................................................. ..16 g (38% of calories)
        Protein ............................................................... ...4 g (5% of calories)
        Carbohydrates ................................................... ..53 g (57% of calories)
        Cholesterol .......................................................... .....1 mg
        Sodium ................................................................ 197 mg
        Fiber .................................................................... ....0 g
```

Canned Berry Pie

Serves 8

Remember to bake your pie shell in the microwave. Pie shells are very flaky and the browning will never be missed (See Bread, Cake, Dessert, Pie). Also, you may use any type of berries or fruit for this recipe. Use juice from berries or fruit if desired. Then add enough liquid or juice to make 1 cup.

2 1/2 cups canned berries
1 cup unsweetened fruit juice
1 tablespoon cornstarch
3/4 cup sugar
1/2 teaspoon ground cinnamon
1 baked (9 inch) pie shell
1 tablespoon lowfat margarine
1/2 cup cookie crumbs

Drain berries and set aside. In large measure, mix fruit juice, corn-starch, sugar and cinnamon. Cook 3-4 minutes, stirring once, at 100% power until thickened. Gently stir in fruit and place in pie shell. Sprinkle with crumbs and dot with margarine. Microwave for 15-18 minutes at 70% power until pie is thickened and bubbling.

```
Nutrition (per serving): 257 calories
        Saturated fat .......................................................... ....2 g
        Total Fat ............................................................. ...9 g (33% of calories)
        Protein ............................................................... ...2 g (3% of calories)
        Carbohydrates ................................................... ..41 g (64% of calories)
        Cholesterol .......................................................... ....2 mg
        Sodium ................................................................ 172 mg
        Fiber .................................................................... ...0 g
```

Chocolate Mousse Pie

Serves 8

2 cups graham cracker crumbs
6 tablespoons lowfat margarine
2 teaspoons sugar
4 ounces German sweet chocolate
1/3 cup skim milk
2 tablespoons sugar
1 (3 oz.) package light cream cheese, softened
8 ounces frozen dessert topping, thawed

Mix graham cracker crumbs and sugar in pie plate. Top with margarine and microwave for 1-1 1/2 minutes at 100% power until margarine is melted. Mix well and press into pie plate to form a well shaped shell. Bake for 1 1/2 minutes at 100% power. Place chocolate and milk in small microwave measure. Heat for 1-3 minutes at 50% power or until chocolate is melted. In medium size mixing bowl, beat together sugar and cream cheese. Add chocolate mixture and beat until smooth. Fold in whipped cream topping. Cool and spoon chocolate mixture into cooled crust. Freeze for 4 hours before serving.

```
Nutrition (per serving): 346 calories
    Saturated fat ........................................................ ..12 g
    Total Fat ............................................................. ..21 g (55% of calories)
    Protein ................................................................ ....4 g (5% of calories)
    Carbohydrates .................................................... ..35 g (41% of calories)
    Cholesterol ......................................................... ....8 mg
    Sodium ............................................................... 302 mg
    Fiber ................................................................... ....0 g
```

Custard Pie

Serves 8

Filling may be slightly "wobbly" in center when shaken, but will become firm when cooled. For richer pie, substitute 1 cup of whipping cream for 1 cup of milk.

2 cups evaporated skim milk
3 eggs
2 egg yolks
1/2 cup sugar
2 teaspoons vanilla

1 dash nutmeg
1 baked 9 inch pie crust

Place milk in 4 cup microwave measure. Heat at 100% power for 4-5 minutes until extremely hot, but not boiling. While milk is heating, beat eggs thoroughly and stir in sugar and vanilla. Gradually add hot milk to egg mixture so eggs will not curdle. Place in baked pie shell and sprinkle with nutmeg. Microwave at 70% power for 9-12 minutes or until pie is set.

```
Nutrition (per serving): 255 calories
     Saturated fat ........................ ................................. ....3 g
     Total Fat .............................................................. ..11 g (38% of calories)
     Protein ................................................................. ....9 g (14% of calories)
     Carbohydrates ..................................................... ..30 g (47% of calories)
     Cholesterol ......................................................... 133 mg
     Sodium ................................................................ 237 mg
     Fiber .................................................................... ....0 g
```

Favorite Liqueur Pie

Serves 8

This is also a wonderful dessert served in dessert glasses and sprinkled with cookie crumbs. Evaporated skim milk may be whipped and substituted for whipping cream to lower fat content.

24 whole sandwich chocolate cookies
4 tablespoons melted lowfat margarine
1/4 cup Kahlua/Creme de Menthe liqueur
1 (6 oz.) jar marshmallow cream
2 cups whipping cream

Reserving 2 tablespoons for garnish, mix remaining crumbs and margarine. Place in pie plate. Press into pie plate to form shaped pie shell and bake for 1 1/2 minutes at 100% power. Blend liqueur of choice and marshmallow cream. Whip cream and fold into marshmallow mixture. Place in pie plate and sprinkle with remaining crumbs. Chill until firm.

```
Nutrition (per serving): 600 calories
     Saturated fat ....................................................... ..17 g
     Total Fat .............................................................. ..34 g (51% of calories)
     Protein ................................................................. ....6 g (4% of calories)
     Carbohydrates ..................................................... ..64 g (43% of calories)
     Cholesterol ......................................................... 105 mg
     Sodium ................................................................ 187 mg
     Fiber .................................................................... ....0 g
```

French Apple Pie

Serves 8

6 peeled sliced apples
1 tablespoon lemon juice
1/2 cup sugar
2 tablespoons flour
1/2 teaspoon ground cinnamon
3/4 teaspoon ground nutmeg, divided
1/2 cup flour
1/4 cup brown sugar
1/4 cup lowfat margarine
1 baked pie shell

Place apples, lemon juice, sugar, 2 tablespoons flour, cinnamon and 1/4 tsp. nutmeg in large bowl. Mix gently and place in pie shell. Mix flour, brown sugar and 1/2 teaspoon nutmeg in small bowl. Cut in margarine until crumbly. Sprinkle evenly over filling. Place wax paper under plate while microwaving. Microwave at 100% power for 8 minutes. Turn and cook another 6-10 minutes until apples are tender.

```
Nutrition (per serving): 337 calories
    Saturated fat ........................................................ ...3 g
    Total Fat .............................................................. ..11 g (29% of calories)
    Protein ................................................................. ...3 g (3% of calories)
    Carbohydrates ..................................................... ..57 g (67% of calories)
    Cholesterol .......................................................... ...0 mg
    Sodium ................................................................ 209 mg
    Fiber ................................................................... ...1 g
```

Fresh Berry Pie

Serves 8

Any type of fresh berry such as blackberry, raspberry or blueberry may be used.

4 cups blueberries
2/3 cup sugar
2 tablespoons cornstarch
1/4 cup fruit juice or water
1 tablespoon lemon juice
1 tablespoon lowfat margarine
1/2 teaspoon ground cinnamon

1 teaspoon sugar
1 baked 9 inch pie crust
Cutouts of baked pie crust

Place berries into large mixing bowl. Mix in remaining ingredients and stir into fruit. Place in baked pie shell. Dot with margarine. In the microwave at 100% power, bake pastry cutouts which have been sprinkled with cinnamon/sugar mixture. Place cutouts on top of pie and bake for 10-15 minutes at 70% power or until mixture is thick and bubbly.

```
Nutrition (per serving): 242 calories
     Saturated fat .......................................................... ....2 g
     Total Fat ............................................................... ...9 g (32% of calories)
     Protein ................................................................. ....2 g (3% of calories)
     Carbohydrates ....................................................... ..39 g (65% of calories)
     Cholesterol ........................................................... ....0 mg
     Sodium ................................................................. 161 mg
     Fiber .................................................................... ....1 g
```

Peach Pie

Serves 8

Other fresh fruit may be substituted if desired.

1 (3 oz.) package light cream cheese, softened
6 ounces pineapple juice
2 ounces orange juice
3/4 cup sugar
2 tablespoons cornstarch
3 drops red food color
4 cups peeled sliced peaches
1 baked 9 inch pie shell

Spread softened cream cheese on bottom of pie shell. Mix juice, sugar, cornstarch and food coloring in 4 cup microwave measure. Whisk thoroughly. Microwave at 100% power, stirring once for 2-4 minutes until mixture thickens. Place peaches in pie shell on top of cream cheese. Pour juice mixture over peaches. Microwave pie at 70% power for 10-12 minutes until mixture is bubbly. Let cool before serving.

```
Nutrition (per serving): 279 calories
     Saturated fat .......................................................... ....3 g
     Total Fat ............................................................... ..10 g (33% of calories)
     Protein ................................................................. ....3 g (5% of calories)
     Carbohydrates ....................................................... ..44 g (63% of calories)
     Cholesterol ........................................................... ....8 mg
     Sodium ................................................................. 181 mg
     Fiber .................................................................... ....1 g
```

Pecan Pie

Serves 8

Try substituting Grapenut cereal for the pecans if you want a lower fat/calorie dessert. Also, egg substitute may be used, and low fat butter or margarine.

3 eggs, well beaten
1/3 cup brown sugar
1 cup light corn syrup
3 tablespoons melted lowfat margarine
1 teaspoon vanilla
1 1/2 tablespoons flour
1 1/4 cups chopped pecans
1 baked 9 inch pie crust

Mix all ingredients and cook for 2 minutes at 70% power. Put mixture into baked pie shell. Microwave pie for 9-10 minutes at 70% power.

```
Nutrition (per serving): 433 calories
    Saturated fat ........................................ ....4 g
    Total Fat ............................................. ..24 g (49% of calories)
    Protein ............................................... ....5 g (5% of calories)
    Carbohydrates ..................................... ..50 g (46% of calories)
    Cholesterol .......................................... ..80 mg
    Sodium .............................................. 243 mg
    Fiber .................................................. ....0 g
```

Pumpkin Pie

Serves 8

The pie is done when the edges are set and center is still slightly soft. It will firm as it cools. For a crisper crust, bake before filling.

1 (16 oz.) can pumpkin
1 cup packed brown sugar
1 tablespoon pumpkin pie spice
1 tablespoon flour
1 teaspoon salt
1 (12 oz). can evaporated skim milk
2 eggs, well beaten
1 unbaked pie shell

In large microwave measure or 3 quart casserole, blend together all ingredients except for pie crust. Microwave at 50% power for 12-14 minutes stirring every 5 minutes until hot and thickened. Pour hot pumpkin custard filling into unbaked pie shell and bake at 50% power for 22-25 minutes, rotating after 12 minutes. Let stand at room temperature about 15-20 minutes to set and cool before serving.

```
Nutrition (per serving): 250 calories
    Saturated fat ........................................................2 g
    Total Fat ............................................................9 g (33% of calories)
    Protein ...............................................................7 g (11% of calories)
    Carbohydrates ...................................................35 g  (56% of calories)
    Cholesterol .........................................................55 mg
    Sodium ............................................................ 284 mg
    Fiber ...................................................................1 g
```

Strawberry Pie

Serves 8

6 cups fresh strawberries

1 cup water

1 cup plus 2 tablespoon sugar

1/8 teaspoon salt

2 1/2 teaspoons strawberry gelatin

1 teaspoon red food color

3 tablespoons cornstarch

3 tablespoons water

1 cup whipping cream

1 baked 9 inch pie shell

Put 1 cup water, sugar, gelatin and food coloring in medium size microwave measure. Cook for 3-4 minutes until mixture boils and sugar is dissolved. Mix cornstarch and 3 tablespoons water. Add to gelatin mixture and cook for 2-3 additional minutes, stirring occasionally until mixture thickens. Set aside to cool. Brush a small amount of gelatin glaze (about 1/4 cup) on bottom and sides of baked shell. Place whole or sliced berries, stem side down on bottom and sides of pastry shell. Spoon glaze over berries being certain to coat each berry. Arrange remaining berries and spoon on remaining glaze. Chill for 3-4 hours and garnish with whipped cream.

```
Nutrition (per serving): 366 calories
    Saturated fat ......................................................9 g
    Total Fat ............................................................19 g (47% of calories)
    Protein ...............................................................3 g (3% of calories)
    Carbohydrates ...................................................46 g (50% of calories)
    Cholesterol .........................................................41 mg
    Sodium ............................................................ 187 mg
    Fiber ...................................................................1 g
```

notes:

_____
_____
_____
_____
_____
_____
_____
_____
_____
_____
_____
_____
_____
_____
_____
_____
_____
_____
_____
_____
_____

Potpourri—Sauce/Gravy/Gifts/Etc.

DID YOU KNOW?

♥ Don't throw away "flat" club soda. It will add vigor and color to your plants.

♥ Place one or two ice cubes on crushed carpet nap. The next day, after the ice has melted, the nap will be high.

♥ Spray recipe cards with hairspray to keep them clean. Wash your hands in fresh lemon juice to remove onion scent.

♥ Old powder puffs that have been cleaned in soapy water, rinsed and dried, make great polishing pads for silver, copper and brass.

♥ When doing touch up paint jobs, slip your hands into sandwich bags (for mitts) before picking up paint brush.

♥ Plant a few sprigs of dill near your tomatoes to prevent tomato worms.

♥ Effective insecticides for roaches and weevils is baking soda in dark cabinets, and bay leaves in drawers and closets.

♥ Marigolds prevent rodents.

♥ To keep ants out of the house, place whole cloves where they enter. Tuck a few in corners of your kitchen cupboards and under the sink.

♥ Keep birds off fruit trees by attaching plastic film to tree branches.

♥ Ammonia sprayed into garbage sacks will prevent dogs from tearing up the bags before they are picked up.

♥ Colored cottons that have been soaked in strong salt water overnight won't fade.

♥ To drip-dry garments faster and with fewer wrinkles, hang them over plastic dry cleaner bags.

♥ To prevent gravy lumps when making gravy or thickened sauces, mix flour with a bit of salted hot water before adding to sauce.

♥ A pinch of soda mixed into gravy or sauce having grease on top will cause it to mix or blend together.

♥ Add dark percolated coffee to pale gravy. It will add color but won't affect taste.

♥ Pack charcoal briquettes in egg cartons and tie shut. There is no mess. You can light them right in the carton in the barbecue grill.

♥ Instant potatoes will bind and stretch your meat-loaf mixture.

♥ One teaspoon of sugar mixed with one tablespoon of vinegar will help remove salty taste.

♥ Batters made with eggs and water are crisper than those made with milk.

Potpourri—Sauce/Gravy/Gifts/Etc.

Sauces & Gravies

Bar B Q Sauce
Beef Jerky
Cran-Raspberry Sauce
Cumberland Sauce
Dijon Dill Sauce
Easy Gravy
Fudge Sauce
Madeira Sauce
Meat Flavoring
Mushroom Gravy
Mustard Sauce
Picante Sauce
Sun Dried Tomatoes
Teriyaki Marinade/Sauce

Gifts & Etc.

Baby Handy Wipes
Cuticle Softener
Doggie Cookies
Lip Gloss
Liquid Soap
Massage Lotion
Moisture Mask
Play Dough

196

Sauces/Gravies

Bar B Q Sauce

Serves 20

For delicious ribs, place ribs in microwave pan. Sprinkle ribs with crushed red pepper, black pepper and a small amount of salt. Cover with 2 cups of vinegar. Heat at 100% power for 3 minutes. Turn ribs over and lower power to 50% power and cook an additional 10-12 minutes. Drain vinegar and cook ribs as directed (See Main Dish).

12 ounces hot pepper sauce
1 1/2 cups water
2 cups tomato puree
1 tablespoon crushed red pepper
2 tablespoons sugar
1 stalk celery, finely minced
1 green bell pepper, finely minced
1/2 cup finely minced onions
6 tablespoons lemon juice

Make sauce by mixing all ingredients in microwave casserole. Heat for 8-12 minutes at 100% power until mixture is ready to boil. Stir. Reduce power to 50% and simmer for 20-30 minutes, uncovered. (1/4 cup servings)

Nutrition (per serving): 29 calories
Saturated fat ....0 g
Total Fat ....0 g (3% of calories)
Protein ....1 g (11% of calories)
Carbohydrates .... 8 g (85% of calories)
Cholesterol ....0 mg
Sodium .... 57 mg
Fiber ....1 g

Beef Jerky

Serves 20

1 1/2 pounds flank beef steaks
1 1/2 teaspoons salt
1/2 teaspoon garlic salt
1/4 teaspoon freshly ground black pepper

Remove all visible fat from steak. Cut lengthwise with the grain into 1/8 inch thin strips. Mix salts and pepper. Sprinkle over strips and mix to distribute evenly. Arrange half of strips close together on microwave bacon rack. Cover with microwave wrap. Microwave for 20-25 minutes at 30% power. Half way through cooking time, rearrange strips, placing drier strips in center of rack and rotate rack a half-turn. Remove to absorbent paper. Repeat with remaining strips. Cover with absorbent paper and let stand 24 hours. Store in covered container.

```
Nutrition (per serving): 93 calories
      Saturated fat ..................................................... ...3 g
      Total Fat .......................................................... ....6 g (60% of calories)
      Protein ............................................................. .... 9 g (40% of calories)
      Carbohydrates ................................................... 0 g (0% of calories)
      Cholesterol ....................................................... ..31 mg
      Sodium ............................................................. 200 mg
      Fiber ................................................................. ....0 g
```

Cran-Raspberry Sauce

Serves 2

Excellent over chicken breasts or other meat.

1 1/2 tablespoons sugar
1/2 teaspoon red wine vinegar
1/2 cup frozen raspberries
3 tablespoons chicken broth, divided
1 1/2 tablespoons water
1 teaspoon flour
1/2 cup fresh cranberries
1/2 tablespoon green peppercorns

Stir sugar, vinegar, half of broth, water and raspberries together in 4 cup microwave container. Heat, uncovered, at 100% power for 2-3 minutes, stirring once. Continue to boil until mixture reduces to half. Mix remaining broth and flour into smooth mixture. Stir into raspberry mixture. Stir until mixture thickens. Add cranberries and peppercorns. Reduce power to 70% and cook for 2-3 minutes. (1/2 cup)

```
Nutrition (per serving): 129 calories
      Saturated fat ..................................................... ....0 g
      Total Fat .......................................................... ....0 g (2% of calories)
      Protein ............................................................. ...0 g (3% of calories)
      Carbohydrates ................................................... .31 g (95% of calories)
      Cholesterol ....................................................... ....0 mg
      Sodium ............................................................. 138 mg
      Fiber ................................................................. ...2 g
```

Cumberland Sauce

Serves 16

4 tablespoons melted lowfat margarine
3 tablespoons lime juice
1 cup red currant jelly
1 (6 oz.) can frozen orange juice concentrate
4 tablespoons dry sherry
1 teaspoon dry mustard
1/8 teaspoon ground ginger
1/4 teaspoon Tabasco sauce
1 tablespoon Accent seasoning, optional
1 teaspoon salt
1 pinch black pepper

Mix all ingredients. Heat in microwave container for 5-8 minutes at 50% power until jelly is dissolved and mixture hot. Serve hot over chicken breasts or other type meats. (2 1/2 cups)

Nutrition (per serving): 90 calories

Saturated fat	0 g
Total Fat	1 g (15 % of calories)
Protein	0 g (2 % of calories)
Carbohydrates	18 g (79 % of calories)
Cholesterol	0 mg
Sodium	189 mg
Fiber	0 g

Dijon Dill Sauce

Serves 3

Excellent with meats or vegetables.

3 tablespoons nonfat mayonnaise
2 tablespoons Dijon mustard
2 tablespoons lemon juice
1/2 teaspoon dried dill weed

Mix all ingredients. Whisk thoroughly. Serve at room temperature or heat at 10% power for 1-2 minutes until warm, but not boiling. (1/2 cup)

Nutrition (per serving): 26 calories

Saturated fat	0 g
Total Fat	1 g (22% of calories)
Protein	1 g (11% of calories)
Carbohydrates	4 g (67% of calories)
Cholesterol	0 mg
Sodium	429 mg
Fiber	0 g

Easy Gravy

Serves 4

If this recipe is doubled or tripled, whisk several times while cooking. Recipe doubled will cook about 6 minutes, tripled about 7-8 minutes (See Dealing in Multiples). If a thicker gravy is desired , add another tablespoon of flour. Use meat or poultry drippings instead of margarine if desired. Also, for less fat content use Butter Buds.

    2 tablespoons melted lowfat margarine
    2 tablespoons flour
    1 cup low sodium, fat-reduced, chicken broth
    1/2 teaspoon light soy sauce
    1/4 teaspoon celery salt
    1 pinch black pepper

Melt margarine 20-30 seconds at 100% power in 2 cup microwave measure. Blend in flour, then broth and seasonings. Whisk thoroughly. Cook at 100% power for 2-3 minutes, stirring once. (1 cup)

```
Nutrition (per serving): 48 calories
    Saturated fat ............................................................. .....1 g
    Total Fat ..................................................................... .....3 g (57 % of calories)
    Protein ........................................................................ .....1 g (10 % of calories)
    Carbohydrates ........................................................... .....4 g (33 % of calories)
    Cholesterol ................................................................ .....0 mg
    Sodium ....................................................................... 220 mg
    Fiber ........................................................................... .....0 g
```

Fudge Sauce

Serves 20

Serve warm over ice cream or cake. For a low fat version of this recipe ,use evaporated skim milk and 3 tablespoons regular type cocoa plus 1 tablespoon of margarine.

    1 cup semisweet chocolate chips
    1/2 cup lowfat margarine
    2 cups sifted confectioners sugar
    1 1/3 cups evaporated skim milk
    1 teaspoon vanilla

Melt chips and margarine in 8 cup microwave measure for 2-4 minutes at 50% power, uncovered, stirring once or until totally melted. Mix together. Add sugar and milk, mixing well. Cook at 50% power for 4-5 minutes until all is warm and thoroughly blended. Stir in vanilla.

Madeira Sauce

Serves 8

If margarine is omitted, microwave saute. Place vegetable in casserole without margarine, cover and cook until vegetable is softened.

1/2 pound sliced fresh mushrooms
2 tablespoons lowfat margarine
1/2 cup sliced onions
1 cup low sodium beef broth
1/2 cup dry red wine
2 1/2 teaspoons flour
2 teaspoons lemon juice
1 teaspoon beef base concentrate

Place margarine in microwave casserole. Melt for 45 seconds to 1 minute at 100% power. Add mushrooms and onions. Cook, uncovered, for 2-3 minutes at 100% power until vegetables soften. Stir in broth, wine and lemon. Cook for 2-4 minutes at 100% power until mixture is hot. Place flour in small container. Stir a small amount of hot broth mixture into flour. Mix until smooth. Blend flour mixture into mushroom/onion mixture and cook a few more minutes until thickened, stirring once or twice. Serve hot.

Meat Flavoring

Serves 64

A tablespoonful of this mixture in stew, steak or gravy will give not only a fine flavor, but also a rich color.

2 onions, chopped
1 teaspoon crushed red pepper flakes
2 tablespoons brown sugar
1 tablespoon celery seed
1 tablespoon ground mustard
1 teaspoon ground turmeric
1 teaspoon black pepper
1 teaspoon salt
1 quart cider vinegar

Mix first 8 ingredients in a clean quart bottle. Fill with cider vinegar.

Nutrition (per serving): 8 calories

Saturated fat	..0 g
Total Fat	..0 g (6% of calories)
Protein	..0 g (6% of calories)
Carbohydrates	..2 g (89% of calories)
Cholesterol	..0 mg
Sodium	40 mg
Fiber	..0 g

Mushroom Gravy

Serves 8

Remember, a whisk will help keep gravy from becoming lumpy.

1/2 cup sliced fresh mushrooms
2 tablespoons lowfat margarine
1/3 cup meat drippings
1/3 cup flour
1 1/2 cups beef broth
2 tablespoons red wine, optional
1 dash salt
1 dash black pepper

Place mushrooms and margarine in microwave casserole. Cook uncovered at 100% power for 3-4 minutes until mushrooms have softened. Whisk in drippings and flour until smooth. Add broth, wine, salt and pepper. Cook at 100% power for 4-6 minutes, stirring once or twice until thick and smooth.

Nutrition (per serving): 117 calories

Saturated fat	..5 g
Total Fat	11 g (81% of calories)
Protein	..1 g (4% of calories)
Carbohydrates	..4 g (15% of calories)
Cholesterol	..6 mg
Sodium	97 mg
Fiber	. 0 g

Mustard Sauce

Serves 12

Will keep indefinitely in refrigerator. Is delicious with ham. Also makes a nice gift. Egg substitute may be used in this recipe if desired.

1 teaspoon melted butter or margarine
1 tablespoon flour
1/3 cup water
2/3 cup vinegar
1 cup packed brown sugar
2 tablespoons dry mustard
3 eggs, beaten
1 dash salt
1 dash white pepper

Mix all ingredients. Heat, uncovered, at 100% power for 2-4 minutes until thickened, stirring once. Store in refrigerator.

```
Nutrition (per serving): 67 calories
    Saturated fat ........................................................ ...1 g
    Total Fat ............................................................ ...2 g (23% of calories)
    Protein .............................................................. ...2 g (11% of calories)
    Carbohydrates ..................................................... 11 g (67% of calories)
    Cholesterol ......................................................... 54 mg
    Sodium .............................................................. 86 mg
    Fiber ................................................................. ..0 g
```

Picante Sauce

Serves 24

Removing seeds from jalapeños will make them less hot. Also, when working with jalapeño chili peppers, never touch eyes until hands are thoroughly washed. Even then, hands can burn eyes.

8 fresh jalapeño peppers
1/4 cup water
1 large onion
1 (16 oz.) can tomatoes
1/4 teaspoon ground cumin
1/2 teaspoon salt
1/4 teaspoon dried oregano
1/2 teaspoon garlic salt
1/4 teaspoon black pepper

Remove stems from peppers. Place peppers and 1/4 cup water into microwave casserole. Cover and cook at 100% power for about 6 minutes. Finely chop peppers and onion in food processor. Add tomatoes and seasonings. Process another few seconds to mix. Let stand overnight before serving if possible. (3 cups)

```
Nutrition (per serving): 17 calories
    Saturated fat .......................................................0 g
    Total Fat ........................................................... 0 g (6% of calories)
    Protein ...............................................................1 g (15% of calories)
    Carbohydrates ...................................................3 g (79% of calories)
    Cholesterol ........................................................0 mg
    Sodium .............................................................. 83 mg
    Fiber ...................................................................0 g
```

Sun Dried Tomatoes

Serves 12

This is the inexpensive way of preparing a costly, but tasty addition to many recipes. Makes a great gift.

6 plum tomatoes
3/4 cup olive oil
2 cloves garlic
1/2 teaspoon dried rosemary
1/2 teaspoon salt

Wash tomatoes and cut in half lengthwise. Place cut side up, spoke fashion, on layers of paper towel. Sprinkle with salt. Microwave at 50% power for 40-45 minutes, turning once. Tomatoes should be dry to touch, but slightly moist and pliable. Transfer tomatoes to a rack to cool. Let stand at room temperature over night. Peel garlic and quarter. Place olive oil, garlic and rosemary in container with tomatoes. Let marinate for 2 days. Tomatoes will keep for several months stored in a cool, dry place.

```
Nutrition (per serving): 130 calories
    Saturated fat ...................................................... 2 g
    Total Fat ............................................................14 g (94% of calories)
    Protein ...............................................................0 g (1% of calories)
    Carbohydrates ................................................... 2 g (5% of calories)
    Cholesterol ........................................................0 mg
    Sodium .............................................................. 101 mg
    Fiber ...................................................................0 g
```

Teriyaki Marinade/Sauce

Serves 40

1 1/2 cups vegetable oil
1/2 cup low sodium soy sauce
1/2 cup honey
1/4 cup vinegar
2 cloves garlic, minced
3 teaspoons ground ginger
1/4 cup minced green onions including tops
1 1/2 cups teriyaki sauce
1 1/2 tablespoons cornstarch
1 cup water
6 tablespoons sugar

Place all marinade ingredients together and mix well. Heat for 2-4 minutes at 100% power, stirring occasionally until thick. (5 cups)

```
Nutrition (per serving): 102 calories
    Saturated fat ........................................................ ...1 g
    Total Fat ............................................................. ...8 g (72% of calories)
    Protein ............................................................... ...1 g (4% of calories)
    Carbohydrates ..................................................... ...6 g (24% of calories)
    Cholesterol ........................................................ ...0 mg
    Sodium ............................................................. 513 mg
    Fiber ................................................................ ...0 g
```

Gifts/Etc.

Baby Handy Wipes

1 package absorbent paper towels
1 quart water
1 teaspoon baby oil
1 teaspoon baby shampoo

Cut paper towels in half and remove core carefully to expose paper end, pulling from center. Place one half roll in plastic container with cover. Mix water, baby oil and baby shampoo in a microwave casserole. Heat for 5 - 8 minutes at 70% power until liquid is warm. Pour liquid slowly over top of paper towels. Let liquid absorb. Cover container with plastic cover. Cut X shape in top of cover and pull towels through X in cover.

Cuticle Softener

You may make larger batches of this and simply warm when needed. This makes a nice gift.

    1 tablespoon water
    1 tablespoon glycerine
    1/2 teaspoon Knox Unflavored Gelatin
    1/2 teaspoon lemon or almond extract

Mix ingredients in 1 cup measure and microwave at 100% power for 15-20 seconds. Stir again until gelatin dissolves. Soak fingers in warm mixture for 5-10 minutes. Push back cuticles with cuticle stick. Rinse and apply thin layer over both hands.

Doggie Cookies

A great gift for your favorite pet.

    1/2 pound liver
    3/4 cup corn meal
    1/2 cup flour

Cut liver into small pieces and puree in blender or food processor. Mix with cornmeal and flour. Spread about 1/2 inch thick into micro-wave casserole. Microwave, uncovered, at 70% power, turning once, for 5-10 minutes or until firm. Let cool. Cut into pieces.

Lip Gloss

Larger amounts may be made, but heat gently and soften only. Also, any flavor of candy oil may be used to vary taste. For example, chocolate, lemon, peppermint, etc. Placed in a small unique container, this makes a wonderful gift. A brighter color may also be achieved by adding a bit more lipstick.

    2 tablespoons petroleum jelly
    1/4 teaspoon lipstick, any color
    4 drops cinnamon oil

Place petroleum jelly in a small microwave container. Top with lipstick. Microwave for 20-30 seconds at 100% power or until mixture has softened. Blend together. Mix in drops of cinnamon. Store in a small container.

Liquid Soap

Make certain a moisturizer soap is used. Also, if a thicker soap is desired, use less water. Use any fragrance from your favorite perfume to vanilla for scent. A few drops of food coloring will also make this a customized color for any bathroom or kitchen.

3 1/2 ounces bath soap
3 cups water
1/4 teaspoon vanilla extract, or perfume

Grate soap and place in microwave casserole. Add water and mix. Cook at 100% power for 5-8 minutes, stirring occasionally until soap melts and mixture will blend. Stir in scent if desired. Store in pump and use as any other liquid hand soap.

Massage Lotion

This along with cuticle softener, both packaged with instructions make a unique gift for a friend. Larger amounts may be made and heated when ready to use.

1 tablespoon petroleum jelly
1 tablespoon glycerine
1 tablespoon water
1/2 teaspoon almond extract
1/8 teaspoon wintergreen oil

Mix petroleum jelly, water and glycerine in 1 cup measure. Heat, uncovered, for 20-30 seconds at 100% power. Add extract and oil. While warm, rub on skin. Follow with a warm soak in bath tub and cool shower.

Moisture Mask

Remember that many fine beauty products can be made from ingredients we have in our homes.

1 banana, mashed
2 tablespoons cooking oil

Mix ingredients. Microwave at 100% power for 45-60 seconds. Apply to face and leave 10-15 minutes. Relax, elevating feet if possible. Rinse with warm water followed by a cool water splash.

Play Dough

You may also sculpt with this. Will keep for a long time if stored in an air tight container.

1 cup flour
1 teaspoon vegetable oil
1 cup water
1/2 cup salt
2 teaspoons cream of tartar
Food coloring, any color
1/4 cup clear liquid glue
1/4 cup water

Mix flour, oil, water, cream of tartar and food coloring in microwave casserole. Microwave at 70% power for 3-4 minutes, stirring every minute until mixture forms a ball. Stop cooking immediately. Knead gently to make certain mixture is well blended. Cool slightly. Roll out on wax paper. Make cutouts or patterns. Place on microwave tray or cover. Microwave 10-12 minutes at 40%-50% power. Cool. Paint with tempera paint. After paint dries, glaze with glue/water mixture or spray with polyurethane finish.

GENERAL INFORMATION

METRIC CONVERSION

Metric unit for volume is liter in both liquid and dry ingredients. 1000 milliliters (ml) are in 1 liter.

When you have:	Multiply by:	Equals:
Teaspoon	5 ml	# of milliliters
Tablespoon	15 ml	# of milliliters
Dry ounces	28 ml	# of milliliters
Fluid ounces	30 ml	# of milliliters
Cups	236 ml	# of milliliters

GRAMS
Metric unit for weight is grams (g) or kilograms (kg)
Kilogram = 2.2 lbs.
28 grams = 1 ounce
ounces x 28.0 = grams
pounds x .45 = kilograms.

ABBREVIATIONS
Teaspoon = tsp.
Pint = pt.
Tablespoon = Tbsp. or T.
Gallon = Gal.

Cup = c.
Ounce = oz.
Quart = qt.
Pound = lb.

WEIGHTS AND MEASURES
Dash = less than 1/8 teaspoon
3 teaspoons = 1 Tablespoon
4 tablespoons = 1/4 cup
2 tablespoons = 1 liquid ounce
8 tablespoons = 1/2 cup
10 tablespoons + 2 teaspoon = 2/3 cup
12 tablespoons = 3/4 cup
16 tablespoons = 1 cup
8 ounces liquid = 1 cup
16 ounces = 1 pound
2 cups liquid = 1 pound
2 cups = 1 pint

4 cups = 1 quart
4 quarts = 1 gallon
8 quarts = 1 peck
4 pecks = 1 bushel
1 ounce = 28.35 grams
1 gram = 0.035 ounce
1 quart = 946.44 milliliters
1 liter = 1.06 quarts

Use standard measuring spoons and cups for liquid and dry measurements. Measurements are level.

HOW MUCH AND HOW MANY (YIELDS)

Baking powder
1 cup = 5 1/2 ounces

Butter (or Margarine)
1 stick = 1/2 cup

2 cups = l pound

Cabbage
1 pound = about 4 cups shredded

Cereals/Pasta/Rice
1 cup raw cereal = 2 cups cooked

4 ounces macaroni (1 1/4 c.) = 2 1/4 cups cooked

4 ounces noodles (1 1/2 - 2 c.) = 2 cups cooked

7 ounces spaghetti = 4 cups cooked

1 cup precooked (instant) rice = 2 cups cooked

1 cup raw rice = 3-4 cups cooked

Chocolate
1 square bitter = 1 ounce

Cocoa
1 pound = 4 cups ground

Coffee (ground)
1 pound = about 46 six-ounce cups brewed

Cornmeal
1 pound = 3 cups

1 tablespoon = 2 tablespoons flour

Crackers/Bread
1 pound loaf = 10 cups small bread cubes

1 1/2 slices bread = 1 cup soft crumbs

1 slice bread = 1/4 cup dry crumbs

23 soda crackers = 1 cup

15 graham crackers = 1 cup

22 vanilla wafers = 1 cup

Cream/Cheeses
1 cup whipping cream (heavy, 40%) = 2 cups whipped cream

1 lb. American/cheddar cheese, shredded = 4 cups or 2 2/3 cups, cubed

4 ounces cheese = 1 cup shredded

4 ounces blue cheese, crumbled = 1 cup

Eggs (large grade)
1 egg = 4 tablespoons liquid

4-5 whole eggs = 1 cup

7-9 whites = 1 cup

12-16 yolks = 1 cup

Flour
1 pound all-purpose = 4 cups

1 pound cake flour = 4 1/2 cups

1 pound graham or wheat flour = 3 1/2 cups

Fruits and Vegetables
Juice of 1 lemon = 2-3 tablespoons

Bananas, 2-3 medium = about 1 cup mashed

Peel of 1 lemon = 1 teaspoon, grated

5-8 medium lemons = 1 cup juice

Juice of 1 orange = 1/3-1/2 cup

Grated peel of 1 orange = 2 tsp.

1 medium apple, chopped = 1 cup

1 medium onion, chopped = 1/2 cup

Gelatin
3 1/4 ounce package flavored = 1/2 cup

1/4 package unflavored = 1 table-spoon

Nuts
1 pound walnuts or pecans in shell = 1 1/2 - 1 3/4 cup, shelled

1 pound almonds in shell = 3/4 - 1 cup, shelled

Shortening

1 pound = 2 cups

Sugar
1 pound brown = 2 1/2 cups

1 pound cube = 96-160 cubes

1 pound granulated = 2 cups

1 pound powdered = 3 1/2 cups

WHAT ABOUT HERBS AND SPICES ?

All herbs and spices will keep longer if sealed tightly in a non-translucent container. Spices generally will last about six months (sometimes longer) when in ground form and indefinitely if whole. Dry celery tops, onion tops and green pepper pieces in the microwave and store in freezer for use later.

When using herbs, the conversion rule is 1/2 teaspoon of dried herbs equal 1 teaspoon of fresh.

EMERGENCY SUBSTITUTIONS AND EQUIVALENTS

BAKING POWDER = 1 teaspoon cream of tartar plus 1/4 teaspoon baking soda

BAKING POWDER = 1 teaspoon will leaven 1 cup flour

BAKING POWDER AND SWEET MILK = Each half teaspoon of soda with 1 cup sour milk takes the place of 2 teaspoons baking powder and 1 cup sweet milk

BREADCRUMBS 1/3 cup = 1 slice of bread

BUTTER or margarine, 2 tablespoons = 1 ounce

BUTTER, 1 cup = 7/8 cup lard with 1/2 teaspoon salt or hydrogenated fat is 1 cup with 1/2 teaspoon salt

CATSUP or CHILI SAUCE, 1 cup = 1 cup tomato sauce plus 1/2 cup sugar plus 2 T. vinegar

CHOCOLATE, unsweetened, 1 square = 1 ounce or 1 square = 3-4 tablespoons cocoa plus 1 tablespoon shortening

CORNSTARCH, 1 tablespoon = 2 tablespoons flour or 4 teaspoons quick cooking tapioca (thickening)

CREAM, heavy (40%), 1 cup = 3/4 cup milk plus 1/3 cup butter

CREAM, light (20%), 1 cup = 7/8 cup milk plus 3 tablespoons butter

EGGS, 1 whole egg = 2 egg yolks or 2 tablespoons dried whole egg with 2 1/2 T. water

EGGS,   Whole, 4 to 6 = 1 cup

          Whites, 9 to 11 = 1 cup

          Yolks, 12 to 14 = 1 cup

FLOUR, *Cake*, 1 cup = 1 cup plus 2 tablespoons all purpose flour

All-purpose, 1 cup = 1/2 cup bran/wheat or cornmeal plus balance of all purpose to fill 8 oz. c.

Self-rising, 1 cup = 1 cup all-purpose flour, 1 1/2 tsp. baking powder, 1 tsp. salt (sift for less coarse texture)

GARLIC, 1 clove = 1/4 teaspoon minced garlic or 1/8 teaspoon garlic powder

GELATIN, 1 tablespoon = 1 envelope.

HERBS, fresh, 1 tablespoon chopped = 1 teaspoon dried. Basil, fresh = 1/4 cup fresh parsley plus 1 tablespoon dried basil for every 1/4 cup fresh parsley

LEMON, 1 teaspoon juice = 1/2 teaspoon white vinegar. 1 teaspoon grated peel = 1/2 teaspoon lemon extract

MILK, *1 cup whole* = 1/2 cup evaporated plus 1/2 cup water or 1 cup reconstituted non-fat dry milk plus 2 1/2 teaspoon butter or margarine or 1 cup dry whole milk (4 tablespoons plus 1 cup milk or water)

1 cup sour milk or buttermilk = 1 tablespoon lemon juice or vinegar plus sweet milk to make 1 cup (let stand 5 minutes) or 1 3/4 teaspoons cream of tartar

1 cup skim milk = 4 tablespoons nonfat dry milk plus 1 cup water

MUSHROOMS, 1 pound fresh = 12 ounces canned, drained

MUSTARD, 1 tablespoon prepared = 1 teaspoon dry mustard

SUGAR, *Granulated,* 2 1/4 cups = 1 pound

Superfine, 2 1/3 cups = 1 pound

Brown, about 2 1/4 cups firmly packed = 1 pound

Granulated brown, about 3 1/8 cups = 1 pound

Confectioners', about 3 1/2 = 1 pound

SYRUP, *corn or maple,* about 1 1/2 cups = 1 pound

Corn or honey, 1 cup = 1 1/4 cups granulated sugar plus 1/4 c. water or milk

TOMATO JUICE, 1 cup = 1/2 cup tomato sauce plus 1/2 cup water

YOGURT, 1 cup = 1 cup buttermilk

BASICS OF SAFE FOOD

1. Wash your hands. Keep them free of bacteria. Wash hands after handling raw meat or poultry

2. Use clean utensils. Avoid cross contamination. **Do not** allow raw meats to come in contact with cooked foods. **Do not** carry cooked meat from grill on the same plate as the raw meat was carried. Set some fresh, unused marinade sauce aside for use later if it is to be used as basting. **Do not** spread bacteria from raw meat and poultry to other foods. Use fresh plates/utensils for each food.

3. Heat foods thoroughly. High food temperatures (165-212 degrees F.) kill most food poisoning bacteria. Thoroughly cook raw meats, poultry and fish. Make certain poultry reaches an internal temperature of 165-170 degrees; pork internal temperature should reach 160-165 degrees. If delay in serving or reheating food is required, food should be heated and held 140-165 degrees for safety.

4. Refrigerate food as soon as possible after serving to prevent food poisoning. Do not leave food out more than two hours. Make certain your refrigerator registers a safe 40 degrees or lower and freezers set at zero degrees as 15 degrees or higher can reduce some vitamins. Cool foods in small batches. Large batches require too long to chill thoroughly. Bacteria lurking in the center of the large batch can multiply as they have the warm environment they need to flourish, therefore raising the possibility of food poisoning. Cool rapidly to below 50 degrees.

5. Keep foods hot or cold, not room temperature or just warm. The ideal breeding climate for bacteria is 50-125 degrees.

SPECIAL CARE FOR SAFE FOOD

Thoroughly clean leeks and other root vegetables as soil is one of the main sources of a certain type of food poisoning.

If you have lead pipes, let water run for at least 10 minutes the first thing in the morning to protect against lead poisoning.

Never stuff poultry the night before roasting. Stuffing may not heat to high enough temperatures to kill bacteria. Stuff a few minutes before cooking.

Uncooked poultry juices containing bacterial can seep into the dressing. Make certain stuffing is hot enough to kill bacteria. Refrigerate leftover poultry and stuffing. Stuffing should always be removed from the bird.

Use cracked eggs only if thoroughly cooked to kill bacteria.

Special care foods are poultry, fish, seafood, meat, creamed mixtures, mayonnaise, puddings and stuffings.

When partially cooking meat in the microwave or any other way to shorten grill time, make certain food goes directly on grill from microwave and is not allowed to stand and cool as this will encourage bacterial growth.

STORING OUR FOOD

MEAT STORAGE (Refrigerator)

BEEF
Roasts .... 5-6 days
Steaks .... 3-5 days
Ground beef, stew meat .. 2 days

PORK
Roasts .... 5-6 days
Hams, picnics, whole .... 7 days
Bacon .... 5-7 days
Chops, spareribs .... 3 days
Pork sausage .... 2-3 days

VEAL
Roasts .... 5-6 days
Chops .... 4 days

LAMB
Roasts .... 5 days
Chops .... 3 days
Ground lamb .... 2 days

POULTRY
Chickens, whole .... 2-3 days
Chickens, cut up .... 2 days
Turkeys, whole .... 4-5 days

COOKED MEATS
Leftover cooked meats .... 4 days
Cooked poultry .... 2 days
Ham/picnics .... 7 days
Frankfurters .... 4-5 days
Sliced luncheon meats .... 3 days
Unsliced bologna .... 4-6 days

FISH
Fresh .... 24 hours
Marinated .... 1-2 days

STORAGE AND BUYING GUIDE
Vegetables

Type	Refrig. Time	Tips
Asparagus	4-6 days	Tips close, compact. Choose tender, firm with very little white.
Beans	2-5 days	Small seed in pods best. Should not look dry
Broccoli, Brussels Sprouts, Cauliflower	3-7 days	Flower clusters tight and firm and Cauliflower firm.
Celery	7-14 days	Leaves should be green and not wilted. Rigid crisp ribs
Cucumbers	4-5 days	Long and slender.
Mushrooms	**4-5 days**	**Light in color; smooth with cap hugging stem (At peak; most robust stage before cap opens). Brown bag in single layer**
Root Vegetables (carrot, turnip radish, beet, etc.)	**4-5 days**	**Smooth and firm, medium size.** Large can be pithy.
Peppers	4-5 days	Firm, crisp. Avoid wrinkled skin. Gloss and unblemished.

	Will Keep	Tips
Potatoes	2 mo. (mature). 2 weeks (new)	Smooth, well shaped. Tight fitting skin.

Fruits

Type	Ripen at Room Temp.	Refrig. Time	Tips
Apples	yes	2-4 d.	Pick type that suits your need. Intense color for variety.
Berries	no	1-2 d.	Plump, solid with good color. Avoid stained container indicating leakage of berries.
Cantaloupes	yes	7-10 d.	Stem scar completely smooth circular indentation with no ragged edges. Yellow beneath coarse netting, fruity odor.
Watermelon	no	1 week	Deep colored rinds. Bottom that was against ground is yellow rather than pale white or green
Grapes	no	3-5 d.	Firmly attached to stem.
Oranges, Limes, Grapefruit, Lemons	no	10-14 d.	Firm, heavy for size. Skin smooth, fine grained.

LABELING... WHAT IT MEANS

Expiration date   The date after which the food will begin to decrease in quality.

Sell by Date   The last date the product may be sold.
Last Sale Date   Date allows time for use.
Buy Before Date
Pull Date

FREEZER BASICS

The most effective long term frozen food storage temperature is zero degrees or lower.

Freezing works as a food storage method because the low temperature slows down food spoilage. Bacterial growth and enzyme action is also retarded by freezing.

TECHNIQUES FOR FREEZING

1. Freeze only top quality foods as food cannot be improved by freezing.

2. Prepare the food properly for freezing. Cleaning, blanching and cooling food are necessary for good product.

3. Package food properly. You may want food in individual portions as well as family size portions.

4. Label the packages properly. Color code packages in freezer. For example: Red for meat, green for vegetables, etc. You may date packages, but you might rather consider marking them with "use by" dates instead.

5. Freeze foods as rapidly as possible after preparation.

6. Use frozen foods within a reasonable length of time.

BLANCHING VEGETABLES

The microwave gives you the perfect way to blanch fresh vegetables for freezing. Microwave blanching reduces loss of Vitamin C, retains color and texture of the vegetable. Blanch or cook food, covered very tightly for 3 minutes per pound. Next, place vegetables in ice water for rapid cooling and to stop the cooking process. The vegetables are then ready for packaging, cooling and freezing.

PACKAGING FOR THE FREEZER

All freezing materials should be moisture proof to hold food moisture inside and cold air outside.

Vapor proof to seal out cold air and prevent flavor and odor transfer.

Sturdy enough to hold up to stress and the shape of the food being wrapped.

STORAGE TIME FOR FROZEN FOODS

Below are suggested Maximum times for foods held at approximately zero degrees Fahrenheit

MEATS

Beef:
Hamburger .... 4 months
Roasts .... 12 months
Steaks .... 12 months

Lamb:
Ground .... 4 months
Roasts .... 12 months

Pork:
Cured Pork .... 2 months
Fresh Pork Chops ..... 4 months
Sausage .... 2 months
Roasts .... 8 months

Veal:
Chops .... 9 months
Cutlets .... 9 months
Roasts .... 9 months

Cooked Meat:
Pies, dinners, etc. ..... 3 months

POULTRY

Chicken
Whole .... 12 months
Cut up .... 9 months
Livers and Gizzards .. 3 months

Ducks and Geese:
Ducks and Geese ..... 6 months

Turkey:
Whole .... 12 months
Cut up .... 6 months

Cooked Chicken and Turkey:
Dinners, sliced
or Pot Pies .... 6 months
Fried .... 4 months

FISH AND SHELLFISH

Fish:
Fillets .... 6 months
Steaks
(such as salmon) ...... 2 months
Whole .... 3-4 months
Cooked Fish .... 2-3 months

Shellfish:
Shrimp .... 12 months
Clams and
Dungeness Crab .... 3 months
King Crab .... 9-10 months
Shucked Oysters ...... 3-4 months
Cooked Shellfish .... 2-3 months

VEGETABLES AND FRUITS

Fruits and Juice
Concentrates .... 12 months
Vegetables .... 8 months

BAKED GOODS

Breads and Rolls .... 2-3 months
Sweet rolls, Doughnuts,
Danish .... 2-3 months
Angel, Chiffon Cake .... 2 months
Pound, Layer Cake .... 4-6 months
Pies (baked) .... 6 months
Pies (unbaked) .... 8 months

216

EGGS IN THE FREEZER

Freeze egg white in ice cube trays. 1 cube = approximately 1 Tbsp. or the equivalent to 1 egg white. Store in air tight container.

Whole and yolks must be stabilized before freezing. Break yolks and blend in 1/8 tsp. (for savory dishes) and 1 1/2 tsp. (for sweet dishes) of sugar or corn syrup per two whole eggs or 4 egg yolks. Then freeze in ice cube trays and transfer to air tight container. These will keep for up to 1 year.

REFREEZING

You may virtually refreeze any partially thawed food as long as it still has ice crystals and held in refrigerator 1-2 days. Baked goods and ice cream, however, deteriorate.

Meat, fish and poultry thawed in the refrigerator may be refrozen within 24 hours of defrosting. Combination dishes such as pies, casseroles, etc. that have been thawed should NOT be refrozen.

About the Author

♦   Carolyn Dodson has the distinction of being one of the first people in the country to demonstrate the microwave oven. The year was 1957, when her home economics class was chosen to demonstrate Raytheon's first in-home microwave as it toured the United States. Never mind that it resembled a refrigerator... a full five feet tall. A love affair was born.

♦   Since that first demonstration, Carolyn has helped make this "wonder cooker" into a household word. She has lectured throughout Europe, Asia Pacific, Canada and the United States. She has consulted for the Tupperware Company worldwide coming to bear on the design and development of microwave products as well as assisting with recipe conversion, training videos and cookbook development.

♦   For the last 10 years, Carolyn has been making regular appearances on national and syndicated celebrity talk shows and on local and Midwestern programming. She has produced and appeared in more than 350 microwave cooking segments for local and national cable television. Carolyn also has been featured on numerous radio shows and provides print copy for newspaper and magazine.

♦   *Definitive Microwave Cookery II*, is the second in a series of cookbooks aimed at making the microwave every cooks best friend. Other than her own two books, Carolyn has collaborated on numerous other books, conducted microwave cooking classes for most microwave oven manufacturers and lectured to thousands of individuals at trade shows, schools and corporations throughout the world.

♦   Carolyn is a member of The International Microwave Power Institute, The International Association of Culinary Professionals and Who's Who Worldwide.

ARTHUR'S LOST PUPPY

LeapPad Early Reader

This fun-filled activity book teaches core early reading skills!

Based on a teleplay by JOE FALLON.

Arthur and D.W. took Baby Kate to the **street fair**. Pal came along too.

3

There was lots to do. Arthur gave Kate a ride in a little fire truck that went around and around.

GO

STOP

Say It

Spell It

4

💬 D.W. got her face painted. "Look, Kate!" she said. "I'm a cat!" But Kate was looking at something else.

Suddenly, Kate began to cry. "Are you hungry?" asked Arthur. "Here's your bottle." But Kate did not want her bottle. "Wah! Wah! Wah!" she cried.

GO

STOP

Say It

Spell It

6

Arthur **lifted** the baby from her stroller.

He rocked her in his arms.

He tickled her tummy.

He made funny faces.

But still she cried.
"Wah! Wah! Wah!"

GO

STOP

"Kate loves ice cream," said Arthur. "Run to the store, D.W., and get her a cone."

Say It

Spell It

game

repeat

D.W. tied Pal's **leash** to a **bench** and went into the store. A clown with balloons walked by. Pal barked at him. "Woof! Woof! Woof!"

NO DOGS ALLOWED

CREAM

When D.W. came out of the store, Pal was gone! She looked up and down the street and then ran to tell Arthur.

"Oh no!" cried Arthur.
"Why would Pal run away?"
"Maybe he's mad at you,"
said D.W. "You yelled at him
today for chewing your slippers."
Arthur looked very sad.
Then Arthur said, "D.W., take
Kate home. I need to find Pal."

Arthur passed the **ring-toss** table, the **bob-for-apples** table, and a table with pumpkin pies, chocolate cakes, and cookies.

GO

STOP

Say It

Spell It

game

repeat

Arthur wished there was a table with hamburgers. Pal would be sure to be **hanging around** it!

PIES, CAKES and COOKIES

DRINKS

"Have you seen a lost puppy?" Arthur asked a police officer. "Yes, one was taken to the school." "Oh, thank you!" said Arthur and he ran to the school.

Say It

Spell It

 But the puppy was not Pal.
Arthur sadly walked home.

Back at the street fair, the clown with the balloons **tripped** over his big **floppy** shoes. **CRASH!** Down he went.

Say It

Spell It

game

As he fell, he let go
of his balloons. A little brown
puppy jumped up and **grabbed**
the balloon strings with his
teeth.

The balloons rose higher and higher. Over the roofs, over the trees, up, up, up they went. And so did Pal!

Then **suddenly—**
BANG! POP! BANG!
The balloons hit a
tall tree. One by one
they all **burst**. Pal
floated slowly down.

Say It Spell It happy sad mad

 When he got home
he still had one **beautiful**
red balloon.

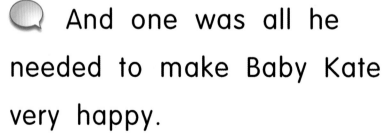 And one was all he needed to make Baby Kate very happy.

 Say It

 Spell It

Dear Diary...

STREET FAIR

PIZZA

25¢ a slice

FACE PAINTING

game

repeat

25

Arthur's Word Round-Up

bang

beautiful

bench

bob
for apples

burst

hanging
around

leash

lifted

pop

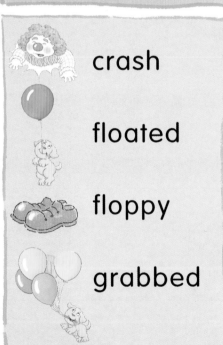

crash

floated

floppy

grabbed

ring toss

street fair

suddenly

tripped

 STOP

 Say It

 Spell It

 game

 repeat

The·End

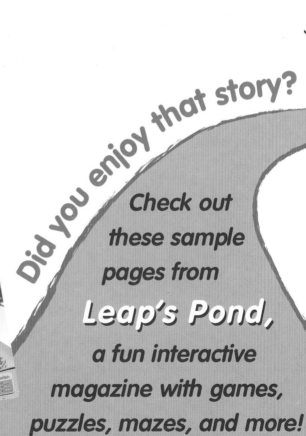

Did you enjoy that story?

Check out
these sample
pages from

Leap's Pond,

a fun interactive
magazine with games,
puzzles, mazes, and more!

Word Wizard

Create a fun sentence! Touch a blue word, a purple word, and a green word.

Wet

fly.

pups

Fuzzy

nap.

hippos

Wobbly

jump.

frogs

STOP

 game say it spell it sound it

Word Bubbles!

Find the words hidden in the bubbles.

GO

N	E	T	M	A	T
H	Y	R	C	D	F
N	A	P	T	A	P
H	O	T	S	U	B
A	L	B	T	U	B
E	W	E	T	O	P

NET
MAT
TUB

TAP
HOT
NAP

WET
SUB
TOP

TEN
PAT
PAN

BUS
BUT
POT

 game   say it   sound it   ∨ ∧

Welcome to the LeapPad® Library!

LeapFrog® LEAP•START
Preschool-K • Up to Age 5

LEAP•START Books:
Reading readiness and simple activities. Letters, phonics, rhymes, matching and music.

Leap's Friends From A to Z | The Birthday Surprise | Tad Goes Shopping | Richard Scarry's Things To Know
© 1991 Richard Scarry

LeapFrog® LEAP•1
Preschool-Grade 1 • Ages 4-6

LEAP•1 Books:
Phonics, learning to read and introduction to simple subjects.

Scooby-Doo and the Disappearing Donuts
TM & © Hanna-Barbera
TM & © Cartoon Network (s02) | Bounce, Tigger, Bounce © 1999 Disney | Monster Money © 1998 Scholastic | Mother Goose Songbook

LeapFrog® LEAP•2
Grades 1-3 • Ages 6-8

LEAP•2 Books:
Reading practice and school-related subjects like math and science.

Arthur and the Lost Diary © 1998 Marc Brown | Arthur Makes the Team © 1998 Marc Brown | Disney/Pixar Monster's Inc. © 2001 Disney/Pixar | The Great Dune Buggy Race

LeapFrog® LEAP•3
Grades 3-5 • Ages 8-10

LEAP•3 Books:
Reading comprehension and reading to learn. Geography, science and more!

   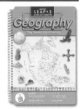

Search the City | The Human Body | The Wind in the Willows | The Seven Continents

Many more titles available!

 Introducing LeapsPond™ magazine!
Join the LeapFrog® Never-Ending Learning™ Club for more learning fun for your **LeapPad** player.
Go to: www.leapfrog.com for information on how to join!